D1189513

A FIELD GUIDE TO

HUMMINGBIRDS

OF NORTH AMERICA

THE PETERSON FIELD GUIDE SERIES ®

A FIELD GUIDE TO

HUMMINGBIRDS

OF NORTH AMERICA

S H E R I L. W I L L I A M S O N

SPONSORED BY
THE NATIONAL WILDLIFE FEDERATION
AND THE ROGER TORY PETERSON INSTITUTE

HOUGHTON MIFFLIN COMPANY
BOSTON   NEW YORK   2001

For information about permission to reproduce selections from
this book, write to Permissions, Houghton Mifflin Company,
215 Park Avenue, New York, New York 10003.

Visit our Web site: www.houghtonmifflinbooks.com.

PETERSON FIELD GUIDES and PETERSON FIELD GUIDE SERIES
are registered trademarks of Houghton Mifflin Company.

Library of Congress Cataloging in Publication Data

Williamson, Sheri.
A field guide to hummingbirds of North America /
Sheri L. Williamson.
p. cm. — (The Peterson field guide series)
ISBN 0-618-02496-4
1. Hummingbirds — North America —
Identification. I. Title. II. Series.
QL696.A558 W5   2002
598.7'64'097—dc21   2001024473

Book design by Anne Chalmers
Typeface: Linotype-Hell Fairfield; Futura Condensed (Adobe)

Printed in Singapore

TWP 10 9 8 7 6 5 4 3 2 1

To Tom

and the wild things

that make our hearts sing

CONTENTS

LIST OF PLATES

A FIELD GUIDE TO

HUMMINGBIRDS

OF NORTH AMERICA

The legacy of America's great naturalist, Roger Tory Peterson, is preserved through the programs and work of the Roger Tory Peterson Institute of Natural History. The RTPI mission is to create passion for and knowledge of the natural world in the hearts and minds of children by inspiring and guiding the study of nature in our schools and communities. You can become a part of this worthy effort by joining RTPI. Just call RTPI's membership department at 1-800-758-6841, fax 716-665-3794, or e-mail (webmaster@rtpi.org) for a free one-year membership with the purchase of this Field Guide.

INTRODUCTION

Hummingbirds are among the few birds capable of inspiring equal fascination among birders and nonbirders alike. Their jewel-like colors, astounding powers of flight, and fearless nature have captured the imagination of people around the world, many of whom have never come into direct contact with these uniquely New World birds. These charismatic creatures are also an increasingly conspicuous part of both rural and urban landscapes in the continental United States and southern Canada as feeding and gardening for hummingbirds grow in popularity.

But hummingbirds are more than just pretty faces. As migratory birds, they are part of the Earth's circulatory system, transporting energy and other resources between tropical and temperate ecosystems thousands of miles apart. As pollinators, they shape the landscapes they visit in these travels. Plants, from wildflowers to trees, benefit from the pollination services of hummingbirds; many are so specialized as to be unable to reproduce without the birds' assistance. The shape and color of familiar flowers such as trumpet creeper, cardinal flower, fuchsia, and even Christmas cactus are due in large part to their relationships with hummingbirds. These interdependencies between the birds and the plants they pollinate have contributed significantly to the structure and composition of the forests, woodlands, deserts, and alpine meadows of the Americas and to the diversity of animals and plants that share these habitats.

Despite their familiarity, hummingbirds are far more challenging to identify than most people realize. Females and immature males of closely related species are often extremely difficult, if not impossible, to separate visually. Even adult males may present a challenge if viewed under less than ideal conditions. Unfortunately, space limitations prevent most general field guides from adequately addressing the more complex identification issues, and few of the many specialty books on hummingbirds cover identification in any but the most elementary way. The inadequacies of existing resources result in frustration for birders from entry level to expert and limit the ability of lay observers to contribute to our understanding of hummingbird migration and distribution. The goal of this guide is to fill this void and take some of the mystery out of hummingbird identification for enthusiasts at all levels of skill and interest.

Traditional field guide illustrations have seldom done justice to hummingbirds. Creating convincing depictions of both the chameleon-like quality of iridescence and the rapidly moving wings of these birds has sorely challenged the skill and creativity of illustrators. Photographs avoid the potential pitfalls of artistic interpretation, but as records of fleeting moments in the lives of individual birds they are of limited value in general field guides. In a tightly focused guide such as this, however, a gallery of carefully selected photographs can surpass traditional paintings in depicting plumage variation within and between species. The majority of photos used to illustrate this guide are of free-living wild birds, though a few are of long-term captives on exhibit in public institutions such as the Arizona-Sonora Desert Museum. Most close-ups of heads, tails, and wings were taken during banding sessions that are part of ongoing monitoring programs. No birds were captured solely for purposes of photography.

The information presented in this guide comes from a variety of sources, both published and unpublished. The most valuable published resource on the biology and natural history of North American hummingbirds is the Birds of North America series, a joint project of the American Ornithologists' Union, the Academy of Natural Sciences of Philadelphia, and the Cornell Laboratory of Ornithology. The series consists of individual species accounts summarizing the life histories of birds that breed in the United States and Canada, including 14 of the 17 species of hummingbirds that have bred there. Each account includes an exhaustive bibliography of published references as well as previously unpublished information. The Birds of North America series is the most recent successor to the classic 20-volume series by Arthur Cleveland Bent; his *Life Histories of North American Cuckoos, Goatsuckers, Hummingbirds and Their Allies* (1940) contains firsthand accounts from a wide variety of sources assembled into narratives covering 17 hummingbird species and one probable hybrid. Other valuable references on hummingbirds, especially those species peripheral to or outside the geographic area covered in this guide, include *Handbook of the Birds of the World*, vol. 5, edited by Josep del Hoyo, Andrew Elliot, and Jordi Sargatal (1999); *The Hum-

mingbirds of North America, second edition, by Paul A. Johnsgard (1997); *A Guide to the Birds of Mexico and Northern Central America,* by Steve N. G. Howell and Sophie Webb (1995); *A Guide to the Birds of the West Indies,* by Herbert Raffaele, James Wiley, Orlando Garrido, Allan Keith, and Janis Raffaele (1998); *A Guide to the Birds of Colombia,* by Steven L. Hilty and William L. Brown; and *A Guide to the Birds of Venezuela,* by Rodolphe M. de Schauensee and William R. Phelps Jr.

Basic distributional data for most species was drawn from the sources listed above, especially the Birds of North America accounts. For records of occurrence outside the "normal" range for a species, the primary reference was the journal known at various times as *Audubon Field Notes, American Birds, Field Notes,* and *North American Birds.* By any name, this is one of the best examples of citizen science. The wealth of data contained in each issue was contributed largely by recreational birders and amateur ornithologists. The regional reports were a major source for data used in the range maps, and searching more than a decade's worth of back issues revealed interesting patterns in both hummingbird distribution and birder awareness. State bird record committee reports and annotated checklists provided additional documentation for many unusual records.

The bulk of the data used to compile the species accounts came from countless hours of field observations plus documentation of tens of thousands of living birds during banding studies. Much of this information is unpublished and was made available courtesy of individual ornithologists, banders, and birders. The Internet was an indispensable resource, with some references available on-line and others just an e-mail request away. Among the Internet resources most valuable in the creation of this guide were virtual communities such as Humnet, a discussion group of dedicated hummingbird enthusiasts concentrated in the southeastern United States but with participants scattered from Canada to Ecuador. Correspondents' reports provided up-to-date information on breeding and winter ranges, migration patterns, extralimital occurrences, and identification as well as behavior, backyard habitat, conservation issues, and other matters.

Despite this wealth of information from living birds, the less familiar species could not have been accurately profiled without access to museum specimens. I gathered essential information from hundreds of specimens in collections at the Field Museum in Chicago, the Museum of Natural Science at Louisiana State University in Baton Rouge, the Moore Laboratory of Ornithology at Occidental College in Los Angeles, the San Diego Natural History Museum, the Natural History Museum of Los Angeles

County, the Academy of Natural Sciences in Philadelphia, and the American Museum of Natural History in New York. Though the future of ornithology lies in innovative, low-impact methods of data collection, we owe it to generations of researchers to come, as well as to those birds who died to further our knowledge, to provide these and other scientific collections with public and private support worthy of the treasure houses they are.

GEOGRAPHICAL SCOPE

This guide covers 31 species of hummingbirds, including 26 species recorded in continental North America north of the border between the United States and Mexico as well as 5 additional species found in northern Mexico but as yet unrecorded north of the border. Antillean Crested, Bumblebee, and Rufous-tailed Hummingbirds are often included as part of the fauna of the United States based on limited and sometimes dubious evidence; these records have been given the benefit of the doubt. Wedge-tailed Sabrewing, Amethyst-throated Hummingbird, Azure-crowned Hummingbird, Canivet's Emerald, and Golden-crowned Emerald are included because of the proximity of their known ranges to the United States and the potential, however slight, for accidental occurrence. These species bear at least superficial resemblance to more common species and might be misidentified if omitted from this guide. Additionally, several species native to the Caribbean and Central and South America, for which full coverage was not warranted, have been mentioned in the text under similar species. These may occur in the United States or Canada as escapes from captivity, ship-assisted visitors, or legitimate strays following hurricanes.

WHAT IS A HUMMINGBIRD?

Hummingbirds are among the most instantly recognizable of all birds. When asked to describe a hummingbird, the average person will mention small size, colorful male plumage, and a long rapier-like bill and hovering flight for harvesting nectar from the flowers it pollinates. In reality, these characteristics vary considerably. The Bee Hummingbird (*Mellisuga helenae*) of Cuba is among the smallest of all warm-blooded animals, but the Giant Hummingbird (*Patagona gigas*) of South America outweighs many songbirds. Male and female hummingbirds may be equally drab in plumage, as in the Plain-capped Starthroat, or equally gaudy, as in the Green Violet-ear. Bill length ranges from scarcely longer than that of a warbler in the Purple-backed Thornbill (*Ramphomicron microrhynchum*) to more than half the bird's total length in the Sword-billed Hummingbird (*Ensifera ensifera*). The bills of most hummingbirds are straight or nearly so but range from deeply decurved in the White-tipped Sicklebill (*Eutoxeres aquila*) to upturned at the tip in the Fiery-tailed Awlbill (*Anthracothorax [Avocettula] recurvirostris*). Their dependence on flower nectar also varies. Larger species tend to be more insectivorous, but in lean times even smaller species may subsist primarily on insects and other invertebrates for long periods. Not all hummingbirds pollinate the flowers from which they feed; some short-billed species routinely bypass the pollination mechanism by inserting their bills between the bases of the petals or through holes created by insects or other birds.

Of these characteristics, the one that sets hummingbirds apart from all other birds is their hovering, insectlike flight. Many birds, from ospreys to warblers, can remain stationary in midair for a few wingbeats, but only hummingbirds have the ability to do so almost indefinitely, as well as to fly backward, straight up and down, and side to side. Though all hummingbird species can

Hummingbirds do not always pollinate the flowers they visit. (Broad-billed Hummingbird at Sultan's Turban Hibiscus)

hover, some find this ability less useful than others. On the high slopes of the Andes Mountains of South America, where the thin air makes even normal flight difficult, hummingbirds such as the Bearded Helmetcrest (*Oxypogon guerinii*) feed while clinging to flowers and even hunt insects on the ground.

Based on similarities in anatomy and biochemistry, the hummingbird family, Trochilidae, is usually placed in the order Apodiformes with the swifts (family Apodidae), extraordinary aerialists in their own right. This is still a subject of debate, however, and a few authorities, including Monroe and Sibley (1993), place hummingbirds in their own order, Trochiliformes. The family Trochilidae is what taxonomists refer to as a "natural" family, one in which all members are clearly related to one another. Its approximately 340 species are divided into two subfamilies: hermits and their relatives (Phaethornithinae) and typical hummingbirds (Trochilinae). The hermits, approximately three dozen species found mostly in tropical lowlands from southern Mexico to northeastern Argentina, are the least colorful and perhaps the most primitive of hummingbirds. Many members of this subfamily sport dramatically decurved bills, pointed tails, and bold face markings, and males of many species gather at communal courtship sites known as leks to sing and display for females.

The members of the subfamily Trochilinae are far more numerous and diverse, encompassing extremes of size, shape, plumage color and ornamentation, sexual dimorphism, and habitat. They include such remarkable species as the Andean Hillstar (*Oreotrochilus estella*), which roosts and nests in caves to survive the bitter cold of its high-mountain habitat, and the rare Marvelous Spatuletail (*Loddigesia mirabilis*), whose long, wiry outer

The sunbirds of the Old World tropics fill an ecological niche similar to that of hummingbirds but are unable to hover at flowers. (Variable Sunbird, Nectarinia venusta)

tail feathers curve gracefully over each other in nature's own version of art nouveau.

Members of the family Trochilidae go by a variety of names around the world. Many of these are based on the sound of the birds' wings, including the Mayan *tz'unun* and Spanish *zumbador* as well as "humbird," the name coined by early English colonists. Some, such as the Spanish *chuparosa,* Portuguese *beijaflor,* and French *suce-fleur,* were inspired by the birds' relationship with flowers. A few even refer to the birds' small size and insectlike flight, such as the French *oiseau-mouche* and Spanish *pájaro mosca,* both of which mean "fly bird." Europeans were first introduced to hummingbirds by native people of the Caribbean, and versions of the Arawak word *colibrí* have been adopted by speakers of German, Portuguese, French, and Spanish.

The English language has only a single word relating to hummingbirds in general, but different groups within the family have earned more varied and exotic names. The dazzling variety of shapes and colors of tropical hummingbirds inspired such evocative group names as topaz, sapphire, starfrontlet, woodnymph, coquette, metaltail, puffleg, firecrown, and sunangel. Far less imagination went into the naming of most North American hummingbirds, and these lackluster labels prevail even where justifiable alternatives exist. For example, the Blue-throated and Amethyst-throated Hummingbirds are members of the same genus as the mountain-gems but have never shared this charming name.

NATURAL HISTORY OF
NORTH AMERICAN HUMMINGBIRDS

The 17 species of hummingbirds that have bred in the United States and Canada represent approximately 5 percent of the world's hummingbird species. They are mostly small generalists, likely of relatively recent evolutionary origin as ranges expanded northward following the end of major glacial periods. Their nectar plants, too, are less specialized than hummingbird-pollinated plants of the tropics, suggesting recent divergence from insect-pollinated ancestors.

The distribution of species in North America reflects both the geographic challenges to migration and the opportunities created by diverse habitats. The formidable migration barrier of the Gulf of Mexico, combined with the relative monotony of the primeval eastern forests, explains the presence of a single breeding species, the Ruby-throated Hummingbird, east of the Mississippi River. The varied topography and habitat types of the West and its overland migration routes led to the evolution of a wider diversity of hummingbird species to exploit them. The diversity of breeding species increases dramatically along the Mexican border between western Texas and southeastern Arizona, thanks to the variety of elevations and habitats within a small geographic area and proximity to the tropics, the ancestral home of all hummingbirds.

HUMMINGBIRD GENERA

Our concepts of the relationships among the species of North American hummingbirds have remained relatively stable in recent times. Recent advances in the study of DNA are providing evidence that may result in changes in the total number of recognized genera and species in coming years, but these changes are unlikely to affect North American hummingbirds at the species level.

The 31 species of hummingbirds covered in this guide are currently placed in 18 genera. Some of these, particularly among the "flame-throated"group, are recognized as closely related and may be combined in the future. Others, such as *Amazilia* and *Hylocharis,* are collections of superficially similar species that may belong in two or more genera. With minor exceptions, both the genus and species names used in this guide and the order in which they are presented are based on the *American Ornithologists' Union Check-list,* seventh edition (1998) and its supplements. Taxonomists do not always agree on the evolutionary relationships between hummingbird genera and species, and alternative views of these relationships are discussed briefly.

Campylopterus (Wedge-tailed Sabrewing): A genus of large tropical hummingbirds, most of which are called sabrewings because of the dramatically flattened and thickened shafts of the outer primary feathers in adult males. Bills range from straight to slightly decurved, and tails are long, often with conspicuous white markings. The sexes may be either similarly subdued in plumage, as in the Wedge-tailed Sabrewing, or dramatically different, as in the Violet Sabrewing *(Campylopterus hemileucurus).* Males of some species are noted for their complex songs and accompanying wing-waving displays. The modified primaries inspired the genus name, which comes from the Greek for "curved wing."

Colibri (Green Violet-ear): Known as violet-ears for the patch of elongate blue-violet to violet feathers below and behind the eye, these medium to large hummingbirds live on tropical mountain slopes. This is one of the few groups of hummingbirds for which evidence suggests that males may have some involvement in nesting and rearing of young, though confirmation of this is complicated by the difficulty of distinguishing between the sexes by plumage alone. The genus name comes from the Arawak language spoken by indigenous peoples of the Caribbean.

Anthracothorax (Green-breasted Mango): These large hummingbirds, found from Mexico through Central America and the Caribbean to South America, are called mangos for their attraction to the flowers of a common tropical fruit tree. Adult males are richly iridescent both above and below, usually with a patch or vertical stripe of velvety black on the underparts, while in most species adult females and immatures of both sexes have mostly white underparts divided by a narrow, dark vertical stripe. The genus name is derived from Greek words meaning "coal breast."

Orthorhyncus: The single species in this genus, the Antillean Crested Hummingbird, is endemic to the eastern Caribbean islands, though its closest relatives are found in northern South America. The pointed metallic green crest of the adult male is unique among hummingbirds recorded north of Mexico. It is apparently most closely related to another monotypic genus, *Chrysolampis*, though it also shows affinities to other crested hummingbirds of northern and central South America. DNA evidence suggests a fairly close relationship with the emeralds (*Chlorostilbon*) and sabrewings (*Campylopterus*). Its bill shape inspired the genus name, which in Greek means "straight nose."

Chlorostilbon (Cuban, Canivet's, and Golden-crowned Emeralds): This widespread genus of small long-tailed hummingbirds, most of which are known as emeralds, is the subject of some taxonomic controversy, with disagreement on the total number of species. Continental populations distributed from central Mexico through Central and South America are distinguished from one another primarily by slight differences in length and coloration of tail and bill and may represent between two and eight species. Insular forms such as the Cuban Emerald also show slight differences from one island group to the next but because of their isolation are generally accepted as full species. The genus name translates from Greek as "glittering green." "Emerald" is also used as a group name for a few species in the genera *Amazilia* and *Elvira*.

Cynanthus (Broad-billed Hummingbird): These small active hummingbirds are primarily Mexican in distribution, with only one of two species entering the southwestern United States. Plumage characteristics, voice, and bill color suggest a close relationship to the emeralds of the genus *Chlorostilbon*. The name, perhaps inspired by the plumage and body language of the male Broad-billed Hummingbird, apparently combines a misspelled Greek root meaning "blue" with the genus name of the tail-bobbing American Pipit (*Anthus rubescens*).

Hylocharis (White-eared and Xantus's Hummingbirds): This group of small hummingbirds with red and black bills includes two distinct groups that likely belong in different genera. The two northernmost species share bold white eye-stripes and other features lacking in other members of the genus and are often separated into the genus *Basilinna*. *Hylocharis* translates as "woodland loveliness," while *Basilinna* refers to a ruler or monarch.

Amazilia (Berylline, Rufous-tailed, Cinnamon, Azure-crowned, and Violet-crowned Hummingbirds): The largest of all hummingbird genera is represented in the United States and northern Mexico by six species. All are medium-sized birds with few differences between male and female, even in size and bill length. These largely sedentary birds are common in the humid tropics from Mexico to South America. Within this genus are four distinct groups, each probably worthy of generic status in its own right. Three of these groups include northern species: *Amazilia*, characterized by tails that are largely rufous or cinnamon with some green or bronze iridescence; *Agyrtria*, with largely white underparts and dull green or bronze tails; and *Saucerottia*, in which tail color is red-brown to blackish overlaid with blue to purple iridescence. The genus was apparently named after the fictional Inca heroine of an eighteenth-century novel set in Peru.

Lampornis (Amethyst-throated and Blue-throated Hummingbirds): These medium to large hummingbirds of mountain forests sport bold white eye-stripes. The two rather dull colored northern species are closely related and bear far more resemblance to each other than either does to the more southerly species. The Central American species are known as mountain-gems. The name is derived from Greek words meaning "torch bird" or "radiant bird."

Eugenes (Magnificent Hummingbird): This genus of large, long-billed mountain hummingbirds may contain either one widespread species or two closely related ones. Sexual dimorphism is dramatic: adult males are dark with brilliantly iridescent gorget and crown, while females resemble overgrown Ruby-throated or Black-chinned females. Immature males wear a unique plumage intermediate between those of females and adult males. Its place in the hummingbird family tree is uncertain, but its closest relatives may be the brilliants *(Heliodoxa)* of Central and South America or the mountain-gems *(Lampornis)* of Mexico and Central America. The name means "well born" in Greek.

Heliomaster (Plain-capped Starthroat): Known as starthroats because of the gorget pattern of the southernmost species, the four members of this genus all have very long bills. As in *Lampornis*, the least colorful member of this group of large hummingbirds is also the most northerly in distribution and the only one to reach the United States. The two most northerly species are sometimes separated into the genus *Anthoscenus*. *Heliomaster* translates as "sun seeker."

Calliphlox (Bahama Woodstar): The status of this genus within the woodstar-sheartail group is uncertain. It may include as few as one or as many as 11 species. Though currently assigned to *Calliphlox*, the Bahama Woodstar and two close relatives are sometimes separated into the genus *Philodice*. The name is compounded from the Greek roots *kalos*, "beautiful," and *phlox*, referring to a flame or a type of flower.

Calothorax (Lucifer Hummingbird): This genus consists of two small slender species with slightly decurved bills that suggest mild feeding specialization. Males have long forked tails and purple gorgets with elongated feathers. *Calothorax* is part of the woodstar-sheartail group, which includes 9 other species of small long-tailed hummingbirds currently placed in 5 genera. These genera form a subset of the "flame-throated" hummingbird group that includes most familiar North American genera. The unusually long gorget inspired this genus name, which means "beautiful breast" in Greek.

Archilochus (Ruby-throated and Black-chinned Hummingbirds): These small "flame-throated" hummingbirds are characterized by adult males with notched tails, modified inner primaries, and iridescent gorgets bordered at the top by velvety black. Females and immature males have tails that are banded at the corners in gray-green, black, and white. The two species are east-west counterparts and largely to completely migratory, specialists in taking advantage of the short-term bounty of northern summers. Their medium-length to long bills show no specialization for particular flowers or foraging style. Males perform dramatic display flights that function both in territoriality and courtship. This genus is closely related to both *Calypte* and *Selasphorus*; some authors have suggested merging the three into one. The genus was named for an early Greek poet famous for biting satire and cowardice in battle.

Calypte (Anna's and Costa's Hummingbirds): Like *Archilochus*, this genus of "flame-throated" hummingbirds contains just two species, but they are separated more by habitat preference than geography. Males are unusual among North American hummingbirds in having brilliantly iridescent crown patches the same color as their gorgets. Females are similar to *Archilochus* but often have irregular patches of metallic iridescence in the gorget. The tail feathers of adult males are partly translucent, the outer pair narrow and slightly curved. In both species, territorial males sing and perform dramatic display flights. The name, which means "covered" in Greek, may refer to the mythical sea nymph Calypso.

Stellula (Calliope Hummingbird): The single member of this genus is the smallest bird to breed in the United States. The plumage shows strong affinities to *Selasphorus*, though outer primaries of adult males show no modification for sound production. The male's gorget of narrow iridescent rays on a white background is unique among North American hummingbirds. The name means "little star" in Latin.

Atthis (Bumblebee Hummingbird): The two tiny species in this genus are unusual in that adult males have "femalelike" banding of rufous, black, and white at the corners of the tail. Their flight behavior mimics that of a large bee, which may help foraging individuals avoid detection in territories held by larger, more aggressive hummingbirds. As in most *Selasphorus*, adult males have narrowed outer primaries that create a distinctive sound in flight. The significance of the name is obscure, but it apparently refers to a citizen of the Greek city of Athens.

Selasphorus (Broad-tailed, Rufous, and Allen's Hummingbirds): The second most widespread hummingbird genus in the United

States consists of six small to medium-sized species found from south coastal Alaska to Panama. All species show significant rufous color in at least some plumages, and adult males of all but one have modified outer primaries that create trilling or whining sounds in flight. The three North American species range from highly migratory to sedentary within part of the range. The name is derived from Greek words meaning "light bearer."

HYBRIDIZATION

The polygamous nature of hummingbirds and the increasing overlap of ranges and habitats contribute to the occurrence of hybrids. Twenty-four hybrid combinations have been identified among 18 of the 31 species covered in this guide. This unusually high level of hybridization is made all the more remarkable by the fact that the vast majority of known hummingbird hybrids are between species in different genera. Most combinations involve similar species in closely related genera, and it has been argued from the frequency of hybridization that not all of these genera are valid. However, many intergeneric pairings involve species exhibiting dramatic differences in size, plumage, behavior, and even habitat. Intergeneric hybrids are presumed to be sterile, but hybrids between Anna's and Costa's Hummingbirds, both in the genus *Calypte*, have backcrossed to both parent species in captivity.

Hybridization can explain some, but certainly not all, ambiguous hummingbirds. Typical hybrids blend elements of the two parent species in both physical and behavioral attributes, but the results are not always predictable. Identification has traditionally been scholarly but speculative, based on comparisons of characteristics observed in the hybrid with those of possible parent species. Modern techniques for analyzing genetic material promise to verify these tentative identifications, but until this technology becomes widely available, suspected hybrids should continue to be carefully documented by a combination of more traditional techniques, including still photography, videography, audio recording, and in-hand measurements taken during banding.

PLUMAGE AND MOLT

Iridescence is the dominant component of the plumage color of most hummingbirds. These shimmering, changeable hues are created by the common pigment melanin, which normally absorbs light to produce blacks, grays, and browns. In the iridescent plumage of hummingbirds, melanin becomes a structural ele-

The plumage colors of hummingbirds are the result of both pigments and iridescence. (Close-up of rump of Rufous Hummingbird)

ment used to reflect and refract light. The pigment occurs in flattened particles called *platelets,* each of which encloses minute air bubbles that act like tiny prisms, breaking white light into its component colors before reflecting it back out of the feather. The platelets are arranged in 7 to 15 tightly packed parallel layers beneath the cortex, the transparent outer layer of the feather's barbules. As different wavelengths of light pass through and reflect off these layers, interference effects cause some to reinforce each other while others are canceled out, leaving a narrow range of wavelengths to be reflected back to the observer's eye. The thickness of the platelets and the size of the enclosed air bubbles determine the range of wavelengths, and therefore the colors, of the light reflected, while the number of layers influences the intensity of the iridescence.

In the body plumage of hummingbirds, the surfaces of the barbules are curved to capture and reflect light from many directions, resulting in a satiny iridescence visible from most angles. In the "metallic" feathers most commonly seen in the gorget and crown, however, the reflecting surface of each barbule is flat and aligned in the same plane as other barbules in the feather to create a mirrorlike flash of color. In courtship displays, many male hummingbirds use this characteristic to best advantage by fanning the gorget to keep the plane of the feathers perpendicular to the female's line of sight.

A hummingbird's iridescent colors are artifacts of the moment, changing with the relative positions of feather, viewer, and light source. This is especially true of the highly specialized metallic colors. From different angles, the gorget feathers of an adult male Rufous Hummingbird may appear scarlet, red-orange, yellow-orange, golden yellow, chartreuse, or dull blackish. Iridescent colors

Understanding molt cycles can be an aid to identification. This hybrid Anna's × Calliope molted in mid-summer like its Anna's parent.

tend to shift toward the violet end of the spectrum as the angle between the feather's surface and the viewer's line of sight decreases. This phenomenon makes blue and violet the most elusive of iridescent colors, as from most angles such feathers appear black.

In its more normal role, pigment also produces blacks, grays, browns, tans, and earthy reds and oranges in the plumage of hummingbirds. Though these colors do not change with the angle of the light, the surface structure of the feather may create a subtle overlay of iridescent color. Carotenoid pigments, which create the brilliant reds, oranges, and yellows of birds such as warblers, orioles, and goldfinches, play little or no role in the plumage color of hummingbirds. Experiments demonstrating that some hummingbirds can see ultraviolet light suggest that there may be colors and patterns in their plumage that are invisible to the human eye.

The most common color abnormalities recorded in North American hummingbirds are forms of albinism, in which pigment in the feathers, skin, and other parts is reduced or absent. The white feathers of affected birds do not show a pearly iridescence, because the missing pigment is needed to create the structures that produce the iridescent colors. A total lack of pigment in all parts of the body results in entirely white plumage and pink or reddish eyes, bill, and feet, a rare condition known as *complete, total,* or *perfect albinism. Incomplete albinism* is a more common mutation in which pigment is missing from some combination of plumage, eyes, and skin but not all three. Such a bird might have pure white feathers but normally pigmented eyes, bill, and feet. In *imperfect albinism* or *leucism,* pigment production is drastically reduced or one type of pigment is missing altogether, creating a faded or pastel appearance. Leucistic birds often show "shadow markings" of gray, tan, beige, or pale rufous, especially in the tail, which may aid identification. Birds with complete, incomplete, and imperfect albinism probably seldom survive to reproduce. Not only are they more conspicuous to predators, but the absence or deficiency of pigment can impair eyesight, interfere with regulation of body temperature, and cause feathers to wear more quickly, reducing flight efficiency and insulation.

Perhaps the most common plumage abnormality is *partial albinism,* in which white feathers occur individually or in patches among normally colored feathers. Through selective breeding, similar mutations have produced distinctive strains of domesticated animals, from goldfish to horses. Partial albinism is not always a hereditary, or even congenital, condition, however. Mature hummingbirds will occasionally acquire a few to many white or partially white feathers, perhaps as a consequence of aging, autoimmune disorders, or external factors such as environmental contaminants, chronic skin irritation, or dietary deficiencies.

Rarer and less obvious than albinism is *melanism,* an excess of pigment that results in overall darker colors, often imparting bronzy or coppery tones to normally green iridescence. Though rare in North American hummingbirds, melanism occurs regularly in a few tropical species. Less drastic mutations can produce subtle but noticeable color differences. This phenomenon has given rise to different colors of gorgets in isolated populations of the Volcano Hummingbird (*Selasphorus flammula*) in Costa Rica, but it is also occasionally seen in North American species. Wear and exposure to sunlight can produce similar changes in feather color. The gorget feathers of male Anna's Hummingbirds are rose red when fresh but may turn coppery red or reddish bronze before the summer molt.

Physical differences between males and females are known collectively as *sexual dimorphism,* and in hummingbirds these differences are usually most conspicuous in the plumage. In species in which adult male and female are dramatically different in appearance, the plumage of immature males is usually most similar to that of adult females, with both showing more specialization in feather shape and color than the plumage of immature females. In species in which the adult male displays an iridescent gorget, immature males often have broad dusky or dully iridescent centers to the feathers of the gorget area, creating a "five o'clock shadow." The shape of this dusky area, particularly its lower border, can help determine the species of young males even when no iridescent feathers are present. Adult female Black-chinned and Ruby-throated Hummingbirds often show similar markings on the throat, though typically concentrated toward the center of the gorget. In Rufous, Allen's, and Anna's, adult females typically have a few to many iridescent feathers in the gorget and may be mistaken for young males; however, each feather is smaller and has a more limited area of iridescence, unlike the broad mirror-like feathers characteristic of males. These scaled-down gorget feathers are also seen less consistently in Costa's, Broad-tailed, and Calliope.

Molt is the periodic loss and replacement of a bird's feathers, usually the entire set in a single cycle. Understanding how molt cycles vary by species and age can be useful in identification. Unlike some colorful songbirds such as the Indigo Bunting and American Goldfinch, hummingbirds do not have different breeding and nonbreeding plumages and molt only once per year. Because this process is stressful, birds usually molt during periods when they are neither breeding nor migrating. Most North American hummingbirds undergo the process in winter in the tropics, out of sight of northern observers, but a few molt on different schedules. Anna's and Costa's breed early, beginning in winter, and molt during their late summer nonbreeding season. The nesting season for Violet-crowned Hummingbirds is divided between early spring and the summer rainy season, and molt takes place between the two.

Young birds typically molt later than adults, often not completing the change into adult plumage until well into the following year's nesting season. In most North American hummingbirds the first molt produces a plumage indistinguishable from that of older adults. However, in a few species this molt is incomplete or full color is not attained until the second molt, allowing some birds to be accurately aged well into their second year of life. Accidental loss of feathers can result in premature acquisition of adult characteristics. It is not uncommon to see young males with tail feathers that are completely adult in shape and color or intermediate between immature and adult.

The soft contour feathers that cover the body are lost and replaced throughout the molting process, with the feathers of the male's gorget usually among the last to be replaced. The 10 primary feathers of the wing are typically replaced in order from innermost toward the wingtip, with the exception that the outermost primary (P10) is next to last to be replaced. The five pairs of tail feathers, or rectrices, are also molted in a specific sequence, from the center of the tail (R1) to the outside (R5), usually beginning after wing molt is well under way or complete. Replacement of wing and tail feathers is normally symmetrical on each side of the body, which helps retain balance in flight. Wing or tail feathers missing from one side only or large sections of missing body feathers indicate accidental loss during combat or close encounters with predators rather than normal molt. Feathers lost accidentally are replaced within a few weeks, while those that are damaged but not lost are replaced during the next normal molt.

Birds in fresh plumage often show pale, fringelike feather edges. These edges are broader and more conspicuous in young birds and wear away over time, making them a useful clue to a bird's age. In most species these edges are buff to pale grayish, contrasting with the green iridescence of the upperparts and giving the back a scaly appearance. However, in a few species, including Rufous and Allen's, these edges are rusty to cinnamon and may be difficult to see against the normal rufous tones of the plumage.

HABITATS

North American hummingbirds have adapted to a wide variety of environments, including desert scrub, shady forest edges, coastal chaparral, and alpine meadows. For at least part of the year, these habitat types meet the birds' basic daily needs for nectar, insect prey, and protection from weather and predators as well as providing safe nesting sites and sufficient food for raising young. The less critical demands of the nonbreeding season allow more latitude in habitat selection, and even grasslands, marshes, and coastal dunes may be visited during migration.

The diversity of habitats found across North America enables similar hummingbird species to coexist through specialization. Ruby-throated and Black-chinned Hummingbirds are closely related and so similar as to be difficult to tell apart in some plumages. In the narrow zone where their breeding ranges overlap, however, the Ruby-throated nests primarily in river-bottom forest while the Black-chinned prefers more open uplands. In California and the desert Southwest, the ranges of Costa's and Anna's overlap extensively, but the two species remain largely separate because of the Costa's ability to exploit drier habitats. Habitat requirements tend to become narrower at the fringes of a species' range. Blue-throated and Violet-crowned Hummingbirds show a stronger attraction to lush streamside vegetation within their limited U.S. ranges than they do in Mexico.

Some North American hummingbirds survive and even thrive where human activity has modified or replaced natural habitats. Gardens with nectar plants and artificial feeders provide resources for breeding, wintering, and migrating hummingbirds where natural nectar sources have been lost to development. Suburban and urban landscaping can also create favorable conditions in otherwise inhospitable areas. Anna's Hummingbird has been able to expand its breeding range to the north and east thanks to the shelter, nectar, and water provided by residential and recreational landscapes, and Rufous Hummingbird has become a regular wintering species along the Gulf Coast where feeders and winter-blooming exotic flowers provide reliable food sources. However, life in "civilized" landscapes has its risks, including pesticides, free-roaming cats, windows, air and water pollution, and continuing loss of habitat to urbanization.

EEDING

Their relationships with flowering plants have shaped virtually every part of hummingbirds' lives, from their size, shape, and hovering flight to mating habits and migration. The nectar of hummingbird-pollinated flowers is rich in sugars, especially sucrose (also found in sugar cane and sugar beets), and it is these energy-rich compounds that fuel the high metabolic rates necessary to achieve hovering flight. The reduction in body size that helps to optimize flight performance also results in a higher rate of heat loss, requiring enormous caloric intake simply to maintain the birds' normal body temperature.

A hummingbird's daily nectar requirement depends on a variety of factors, including activity level, air temperature, quality of available resources, and time of year. The nectar of hummingbird-pollinated flowers contains less than 30 percent sugar on average, and a bird may need more than one and a half times its body weight in nectar to meet its daily energy needs. The liquid is licked up rather than sucked, moving by capillary action from the forked tip of the tongue through two partial tubes formed by its thin membranous edges before being squeezed into the throat for swallowing. After feeding, a hummingbird may extend its tongue completely several times, an action that helps clear nectar residue from the mouth and also allows the remarkable length of the tongue to be seen.

Digestion of nectar is amazingly rapid and efficient. The liquid passes entirely through the digestive system in less than 20 minutes, during which time the gut can extract virtually all of the sugars. Some of the remaining water is utilized by the body or evaporated through the respiratory system, but the rest must be eliminated as waste. Like lizards, snakes, and other reptiles, most birds have highly efficient kidneys that conserve water by concentrating the waste from protein digestion into uric acid, the whitish semisolid material that gives the droppings their characteristic appearance. Hummingbirds are among the few bird species that must manage a chronic water surplus by excreting liquid urine. When nectar is plentiful, a hummingbird's daily urine output may exceed 80 percent of its body weight.

The relationship between hummingbirds and their flowers is a mutualistic one, with both partners receiving benefits. Many plants are self-sterile and require cross-pollination to produce seed. A hummingbird's voracious appetite and high mobility improve the chances that the pollen it carries on its bill, throat, or crown will be from a different plant of the same species, perhaps from a population miles away. Few insects travel such long distances between feeding sites, and so they are not as efficient at maintaining the genetic diversity of their nectar plants. Hummingbirds are also superior pollinators in environments where cool, cloudy, or rainy conditions hamper insect activity.

In the process of coevolution, plants have developed characteristics that accommodate the needs of their pollinators while limiting competition from nonpollinating species. These adaptations include nectar output and composition as well as specialized flower shape, position, and color. Typical hummingbird-pollinated flowers have horizontal or downward-facing tubular corollas in shades of red, orange, or bright pink. That these "warm" colors are also common in the iridescent plumage of male hummingbirds suggests that these birds' vision, like our own, is particularly sensitive in the long-wavelength end of the spectrum. Similarity in flower color and shape may function like the sign of a popular fast-food franchise, triggering instant recognition of an otherwise unfamiliar food source, but it also helps to exclude competitors. Red attracts little attention from bees, whose vision is most acute in the shorter wavelengths, and long narrow flowers provide further protection against nectar theft.

Despite the predominance of certain hues in hummingbird-pollinated flowers, color is far less important in determining a bird's "favorite" nectar source than the quantity and quality of the nectar. When presented with a variety of flowers, hummingbirds will maximize their energy intake by selecting for highest nectar output and richest concentration of sugars, regardless of flower shape or color. Taste also ranks above flower color in nectar selection. Like humans, hummingbirds prefer sucrose over simpler sugars such as glucose and fructose. The nectar of hummingbird-pollinated flowers typically contains a high proportion of this sugar, whereas the simpler sugars dominate in the nectars of most insect-pollinated flowers.

Insects and other invertebrates make up a significant portion of a hummingbird's diet. Nectar is basically a solution of water, sug-

Bright red color and long stamens are common traits in hummingbird-pollinated flowers. (Fuchsia-flowered Gooseberry)

ars, and electrolyte salts, with only trace quantities of the essential nutrients that are abundant in the bodies of invertebrates. Most hummingbirds are enthusiastic and versatile predators, plucking gnats and flies out of the air, searching leaves and bark crevices for aphids and beetles, and even robbing spiders of their silk-wrapped prey. Larger species are often more insectivorous, taking nectar mainly in the morning and evening and during inclement weather. Both egg-laying and providing for rapidly growing nestlings require large quantities of proteins, amino acids, vitamins, minerals, and other nutrients not supplied by nectar, and nesting females spend relatively little time at flowers or feeders.

When nectar is in short supply, hummingbirds may survive on invertebrates alone or seek out other sources of sugar. Ruby-throated and Rufous Hummingbirds arriving on their northern breeding grounds drink tree sap from wells drilled by sapsuckers, a type of woodpecker, until the first flowers bloom. In fall, southbound migrants often gather in groves of oak trees along the Gulf Coast to lick the sap that oozes from acorn cups.

Despite their high metabolism, hummingbirds do not drink their fill at every opportunity. The additional weight of a crop full of nectar increases energy consumption, and frequent short feeding bouts during daylight hours can meet the bird's energy needs while maintaining peak flight efficiency. As night approaches, a hummingbird will feed as heavily as the nectar supply allows, storing as much as a third of its weight in nectar in its balloonlike crop. This reserve is digested as the bird sleeps, enabling it to survive its overnight fast while maintaining its normal resting metabolic rate. Under stressful conditions, such as cold temperatures, long nights, inadequate food supplies, or preparation for

In early spring, before their flowers bloom, hummingbirds may take advantage of the wells drilled by sapsuckers.

migration, a hummingbird may resort to torpor, a hibernation-like state in which breathing, heart rate, and body temperature are dramatically reduced. Though highly effective at conserving energy, torpor also increases the bird's vulnerability by greatly reducing its ability to respond to danger. Tropical hummingbirds apparently enter torpor more routinely than those in temperate zones, where a crop full of nectar can supply enough energy to survive the short summer nights.

AGGRESSION AND TERRITORIALITY

It will come as no surprise to anyone who has spent time observing hummingbirds that they are among the least social of all birds. In fact, much of their behavior is acutely antisocial, ranging from strained tolerance of other hummingbirds to violent confrontation. Most aggressive behavior is aimed at ensuring an adequate supply of nectar, and birds of either sex may defend feeding territories. The size of a feeding territory is largely dependent on the availability of nectar. A hummingbird must be able to defend enough flowers to meet its daily energy needs, and territories can be smaller where flowers are abundant and tightly clustered. Dominant individuals claim flower patches with the highest nectar output or sugar concentration, leaving those of lower quality to less assertive birds. Even a rich flower patch can be costly to

Territorial battles between hummingbirds rarely result in death for either party, but these two male Broad-tailed fatally impaled each other in a midair collision, perhaps when the trajectories of their courtship displays intersected.

defend in terms of the energy required when competitors are numerous, and territorial birds will selectively exclude competitors based on sex and species. Territorial males behave less aggressively toward females of their species, and the femalelike plumage worn by immature males of some species may reduce conflicts with adult males. When nectar is abundant, large hummingbirds such as the Blue-throated will often ignore smaller interlopers while continuing to challenge large competitors.

Some hummingbirds avoid the costs of territorial defense by "parasitizing" patches guarded by other birds. Small territory parasites such as the Bumblebee Hummingbird often feed quietly out of sight of the territory holder, while larger species such as the Magnificent Hummingbird simply ignore threats from smaller territorial birds. Where widely dispersed flowers make it impossible to defend an adequate nectar supply, the most effective strategy may be to travel from patch to patch along a regular foraging route, a behavior known as "traplining." Some species follow a predictable feeding strategy while others are more flexible, varying from territoriality to traplining depending on the abundance, richness, and spacing of nectar sources.

Aggression is not always directed at other hummingbirds. Territorial birds may defend nectar sources from potential competitors such as bees and small songbirds. Potential predators such as hawks, owls, jays, cats, and snakes may be mobbed by several individuals, one of the few examples of cooperative behavior among these nonsocial birds.

COMMUNICATION

Hummingbirds communicate through vocal and mechanical sounds and visual signals. Vocal sounds are divided into two basic groups: calls and songs. Calls are largely innate and communicate information about the bird's species, sex, age, or emotional state. Calls are typically used to intimidate competitors, express pain or fear, or draw attention to danger. Nestlings of most North American hummingbirds are silent, but calling begins within minutes after departure from the nest. The simple, plaintive peeps fledglings use to attract the mother's attention may be retained after independence and are often heard during territorial disputes involving young birds.

Simply defined, songs are those vocalizations that serve to advertise for mates and/or intimidate rivals. These range from relatively simple chips or peeps to varied and complex phrases. Usually it is males who sing, often beginning well before they attain mature plumage. However, the recent discovery that the female Blue-throated Hummingbird sings to advertise her desire to mate, a performance that often attracts several eager suitors, suggests that females of other species may also have songs. Learning often plays a role in the development of complex songs. An individual may copy song elements from neighbors, even other hummingbird species. Among birds, only parrots and songbirds share this ability to learn and repeat sounds.

The wings of most hummingbirds create a humming sound in flight, but a few species have modified primaries that produce distinctive trills, whines, or buzzes. These mechanical sounds are produced mainly by adult males and serve a similar function to

Though Anna's is the best-known vocalist among North American hummingbirds, males of many species sing complex songs.

Male hummingbirds orient their feathers toward rivals and potential mates to best display their brilliant iridescent colors. (Anna's Hummingbird)

songs; in fact, species with distinctive wing sounds usually do not sing. Though the sound-producing structures are typically fully developed only in adult males, adult females and immature males of some species have rudimentary versions of these structures and produce less conspicuous but still distinctive sounds in flight. The best-known wing sounds belong to male Broad-tailed, Allen's, and Rufous Hummingbirds, but male Black-chinned, Ruby-throated, Bumblebee, and Lucifer also have sound-producing structures. Tail feathers may also produce sounds during the spectacular dive displays performed by males of some species, including Costa's and Lucifer.

Visual signals also play an important role in the lives of hummingbirds. Tail movements are commonly used to intimidate rivals and advertise territorial claims. Hummingbirds of many species fan their tails in clashes with other birds over feeding rights. Dominant Blue-throated Hummingbirds call and flick their tails frequently while foraging, while subordinate individuals maintain a low profile to avoid attracting attention. In most North American species, territorial males adopt a conspicuous perch from which they flash their metallic iridescence at both rivals and potential mates.

In many species, the male performs spectacular *dive displays,* ascending to great heights before plunging straight downward toward the object of the display, which is most often a female but may also be a rival male. The more intimate *shuttle display* may precede or follow the dive display. The male approaches the female from directly in front or just above, weaving back and forth in shallow arcs while displaying the brilliant colors of gorget and crown.

The energy-rich diet of hummingbirds allows for successful single-parent families, emancipating males to devote all their energies to mating with as many partners as possible. Nest-building, incubation, and care of the young are entirely the responsibility of the female, and observations of male hummingbirds at nests usually suggest courtship or territoriality. In one remarkable instance, however, an adult male Anna's Hummingbird was observed feeding nestlings whose mother had disappeared.

Females begin nest-building before mating. The location selected may be the site of a successful nest from the previous season. It is not uncommon for a female to build successive nests within inches of one another, either within a season or from one season to the next. The female begins with strands of sticky spider silk, which she adheres to the site with wiping and stitching motions of her bill. Plant fibers such as thistle down and cattail fluff, secured with new layers of silk, are added for insulation and cushioning. The female shapes the developing mass into a cup by stamping her feet, rotating her body, and smoothing the outer edge with her chin. The outside of the nest may be left mostly bare or camouflaged with bits of lichen, tiny leaves, oak catkins, mosses, feathers, or similar material. In urban areas, pet hair, dryer lint, cigarette paper, and paint chips may be incorporated into the nest. The entire construction process typically takes less than a week, but the female will continue to add material to the nest during incubation.

Once the nest is almost complete, the female seeks out a male for mating. Males usually greet prospective mates with singing and dive displays. Unreceptive females may leave the male's territory or respond aggressively, but those that neither flee nor fight become the audience for the more intimate shuttle display. The male closes in on the female, swinging back and forth in pendulum-like arcs in front of or above her, flashing his brilliant colors. Courtship and mating usually take place within the male's territory or in some neutral area nearby, but in some species the male may accompany the female to her nesting territory or seek her out there for mating. The mating act itself is seldom observed but may take place on a branch, on the ground, or in flight. Exactly how a female hummingbird selects a mate is likely to remain a mystery, but the extravagant ornaments worn by males of many species are testimony to untold generations of females acting on innate concepts of male perfection. However, despite the assertiveness of many female hummingbirds in rejecting unwelcome suitors, forcible matings do occur.

Egg-laying takes place shortly after mating. Though the normal clutch size for all hummingbirds is 2, very rare nests contain 3 or even 4 eggs; these may be examples of egg dumping by a second female. The incubation period among North American hummingbirds ranges from 12 to 22 days, depending as much on external factors as on species. Larger species tend to have longer incubation periods, but cool weather or long absences by the female can slow development of the embryos and result in significant delays in hatching. During incubation, the female will spend most of her time at the nest, leaving only to feed, bathe, gather additional material, or defend the nesting territory. Even these short absences leave the nest vulnerable to predators, which are the most common cause of nest failure. Female hummingbirds are quick to attack other animals that present a threat to their eggs or young, including birds of prey, jays, wrens, squirrels, snakes, and lizards. Despite this vigilance, fewer than half of all hummingbird nests successfully produce fledglings.

The blind, helpless hatchlings are nearly naked, with sparse, wispy tufts of down on their backs. After the eggs have hatched, the female begins spending more time away from the nest gathering food. She regurgitates a slurry of partially digested insects into the open mouth of each nestling, appearing to pin it to the nest. Growth is rapid on this high-protein diet. True feathers quickly replace the down, and the young are well feathered and capable of maintaining their body temperature within 9 to 12 days of hatching. At this stage the mother no longer needs to brood the nestlings, and her visits to the nest become shorter. Between 15 and 20 days of age the young begin exercising their wings in preparation for their first flight. By this time the nest is crowded, and one or both nestlings may perch on the rim. The young will leave the nest, or fledge, 18 to 28 days after hatching, attracting their mother's attention with shrill peeps within minutes after taking their first flight. The nest is usually abandoned after the young have fledged, but on rare occasions one or both fledglings may return for a short period.

The young will remain dependent on their mother for one to four weeks as they mature and learn survival skills. She will continue to feed them as they strengthen their wings and learn prey-catching techniques and the locations of nectar sources. Once independent, the young birds will face the challenges of finding food and making their first migration with no assistance and little tolerance from their elders. Behaviors related to territoriality and courtship often develop early. Young males only a few weeks out of the nest may sing and ardently pursue and display for females. These "early bloomers" have little chance of successful mating until they acquire full adult plumage, which may require up to two molt cycles. Though young females typically become sexually mature by the next year's breeding season, their nesting success may not equal that of more experienced females.

Females may nest two or three times in a season, sometimes beginning a second nest even before the young have fledged from the first. After a complete nesting cycle, the nest is usually so fouled with droppings that it is seldom reused as is, but it may become the base for a new nest. Nests that fail early may be dismantled to be incorporated into a new nest in a more secure location. In some areas, prime nesting locations are rare enough that the same nest site may be used by successive generations of females.

MIGRATION

Migration is a way to exploit short-term opportunities in habitats that cannot support year-round populations. For most North American hummingbirds, this means traveling north in spring and south in fall, but the overall picture is far more complicated. Buff-bellied Hummingbirds nest from spring through early fall in southern Texas and northeastern Mexico, but after the breeding season some individuals follow the Gulf Coast north to winter as far east as northwestern Florida. Many Anna's Hummingbirds undertake an altitudinal migration, breeding in lower elevations from winter through spring, then moving to higher elevations by midsummer to take advantage of the abundance of mountain wildflowers. With the onset of fall, the birds begin leaving the higher elevations, and by December most are back on the breeding grounds.

In highly migratory species the timing and direction of migration are instinctive, and young hummingbirds make their first southward migration with no guidance from adults. In some species, apparent variations in the internal compass induce young birds to migrate in directions that hold little or no hope of overwinter survival. Rufous Hummingbirds are particularly prone to this, and young birds regularly stray to the eastern United States and have even been seen heading out over the Pacific Ocean. Individuals that reach the Southeast may be fortunate enough to find gardens and feeders, and these survivors may return to the same garden each winter for years. Those stranded in northern latitudes with no fat reserves on which to travel are doomed. Even if a wayward bird survives "rescue" and transport to an appropriate wintering location, it will likely follow its established migration route the next fall, ending up in the same inappropriate location.

Migration routes are refined through experience, and individual birds may develop different routes for each season. Ruby-throated Hummingbirds wintering in Central America take the most direct route available in spring migration, up the Yucatán Peninsula and across the Gulf of Mexico. This route would be dangerous in reverse, with a significant chance of missing the peninsula, which may be one reason many thousands of southbound Ruby-throateds follow the Gulf Coast through Louisiana and Texas. Rufous and Allen's Hummingbirds migrate mainly through the Pacific Flyway in spring migration, but the bounty of summer wildflowers in the Rocky Mountains and Sierra Madre of Mexico leads many to shift their southward migration inland.

Hummingbird migration is almost entirely diurnal and apparently triggered by changes in day length, or photoperiod. Most birds depart their nesting grounds while nectar is still abundant, strong evidence that weather and food availability have little direct influence on the timing of migration. In late summer, the urge to migrate is accompanied by an increase in appetite. Migrating hummingbirds engage in a virtual feeding frenzy, storing excess energy as fat to fuel the long journey ahead. A well-prepared migrant may double its body weight before departure, refueling along the way as conditions permit. This fuel reserve is particularly important for species that face migration barriers such as deserts and oceans but may also serve as insurance against destruction of habitat in migration corridors and stopover sites.

LIFE SPAN

Despite their diminutive size and high metabolism, hummingbirds can have surprisingly long life spans. A female Broad-tailed Hummingbird banded in Colorado exceeded 12 years of age, and even the tiny Calliope has reached a similar age in captivity. Such extremes are seldom reached, however. Many nestlings are eaten by predators or lost to late freezes or summer hailstorms, and only a small fraction of the young birds that reach independence live through their first winter. Even experienced adults are vulnerable to drought, storms, predators, and accidents. For most North American species, the average life span is three to five years.

Life for male hummingbirds can be particularly difficult. The physical demands of territorial defense and migration, often coupled with more conspicuous plumage and behavior and smaller body size, apparently take a disproportionate toll on males. Banding studies show significantly lower return rates for male Ruby-throated Hummingbirds, resulting in a sex ratio biased toward females. This has little or no impact on reproduction, as it would in species in which both parents cooperate in raising the young. The surviving males simply have more opportunities to pass on their arguably superior genes to the next generation.

RESEARCH

For all their familiarity, hummingbirds have proven to be frustrating subjects for scientific study. Their small size and nonsocial habits make direct observation difficult and challenge both traditional and newer methods of identification and tracking. Banding, a centuries-old marking method used to study thousands of other bird species, has proven to be the most effective means of studying hummingbirds both as individuals and as populations. Few researchers have the skills and patience required for the task of making and attaching tiny metal rings to minuscule feet, but those who have mastered this delicate procedure are contributing greatly to our understanding of hummingbird biology, ecology, behavior, and migration.

Hummingbirds can be captured using the fine nylon "mist nets" that are standard equipment for bird banders, but the more efficient method is to lure the birds into a trap baited with feeders or flowers. Though their intelligence makes hummingbirds more challenging to trap than most other birds, it also seems to minimize the stress they feel during capture and data collection. Some regular study subjects seem to take handling in stride, even reentering the trap within minutes of release.

Once in hand, the bird is fitted with a lightweight aluminum band printed with a unique number that will be its identification code for life. These numbers are assigned by the Bird Banding

Ordinary bird bands are too large and heavy for hummingbirds. (Female Magnificent Hummingbird in a swan-sized band)

Laboratory, a division of the United States Department of the Interior. Banders submit their records to BBL, which uses them to identify banded birds reported by other banders or members of the public. These records have provided invaluable information on longevity, survivorship, migration routes and timing, and site fidelity. (For information on reporting banded birds, see Resources for Hummingbird Watchers, p. 245.)

During its short time in captivity, a bird must be identified as to species, age, and sex, not always a simple task even in hand. Lengths of bill, wing, and tail; weight; plumage condition; and signs of breeding, disease, or parasites may also be recorded, and pollen samples or feathers may be collected for study. Most hummingbird banders offer each bird a drink of sugar water before release to compensate for lost feeding time, and the majority of birds eagerly take advantage of the free meal. The bird is then released to resume its normal activities. With luck, it will live a long life and continue to enhance our understanding of its kind through repeated encounters with researchers.

CONSERVATION

In the history of relationships between wildlife and humans, hummingbirds are virtually unique in being free of the kinds of negative perceptions by humans that have led to the persecution and extinction of so many other species. Their beauty, fearlessness, and near-magical qualities have long attracted human admirers—from the Aztecs, who believed fallen warriors were reborn as hummingbirds, to modern Americans, who view them more as fairy tale characters than as wild animals. Unfortunately, this fascination has its dark side. Native people all over the Americas have traditionally used dead hummingbirds as ornaments and charms, but the real slaughter began with the arrival of the first European explorers. Through the nineteenth and early twentieth centuries, hummingbirds were among the millions of wild birds killed to decorate parlors and ladies' fashions and to satisfy the egos of private collectors. Thousands more were captured alive to fill the demand for exotic aviary subjects. The few that survived capture and export often died on the long oversea passage from the Americas to Europe, and fewer still lived more than a few months in captivity. North American hummingbirds were protected from such exploitation by the Migratory Bird Treaty Act of 1918, but small-scale commercialization of some South American species continues today.

Human activities of less direct but equally lethal nature continue to be a major threat to hummingbirds. Large-scale clearing of natural vegetation for timber, agriculture, and residential and commercial development, whether on breeding or wintering grounds or in important migration corridors, often has devastating effects on hummingbird populations. Such development brings with it unnatural hazards such as pesticides, domestic cats, windows, and transmission towers, which take a continuing toll on even the most adaptable species.

Even parks, wildlife refuges, forest reserves, and other natural areas are not immune to the effects of human activities. Nectar plants thrive in the sunny clearings and rich soil left by natural forest fires, and long-term fire suppression results in a decline in nectar availability as well as loss of habitat to catastrophic wildfires. Extermination of large predators has led to overbrowsing by deer and increased rates of nest predation by smaller predators such as raccoons, squirrels, and jays. Overgrazing by livestock destroys both nectar plants and the shrub cover needed for shelter and nesting. Nonnative plants and animals, whether accidentally or deliberately introduced, crowd out or even kill native species. In the arid West, the demand for lawns, swimming pools, and golf courses is lowering water tables and drying up rivers and streams vital to nesting and migrating hummingbirds. Even the most remote wilderness areas are imperiled by air, water, and noise pollution and the effects of global warming and the destruction of the ozone layer.

Despite the overwhelming scale of these threats, it is possible for individuals to make a difference. Limiting use of pesticides in home and yard, keeping cats indoors, selecting native and noninvasive exotic plants for home and public landscapes, and practicing water conservation are all positive steps toward preserving local ecosystems and wildlife. Supporting community parks and open space preservation, habitat restoration projects, and environmental education programs can have far-reaching benefits for both wildlife survival and human quality of life. Most important of all is sharing one's appreciation of hummingbirds and other wildlife with family, neighbors, and public policy makers.

Watching Hummingbirds

ATTRACTING AND FEEDING

By far the best way to encourage visits by hummingbirds is to create a landscape that meets their basic needs for food, water, and shelter. Unfortunately, the expansive lawns so typical of modern suburbia fail to meet even minimal requirements for hummingbird habitat, and creating a haven from such a landscape may take many years. Fortunately, a growing list of resources is available to the beginning wildlife gardener, from books and videos to specialty nurseries and seed suppliers.

Nectar plants can be used to attract hummingbirds to virtually any setting, even the limited space of a patio, deck, courtyard, or apartment balcony. Colorful blossoms of all types will catch the eyes of passing migrants, but serious hummingbird gardeners choose plants that provide the quantity and quality of nectar the birds prefer. For maximum enjoyment as well as value to the birds, a hummingbird garden should include a variety of species that bloom sequentially over the entire season, from before the earliest spring arrival appears to after the last fall straggler takes its leave.

Many plants favored by hummingbirds are commonly available from mainstream seed companies or nurseries. These include annuals such as scarlet sage, Texas or tropical sage, and cypress vine; perennials such as four-o'clock, canna, pineapple sage, and bee balm; and woody plants such as trumpet creeper, coral honeysuckle, and Gregg sage. Tender plants such as fuchsias, "holiday" cacti, amaryllis, and many bromeliads also produce flowers that attract hummingbirds. (See List of Nectar Plants, p. 242, for scientific names.)

Favorite nectar plants of both hummingbirds and their human hosts vary regionally. In the eastern United States, jewelweed, cardinal flower, bee balm, coral honeysuckle, and trumpet creeper are widely used by Ruby-throated Hummingbirds. The mild climate of Florida and the Gulf Coast is favorable to both wintering hummingbirds and semitropical plants such as Turk's-cap hibiscus, shrimp plant, firebush, and various cupheas. In the western mountains, hummingbird favorites include columbines, Indian paintbrushes, larkspurs, penstemons, and skyrocket. Drought-tolerant plants for desert hummingbird gardens include ocotillo, chuparosa, desert honeysuckle, Gregg sage, and a wide variety of penstemons. Californians have many native nectar plants to choose from, such as bush-penstemons, pitcher sage, fuchsia-flowered gooseberry, and orange bush monkeyflower.

Shelter is a vitally important but often overlooked element in creating hummingbird habitat in the home landscape. A garden full of colorful flowers may attract the attention of passing migrants, but without cover for nesting and protection from weather and predators their visits will be short. Native trees and shrubs require minimal maintenance once established and serve as food plants for the birds' insect prey. Some woody plants, such as trumpet creeper, red buckeye, Mexican buckeye, white and twinberry honeysuckles, and various species of manzanita, provide both shelter and nectar. In coastal and desert regions that host hummingbirds year-round, conifers or broad-leaved evergreens provide essential protection from winter weather.

Hummingbird-friendly landscapes generally require less intensive management than traditional gardens. Native plants adapted to local soil type and rainfall will thrive and bloom without fertilizer, spraying, or heavy irrigation. Avoiding pesticides and other harsh chemicals reduces hazards to hummingbirds and other wildlife and encourages natural predators that keep insect pests in check. Periodic deadheading to remove wilted flowers can help prolong bloom, but pruning of shrubs and trees should be kept to a minimum to avoid removing sentinel perches and disturbing nests. Time saved in chores can be put to good use studying and enjoying the garden's birds, butterflies, and other visitors.

Fortunately for those with "brown thumbs," a junglelike landscape full of colorful flowers is not the only means of attracting hummingbirds. For at least a century, people have accommodated the birds' voracious appetite for nectar by providing sugar-water solutions in artificial containers. In the beginning, these feeders were little more than vials or jars decorated with red paint or a scrap of bright-colored cloth or paper. Though the fundamental principle remains the same, decades of experimentation and innovation have created greatly improved feeder designs. Today's top-of-the-line feeders are made from shatter-proof plastics that will last years in the sun without fading, yellowing, or cracking, with all parts easily accessible for thorough cleaning. Innovative features available in some models include post-mounting sockets, built-in ant moats, and optional barriers impassable to even the tiniest insects.

Hummingbird preferences are relatively unimportant in selecting a feeder, as the birds are adaptable and will learn to drink from virtually any container. More important considerations are durability, ease of cleaning and refilling, and resistance to common problems such as dripping, insects, and larger birds. Though commercial hummingbird feeders range in size from 3 to 96 ounces, smaller models reduce waste and simplify maintenance. A feeder holding 8 fluid ounces (237 ml) of sugar solution will fill the daily energy needs of 40 to 60 birds, a more than adequate supply under most circumstances. In peak activity periods, as during spring and fall migration, multiple feeders permit larger numbers of birds to feed under less stressful conditions. Feeders larger than 20 ounces are recommended only for feeding stations visited by hundreds to thousands of migrants per day.

A solution of four parts water to one part white table sugar is simple to prepare, economical, and remarkably similar to the natural nectar of hummingbird-pollinated flowers. The ratio need not be precise but should fall between three and five parts water to one part sugar. A solution weaker than 5:1 may be ignored by the birds, and one stronger than 3:1 may not provide sufficient water, particularly if no other nectar source is available. The sugar can be dissolved in either hot or cold water. Brief boiling or microwaving may help slow fermentation, but the solution must be cooled thoroughly before serving. Any unused solution should be refrigerated and used within a week.

Adding dye to the solution is both unnatural and unnecessary. Flower nectar is colorless, and the red color of the feeder is enough to attract the birds' attention. Field tests have shown that hummingbirds generally prefer plain sugar water over dyed solutions, and there is concern that chemical additives may be harmful to the birds' health. Substituting other common sweeteners for white sugar is another potential health hazard. Artificial sweeteners do not provide the energy the birds need and could result in starvation, and honey contains spores that can cause fatal infections.

Commercial feeder mixes, usually advertised as "instant nectar," are also not recommended. These come in three forms: pure sugar, sugar with additives such as dyes, preservatives, flavorings, and vitamins, and water with these additives to which sugar must be added. Nothing in these mixes justifies the cost, which is five to eight times that of a homemade sugar solution. Healthy, wild hummingbirds get all the major nutrients they need from their insect prey and do not need enhanced feeder solutions.

Sugar water is more perishable than seed, and hummingbird feeders should be cleaned and refilled with fresh solution every two to three days. At best, the birds will bypass a contaminated solution; at worst, they may drink it and become ill. Feeders may be cleaned in hot water alone or with a small amount of vinegar or bleach added. Soap and detergent should be used with care to avoid leaving residues, and feeders must be thoroughly rinsed before refilling. Specially designed feeder brushes make cleaning easier and more thorough.

Feeding stations in warm areas, including the Gulf and Pacific Coasts and desert Southwest, may have a year-round hummingbird clientele, but in most parts of North America, hummingbird season is all too short. In cooler regions, feeders may be filled and hung as early as a week before the first migrants are expected to arrive in spring and left out until a week or two after the last sighting in fall (see migration information in each species account). Contrary to widespread belief, leaving feeders out in fall will not cause normal birds to delay their migration but may help late migrants when natural food is in short supply.

Occasionally a hummingbird will linger into winter in a climate in which its only chance of survival is through human intervention. These individuals have not been seduced into staying by the presence of feeders but are weak, sick, injured, or disoriented. Depriving these birds of food is more likely to hasten their demise than to force them to move on to more favorable climates. The choice then becomes whether to let nature take its course or make an open-ended commitment to a bird in need. At the very least this entails providing thawed feeder solution up to several times each day, beginning at dawn. Unfortunately, the sense of triumph felt when a wintering bird survives to migrate in spring may last only until it returns to the same location the following fall and its hosts face the prospect of another winter of daily responsibility for its survival. Relocating the bird to a warmer climate, a process requiring federal and state permits and special equipment, has proven to be an unsatisfactory solution in most cases. All too often the capture is delayed until the bird has reached a critically weakened condition, greatly reducing its chances of surviving the stress of capture, confinement, and transport. Those birds that survive relocation may be permanently disoriented.

Though many hummingbird enthusiasts are content to observe and enjoy these fascinating birds in their own yards, most eventually develop an interest in seeing unfamiliar species or larger numbers. Popular tropical destinations such as Mexico, Costa Rica, and Ecuador are rich in hummingbird species, most of which are never seen in the United States. However, hot spots much closer to home offer equally satisfying hummingbird experiences, from incredible numbers of a few species in important migratory corridors to near-tropical diversity in the southwestern border regions.

Following are the best places and times to see hummingbirds in the United States. Actual viewing sites vary from region to region but usually include public parks, botanic gardens, nature preserves, and private homes. State and regional bird-finding guides and wildlife viewing guides are the best sources of information on specific viewing opportunities.

THE SOUTHWEST (southern Arizona, southern New Mexico, western Texas): late April through July in mountain canyons and riparian areas for local breeders, including "specialties" such as Magnificent, Blue-throated, Violet-crowned, and Lucifer; late July through mid-September for breeding species, vagrants, and migrants (up to 15 species).

ROCKY MOUNTAIN FLYWAY (western Colorado, Utah, Nevada, northern Arizona, northern New Mexico): July through August for large numbers of breeding Broad-tailed and Black-chinned, migrating Rufous and Calliope.

PACIFIC FLYWAY (California, Oregon, Washington, southern British Columbia): mid-February through April along Pacific Coast for northbound Rufous and Allen's plus resident Anna's and Costa's; June through September in coastal plain and mountains for large numbers of Rufous, Allen's, Costa's, Anna's, and Black-chinned, occasional Calliope and Broad-tailed; Anna's common to abundant in winter in coastal southern California, Allen's year-round resident on Palos Verdes Peninsula (Los Angeles County) and nearby Channel Islands.

GULF COAST (coastal Texas, Louisiana, Mississippi, Alabama): August through September in wooded habitats for migrating Ruby-throated and Black-chinned; November through February in residential areas for small numbers of western hummingbirds, including Rufous, Black-chinned, Calliope, Broad-tailed, Allen's, plus Buff-bellied and Ruby-throated; Buff-bellied resident year-round in lower Rio Grande Valley of Texas.

MISSISSIPPI FLYWAY (Minnesota, Wisconsin, Illinois, eastern Iowa, Missouri, western Tennessee, western Kentucky, Arkansas, Louisiana, Mississippi): July through September for migration of Ruby-throated through woodlands and river valleys.

ATLANTIC FLYWAY (New Jersey, Pennsylvania south to Carolinas): July through early September for migration of Ruby-throated at Cape May, Hawk Mountain, other major migration corridors.

Many communities and nonprofit organizations in birding hot spots sponsor festivals featuring hummingbirds. Current festivals devoted to hummingbirds or with a significant hummingbird component include:

RUFOUS HUMMINGBIRD FESTIVAL, Ketchikan, Alaska; April

SAGE AND SONGBIRDS FESTIVAL AND GARDEN TOURS, Alpine, California; May

HUMMINGBIRD FESTIVAL, Starsmore Discovery Center, Colorado Springs, Colorado; May

FIESTA DE LAS AVES, Bisbee, Arizona; May

KERN RIVER VALLEY HUMMINGBIRD CELEBRATION, Audubon Kern River Preserve, Weldon, California; July–August

DAVIS MOUNTAINS HUMMINGBIRD ROUND-UP, Fort Davis, Texas; July–August

HUMMER FEST, Golden Pond, Kentucky; August

SUMMER WINGS FESTIVAL, Rio Grande Nature Center, Albuquerque, New Mexico; August

SOUTHWEST WINGS BIRDING FESTIVAL, Bisbee, Arizona; August

XTREME HUMMINGBIRD XTRAVAGANZA, Lake Jackson, Texas; September

HUMMER/BIRD CELEBRATION, Rockport, Texas; September.

How to Identify Hummingbirds

Compared to some birding challenges, identification of North American hummingbirds is relatively straightforward. Geographic variation is limited, and most birds assume complete adult plumage with their first molt. Identification is complicated, however, by the chameleon-like qualities of iridescence, the often nondescript plumages of females and immature males, similarities among closely related species, and hybridization. There is also individual variation, especially in color and pattern of the gorget and tail in females and immature males. As with other birds, wear, staining, molt, and accidental loss of feathers can radically alter appearance. Pollen acquired while feeding at flowers is usually seen as a streak, patch, or wash of color on the crown or throat; these "false field marks" may be white, yellow, orange, or even reddish, depending on the source.

Hummingbird identification is further complicated by the tendency of some species to wander far outside their expected range. Because of lack of both experience and expectation, many birders find themselves ill prepared to face the challenge of distinguishing Rufous from Broad-tailed or Black-chinned from Ruby-throated. Even expert birders have been blinded by assumptions about a bird's identity only to discover their mistake when more open-minded observers raised questions about the original identification.

The most effective means of learning to identify hummingbirds is to spend time studying familiar species. The goal is not only to recognize "something different" at a glance but to use intimate knowledge of common species as a basis for comparison. Too often observers who report a rare species cannot provide convincing details because they do not know the field marks, behavior, plumage variation, and other characteristics of the common local species well enough to rule it out. Keeping a sketchbook or note-

Pollen deposits on the crown, throat, or bill can confuse identification. (Costa's Hummingbird)

book and studying field guide illustrations and descriptions of familiar species in comparison with other possibilities helps to fix the most important characteristics in the mind for instant recall.

When observing a hummingbird, the following characteristics will be most helpful in identification:

- size in relation to other birds, feeders, other objects of known size
- overall proportions of head, tail, and body (usually similar in both adult males and female-plumaged birds)
- shape, pattern, color, and movement of tail
- length, proportions, and color of bill
- shape, pattern, and color of gorget, if present
- calls, songs, and wing sounds
- molt and condition of plumage.

It is often easier to determine a bird's age and sex than its species, and doing so may bring the bird closer to positive identification. In general, immature females are most "generic" and difficult to identify by plumage alone, but behavior and voice prove helpful in many cases.

Sometimes a bird does not seem to fit any particular species. Before giving up, select the species it most closely resembles and consider the following:

- Is any difference in body shape attributable to posture, fat deposits, or fluffing of feathers?
- Are colors influenced by angle of light or reflection from nearby surfaces such as feeders?
- Are anomalous markings due to feather wear or loss, staining, deposits of pollen, or pigment abnormalities such as leucism or partial albinism?
- Is length, shape, or color of tail or wings attributable to wear, molt, or accidental loss of feathers?
- Does the bird show characteristics intermediate between two species, suggesting that it may be a hybrid?

If the bird continues to defy efforts at identification, taking still photos and video recordings to share with knowledgeable persons may shed light on the mystery. However, it is important to accept that not all hummingbirds can be positively identified.

Parts of a Hummingbird

gorget (throat)
breast
side
belly
undertail coverts
flank

upper mandible
nape
back
lower mandible
chin
throat
breast
uppertail coverts
rump
R1
R2
rectrices
R3
R4
R5
secondaries
P1
P2
P3
P4 P5
primaries
P6
P7
P8
P9
P10

crown
hindcrown
forecrown
nape
lore
malar stripe
cheek
eye line (postocular line)

R5
R4
R3
R2
R1
R1
R2
R3
R4
R5

How to Use This Book

This guide is divided into two main sections: plates consisting of multiple photographs accompanied by brief descriptions, and species accounts accompanied by range maps. Both sections should be consulted when working on an identification problem, as the text emphasizes behavior, voice, and other details that may not be obvious in the plates or their legends.

THE PLATES

The plates consist of photographs carefully selected to represent the range of plumages within each species. The familiar arrows of the Peterson System are used to draw attention to important field marks. Most plates are arranged with males on the left, females on the right. Most species are presented in reverse taxonomic order, beginning with the genus *Selasphorus*; this places the more familiar and widespread species at the front of the plates section, though the corresponding species accounts are arranged in the more usual order. Taxonomic order was ignored in a few places in order to group illustrations of similar but distantly related species, and in a few cases space constraints forced dissimilar species to share a plate. Separate plates of heads and tails also group similar species to facilitate comparison. These images are not to scale and are not intended to represent the actual size differences between species.

The legends on the page opposite each plate begin with a summary of basic information for each species followed by descriptions of the plumages illustrated and comparisons with any plumages not pictured. The page number of the corresponding species account and plate numbers of additional illustrations are included for cross-reference.

THE SPECIES ACCOUNTS

ENGLISH AND SCIENTIFIC NAMES: As with all living things, hummingbirds are known to science by their two-part scientific names, which are derived primarily from Greek and Latin. These names are assigned based on the original description of a species but are subject to change as scientists uncover new information on relationships between species. Scientific names are italicized; the first part, the genus, is always capitalized, while the second, the species name, is never capitalized. In addition, English-speaking ornithologists have assigned standardized common names to many hummingbirds, including all the species covered in this guide; these are proper names and are always capitalized. English and scientific names and the order of the species accounts are based primarily on the American Ornithologists' Union *Check-list of North American Birds,* seventh edition (1998), with minor exceptions.

INTRODUCTORY STATEMENT: Each species account begins with a short "character sketch" of the species, summarizing its most prominent attributes. Both total length and lengths of bill and tail are included to give a sense of proportions, particularly useful in making comparisons among similar species. Where applicable, older or alternate names are given in the introductory section of each account, along with the significance of many species names (see Hummingbird Genera for origins of genus names).

DESCRIPTION: This section includes complete physical descriptions by age and sex, beginning with features shared by all members of the species and continuing with specific characteristics distinguishing adult male, adult female, and immatures.

SIMILAR SPECIES: Those species likely to be a source of confusion are covered beginning with the most similar and focusing on those traits that distinguish each species from the subject of the account. In a few instances, species mentioned in this section are not illustrated or described elsewhere in the guide.

SOUNDS: Both vocalizations and mechanical sounds are covered in this section, including calls, songs, and wing sounds as applicable for each species. The descriptions are necessarily subjective, but every attempt has been made to be consistent. Through comparison of the text with actual vocalizations, the differences in tone and quality of sounds should become apparent.

BEHAVIOR: This section includes an overview of the species' behavior, including "body language" such as tail movements, feeding behavior, nectar sources, courtship, nest location and construction, and nesting season.

HABITAT: Since most species covered occur mainly or entirely outside the United States in winter, this section concentrates on breeding habitat within the United States and Canada. Breeding or residential habitat for species not known to nest within the United States is also described; wandering individuals may gravitate toward similar habitat types. Wintering or nonbreeding habitat is described if it varies from breeding habitat.

DISTRIBUTION: Breeding range is described first for highly migratory species, as is resident range for more sedentary species. Little is known about nonbreeding distribution for many species; information presented here is based primarily on the Birds of North America accounts and *A Guide to the Birds of Mexico and Northern Central America*. Variances from the range descriptions in these two sources reflect new information gleaned from numerous sources, including much unpublished data. Timing and routes of migration are described as applicable. Records from outside normal breeding and wintering range and migratory routes are summarized to give a picture of the pattern of vagrancy in the species.

STATUS AND CONSERVATION: Little information is available on the status of most hummingbird populations, but the information available, including factors known or suspected to affect populations, is summarized here. None of the hummingbirds covered in this guide are currently on the federal list of threatened and endangered species.

SUBSPECIES AND TAXONOMIC RELATIONSHIPS: Few North American hummingbirds show any significant geographic variation in plumage color, body size, bill length, and other characteristics used to define distinct populations within a species. The notable exception is Allen's Hummingbird, for which both distinguishing characteristics and range are described. For widespread tropical species, a brief description of the northernmost subspecies is included. This section also summarizes known or suspected relationships to other species, and lists reported hybrid combinations.

PLUMAGE VARIATION AND MOLT: As applicable, individual variations in plumage are covered in more depth here to complement the main plumage descriptions. Timing of molt for adults and immatures is a key element in identification of some hummingbirds; though poorly understood in some species and variable in others, the best available information is summarized here.

REFERENCES: The scientific and popular resources listed at the end of each species account were the most important references used in compiling the accounts and are a starting point for further reading about a species. Most of these are compilations of information gathered from a variety of primary sources, ranging from historical accounts to the most recent revelations of DNA research. Additional references consulted for the species accounts and introductory sections are listed in the Bibliography.

RANGE MAPS: The breeding and nonbreeding ranges and migratory routes of hummingbirds are dynamic, shifting in response to weather, natural forces such as fire, and the effects of human activities such as logging, grazing, farming, and urbanization. The range maps in this guide are based on information from a variety of sources, including the Birds of North America species accounts; *Focus Guide to Birds of North America*; *A Guide to the Birds of Mexico and Northern Central America*; *A Guide to the Birds of the West Indies*; regional reports from *American Birds/Field Notes*; Christmas Bird Count results; state bird record committee reports; breeding bird survey results; breeding bird atlas information; state, regional, and local checklists; and unpublished observations. Though every effort has been made to make these maps and the accompanying text as accurate, precise, and complete as possible, they are at best a general guide to hummingbird distribution and abundance. Local and regional bird-

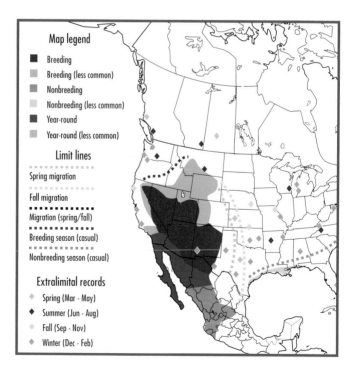

finding guides and checklists are the best resources for more specific information.

The maps employ a variety of colors, shadings, and symbols to depict the distribution and abundance of each species. Solid areas of color represent the normal range of a species during the breeding and nonbreeding seasons and year-round. This differs from the usual field guide treatment in that the breeding and nonbreeding seasons of hummingbirds are not always equivalent to summer and winter respectively. Lighter versions of each color are used on many maps to indicate areas where the species occurs regularly but is uncommon to rare or unevenly distributed ("local"), as is often the case where suitable habitat is scarce. Within the ranges indicated, a species is to be expected only in proper habitat and season (see species accounts for details). Where populations vary seasonally within a species' year-round range, the intensity of shading indicates its abundance in the breeding season.

Migration routes generally cover the entire area between the southern edge of a species' breeding range and the northern edge of its nonbreeding range. To avoid confusion, these routes are not mapped as separate shaded areas. For several well-known species, however, black or gold dashed lines indicate areas where the species is a casual or irregular resident or visitor in the nonbreeding season. Diamond-shaped icons represent vagrants, individual birds sighted or banded outside the usual limits of breeding or nonbreeding range or migratory routes, with colors indicating the period of the year in which the individual was observed. Overwintering vagrants may arrive as early as late summer and remain into early spring but are indicated by blue diamonds regardless of the date of arrival or departure. For most species, only sightings in the last 10 to 12 years are mapped; older records are included in the Distribution section of the species account. Range maps for species considered rare to accidental in the United States display all documented records, a few of which go back more than a century. In some cases, a single icon represents multiple records for the same location. Color-coded question marks indicate areas where status in the season indicated is uncertain.

SPRING MIGRATION MAPS: For a few well-known migratory species, separate migration maps use "isochron" lines to show average spring arrival dates in 10-day increments. These are based primarily on first-hand reports, collected and mapped by Lanny Chambers, with additional information from publications such as *American Birds/Field Notes*. Actual spring arrival varies with weather patterns and may occur earlier or later than indicated on these maps.

PLATES

PLATE 1

ALLEN'S HUMMINGBIRD
Selasphorus sasin

P. 226, PLS. 18, 19, 24

3.2–3.6" (8–9 cm). Common summer resident in coastal Califo
north to southern Oregon, permanent resident locally in south
California. *Similar in all respects to and very difficult to disting*
from Rufous Hummingbird (see text).

ADULT MALE. *Back mostly brilliant green;* rump, uppertail coverts ruf
Crown bright green; cheeks and eyebrows dull rufous. Underp
white with rufous "vest." Gorget brilliant scarlet to orange, appea
golden or even yellow-green from some angles. Black-tipped ruf
tail long, pointed, feathers becoming progressively narrower from
ner to outer pairs. *R5 extremely narrow and stiletto-like; R2 ta
smoothly to sharp point.* Modified wingtips make shrill metallic wh
in flight.

ADULT FEMALE. *Virtually indistinguishable from female Rufous Hummingbir*
the field. Back bright green, underparts white washed rufous on s
and flanks extending onto edges of rump. Face washed rufous. Go
creamy white to ivory, lightly to heavily spangled with green to bro
red-orange to coppery iridescence in center varies from a few sr
spangles to dense ragged-edge triangle or diamond. Rounded tail
tends well past wingtips. Extensive rufous in R3–5, less on R1
white tips on R3–5. R2 tapers smoothly at tip, R5 very narrow.

IMMATURE MALE. Similar to adult female, including *smooth taper of R2
narrowness of R5*, but gorget usually more heavily marked, often v
large mirrorlike metallic feathers in patches throughout gorget are:
concentrated in lower center.

IMMATURE FEMALE. Similar to adult female but with fewer and smaller go
markings (center of throat may be unmarked white), broader outer
feathers with less rufous, white tips on R2–5.

adult male Allen's

adult female Allen's

adult male Allen's

adult female Allen's

immature male Allen's

immature female Allen's

immature male Allen's

immature female Allen's tail

PLATE 2

RUFOUS HUMMINGBIRD
Selasphorus rufus

P. 221, PLS. 18, 19, 24,

3.5–4" (9–10 cm). Breeds in Northwest, common migrant in Paci
and Rocky Mountain Flyways, winters in Mexico and the Southea
vagrant elsewhere. Small, compact, with medium-short all-black b
and extensive rufous in plumage. Pugnacious and vocal, even in m
gration. *Females and immature males virtually indistinguishable fro
Allen's Hummingbird.*

ADULT MALE. *Back solid rufous, rufous with scattered green spangles (typica
or extensively green.* Crown bright green; cheeks and eyebrows dull r
fous. Underparts white with rufous "vest." Gorget brilliant scarlet
orange, appearing golden or even yellow-green from some angle
Black-tipped rufous tail long, pointed, feathers becoming progre
sively narrower from inner to outer pairs. *R5 narrow and knifelike, R
distinctly notched on inner web near tip.* Modified wingtips make shr
metallic whine in flight.

ADULT FEMALE. Bright green above, underparts white *strongly washed with r
fous on sides, flanks, and undertail coverts, extending onto edges
rump.* Face washed rufous. Gorget creamy white to ivory, lightly
heavily spangled with green to bronze; red-orange to coppery irid
cence in center varies from a few small spangles to dense ragged-ed
triangle or diamond. Rounded tail extends well beyond wingtips. E
tensive rufous in R3–5, less on R1–2; white tips on R3–5. *R2 usua
shows shallow indentation near tip,* R5 narrow. Outer primary (P1
tapers to narrow rounded tip (Allen's similar).

IMMATURE MALE. Similar to adult female, including *notched R2,* but usua
with extensive rufous in R1, gorget more heavily marked, often wi
large mirrorlike metallic feathers in patches throughout gorget or co
centrated in lower center.

IMMATURE FEMALE. Resembles adult female but typically with fewer a
smaller gorget markings (center of throat may be unmarked white
outer tail feathers broader with less rufous, small white tip on R2.

RUFOUS × CALLIOPE HYBRID. See Plate 30.

adult male Rufous

adult female Rufous

adult male Rufous

adult female Rufous wing

immature male Rufous

immature female Rufous

immature male Rufous

immature female Rufous

PLATE 3

BROAD-TAILED HUMMINGBIRD
Selasphorus platycercus

P. 216, PLS. 18, 19, 24,

3.75–4.25" (9.5–11 cm). Common breeder in western mountair rare in winter in Southeast, migrant or vagrant elsewhere. Mediui sized, with *long tail*, medium-length black bill.

ADULT MALE. *Gorget brilliant hot pink to rose red, contrasting vividly with wh breast.* Cheeks, edges of chin feathers dull olive-gray; lores dusky. Br liant grass green to emerald green above, white below with gray-gre "vest" and tawny wash on flanks. *Tail long, extending well pe wingtips. Central tail feathers pointed, green or dusky.* R2–4 green blackish, with *narrow to broad rufous edge on outer web.* R5 narro rounded, all dark or with smudgy whitish tip. *Modified wingtips crea bright silvery trill in flight,* like the ringing of tiny bells.

ADULT FEMALE. Bright grass green above, white below washed with pale rufo on sides and flanks. Gorget usually *evenly stippled to spangled wi dusky to bronze,* rarely with a few larger spangles at lower cent reflecting dull rose pink to reddish bronze. *Face dull olive-gray wi* slightly darker cheek, dusky lores. *Long tail shows variable rufous R2–5.* Undertail coverts creamy white washed with cinnamon-buff base. Outer primary (P10) tapers to narrow pointed tip.

IMMATURE MALE. Resembles adult female but sides often washed green or r fous and green; gorget usually more heavily marked with or without few metallic feathers.. Tail feathers more pointed, especially R1– *rufous in R3–5 lightly to heavily mottled with black or dull green.*

IMMATURE FEMALE. Similar to adult female but usually with pale feather edg on upperparts, less rufous in R2–5, small white tip on R2.

BROAD-TAILED × BLACK-CHINNED HYBRID. See Plate 30.

adult male Broad-tailed

adult female Broad-tailed

adult male Broad-tailed

adult female Broad-tailed

immature male Broad-tailed

second-year female Broad-tailed

immature male Broad-tailed

adult male Broad-tailed primaries

PLATE 4

CALLIOPE HUMMINGBIRD
Stellula calliope

P. 208, PLS. 18, 19, 24,

2.75–3.25" (7.5–8 cm). Smallest of all breeding birds in the Unit
States, with *very short black bill, very short tail with unique spad*
shaped central feathers (best developed in adults). Often cocks tail u
ward, perpendicular to body, while hovering at flowers or feeder
Generally quiet.

ADULT MALE. *Gorget wine red to reddish purple iridescence over white bac*
ground; individual feathers very long, narrow, pointed, and convex
corners. Bright green above, creamy white below with green wash o
sides and flanks. *Face dull grayish,* with slightly darker cheek, whitis
moustachial stripe. *Wingtips extend to or beyond tip of very shor*
slightly notched tail. Tail feathers dull gray variably edged in cinn
mon-rufous basally; R1 narrow at base, becoming wider toward tip b
fore abruptly tapering to spade-shaped point.

ADULT FEMALE. Bright grass green to golden green above, creamy white belo
washed with cinnamon-rufous on sides, flanks, and across lowe
breast. Gorget usually evenly stippled to spangled with dusky
brownish bronze, rarely with larger reddish spangles at lower cente
Face grayish. *Slightly notched tail usually falls short of wingtips.* Ce
tral tail feathers green with or without narrow rufous edges at bas
R3–5 (rarely R2–5) tipped white, usually with *narrow edges of cinn*
mon-rufous basally. Undertail coverts washed pale cinnamon, paler
tips. *Bill short, slightly longer than rest of head.* Tip of outer prima
(P10) broad, curved.

IMMATURE MALE. Similar to adult female but gorget usually more heavi
marked, often with random spots, streaks, or patches of wine red ir
descence. R1 always narrowly edged in dull cinnamon-rufous at bas
(difficult to see).

IMMATURE FEMALE. Similar to adult female but with indistinct pale feathe
edges on upperparts. R1 green with blackish tip, *no rufous edges*
base; large white tip on R3, usually small white tip on R2.

ANNA'S × CALLIOPE HYBRID. See Plate 30.
RUFOUS × CALLIOPE HYBRID. See Plate 30.

BUMBLEBEE HUMMINGBIRD
Atthis heloisa

P. 2

2.75–3" (7–7.5 cm). A tiny species of Mexico's Sierra Madre collecte
in southeastern Arizona in 1896. Very small, with *very short black bil*
tail banded in rufous, black, and white on the outer feathers in bot
sexes. Gorget of adult male resembles that of Lucifer in shape an
color without distinct rays or white background of Calliope. Tail e
tends slightly beyond wingtips. See text p. 213.

adult male Calliope

adult female Calliope

adult male Calliope

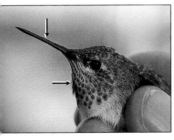

adult female Calliope

Calliope head

immature male Calliope wing

adult male Bumblebee

immature male Bumblebee

PLATE 5

COSTA'S HUMMINGBIRD
Calypte costae

P. 204, PLS. 20, 21, 26, 2

3–3.5" (7.5–9 cm). Common in Pacific coastal chaparral, Mojave an
Sonoran Deserts. Tiny, compact, large-headed, with mostly whitis
underparts; *very short tail; short, thin, straight to slightly decurved bil
Inner primaries all approximately equal width*, unlike Black-chinne
and Ruby-throated. Tail pumped or wagged intermittently in fligh
similar to Black-chinned. Calls include a weak dry *tik*.

ADULT MALE. *Gorget deep purple to violet, with long extensions at corners th
hang down or sweep back over shoulders; crown and separate patch b
hind eye same color as throat.* Green above. Very pale gray or white
breast wraps around side of neck to join whitish eye line, pale eyebro
Sides green, with whitish midline stripe forming a "vest." Wingtips e
tend to or beyond tip of short notched tail. Tail feathers are gray, darke
at edges; *R5 very narrow, curved inward, tapering to point. Bill shor
thin, slightly decurved.* Song is thin shrill *whee-oo*.

ADULT FEMALE. Bright green to golden green above, pale gray to whitish belo
*gorget may be unmarked or show small to large patch of metallic viole
purple feathers at lower center.* Wingtips extend to or slightly beyon
very short, slightly double-rounded tail. Tail feathers rounded; R3–
banded in dull gray-green, blackish, and white. *Bill short, thin, slight
decurved.*

IMMATURE MALE. Similar to adult female but with broad buffy feather edge
when fresh; dusky markings on throat, especially at corners of gorge
Gorget extends downward at corners, often shows extensive patches
metallic purple to violet by late summer. R5 narrower, thin line
black extends into white tip along shaft.

IMMATURE FEMALE. Resembles adult female but with duller upperparts, broa
buffy feather edges when fresh, small white tip on R2.

COSTA'S × ANNA'S HYBRID. See Plate 30.

adult male Costa's

adult female Costa's

adult male Costa's

adult female Costa's

immature male Costa's

adult female Costa's at nest

immature male Costa's

immature female Costa's

PLATE 6

ANNA'S HUMMINGBIRD
Calypte anna

P. 199, PLS. 20, 21, 26,

3.5–4" (9–10 cm). Rare to common year-round resident of Pacif
Coast and Mojave and Sonoran Deserts, visitor or vagrant elsewher
Medium-sized, chunky, with medium-length straight to slightly d
curved black bill, dingy medium to pale gray underparts, medium
length to long tail. *Inner primaries all approximately equal width, u*
like Black-chinned and Ruby-throated. Calls include sharp *tsip o*
tchik notes, rapid *zheega-zheega-zheega* in combat.

ADULT MALE. *Gorget rose red to coppery red, with moderate extensions at co*
ners; crown and separate patch behind eye same color as throat. Brigl
green to bluish green above. *Upper breast medium to pale gray,* usual
slightly mottled. Pale feather edges give green underparts a scaly ap
pearance; pale midline stripe faint or absent. *Long, deeply notched ta*
extends well beyond wingtips. Outer tail feathers gray, darker at edge
bordering paler translucent patches; R5 narrow, rounded at tip. Sor
is series of harsh buzzy notes and chips, often slurred together.

ADULT FEMALE. *Gorget mottled dull grayish, variably marked with bright rose re*
to coppery iridescence. Bright green to bronze-green above, medium t
pale gray below, often mottled dull green to bronze. Slightly notche
to double-rounded tail extends to or beyond wingtips. *Tail feathe*
broad, rounded; R3–5 banded in dull gray-green, blackish, and whit
Bill straight to slightly decurved.

IMMATURE MALE. Resembles adult female but with pale feather edges whe
fresh, heavier mottling in gorget with larger iridescent feathers; *thi*
line of black extends into white tip along shaft of R5, little or no whit
in R3.

IMMATURE FEMALE. Similar to adult female; usually lacks iridescence in gorge
Best distinguished by plumage condition.

COSTA'S × ANNA'S HYBRID. See Plate 30.
ANNA'S × BLACK-CHINNED HYBRID. See Plate 30.
ANNA'S × CALLIOPE HYBRID. See Plate 30.

adult male Anna's

adult female Anna's

adult male Anna's

immature female Anna's

immature male Anna's

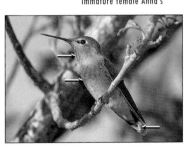

immature female Anna's

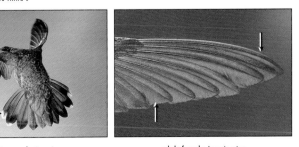

immature male Anna's

adult female Anna's wing

PLATE 7

BLACK-CHINNED HUMMINGBIRD
Archilochus alexandri

P. 194, PLS. 20, 21, 26, 27

3.25–3.75" (8.5–9.5 cm). Western counterpart of Ruby-throated. Small, compact, with medium-length to *long, slightly to moderately decurved* black bill, *dull crown, broad blunt wingtip. Inner primaries graduated in width*, becoming narrower inward. *Usually pumps tail almost constantly in hovering flight.* Calls include soft *tchew, tchip,* or *tchup* notes.

ADULT MALE. *Gorget mostly velvety black, with seldom-visible band of metallic amethyst violet at bottom;* corners rounded. Face blackish, crown dull dusky. Dull green to emerald green above, pale gray to whitish below, becoming dull green on sides. *White "collar" contrasts strongly with dark head.* Tail deeply notched, extends slightly beyond wingtips. Outer feathers pointed, blackish washed bronze-green at tips.

ADULT FEMALE. Dull green to golden green above, *forecrown dull gray to grayish tan*, blending to dull green on hindcrown. Pale gray below, sides washed gray-green, often with tawny to cinnamon patch on lower flank. Cheek dull gray, lores dusky. Throat unmarked or with variable dusky streaking or spotting at center of gorget. Tail square to slightly notched or double-rounded, extends slightly beyond wingtips. Central tail feathers (R1) green, with or without diffuse dark band at tip. R2 gray-green tipped black; R3 like R2 but narrowly tipped white; R4, R5 pointed, broadly tipped white. *Bill long, slightly to moderately decurved.*

IMMATURE MALE. Similar to adult female but with shorter bill, markings on gorget heavier and more extensive, pale buff feather edges visible on upperparts when fresh. Underparts may show a faint cinnamon wash.

IMMATURE FEMALE. Similar to adult female but with pale buff feather edges visible on upperparts when fresh, broader white tip on R3, small white tip on R2, R5 rounded at tip. Underparts may show a faint cinnamon wash.

BROAD-TAILED × BLACK-CHINNED HYBRID. See Plate 30.

ANNA'S × BLACK-CHINNED HYBRID. See Plate 30.

LUCIFER × BLACK-CHINNED HYBRID. See Plate 9.

adult male Black-chinned

adult female Black-chinned

adult male Black-chinned

immature female Black-chinned

immature male Black-chinned

immature female Black-chinned

immature male Black-chinned

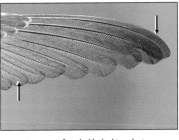

immature female Black-chinned wing

PLATE 8

RUBY-THROATED HUMMINGBIRD
Archilochus colubris

P. 188, PLS. 20, 21, 26, 27

3.25–3.75" (8.5–9.5 cm). The only breeding hummingbird east of the Mississippi River. Small, compact, with *medium-length straight to slightly decurved black bill*, bright green to golden green crown, long tail. *Outer primary (P10) tapers to a narrow rounded tip. Inner primaries graduated in width*, becoming narrower inward. Tail is pumped intermittently in flight, less consistently than in Black-chinned. Calls soft, including *tchew, tchup,* and *tic-tic.*

ADULT MALE. *Gorget mostly ruby red, bordered by narrow black band across top edge; corners rounded. Face blackish.* Bright grass green to emerald green above, pale gray to whitish below, becoming green on sides. White of breast extends around sides of neck, contrasting with gorget and nape. Tail long, *deeply notched to forked;* outer feathers pointed, blackish.

ADULT FEMALE. *Entirely bright grass green to golden green above,* pale gray to whitish below. Throat unmarked or with variable dusky streaking or spotting at center of gorget. Face dusky, contrasting with pale throat and white postocular spot. Sides washed gray-green, often with tawny patches on flanks. *Tail moderately notched to double-rounded, extends well beyond wingtips;* central feathers green, outer feathers (R3-5) tipped white, R5 tapers to dull point.

IMMATURE MALE. Resembles adult female but with shorter bill, pale buff feather edges when fresh. Markings on gorget usually heavier and more extensive. Underparts may show a cinnamon wash.

IMMATURE FEMALE. Resembles adult female but with pale buff feather edges when fresh, small white tip on R2, R5 broad, rounded at tip. Underparts may show a cinnamon wash.

adult male Ruby-throated

adult female Ruby-throated

adult male Ruby-throated

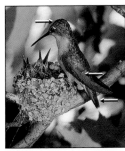

adult female Ruby-throated at nest

immature male Ruby-throated

immature female Ruby-throated

immature male Ruby-throated

immature female Ruby-throated wing

PLATE 9

LUCIFER HUMMINGBIRD   P. 184, PLS. 22, 28
Calothorax lucifer

3.5–4" (9–10 cm). Uncommon and local summer resident of Chihuahuan Desert, "sky island" mountains of western Texas, southwestern New Mexico, southeastern Arizona. Small, slim, with *long black slightly to moderately decurved bill*, short wings, and *long narrow tail*. Often assumes hunched posture when perched, with head thrust forward, shoulders rounded.

ADULT MALE. *Gorget metallic magenta-purple to violet-purple, extending onto upper breast; feathers at corners elongate.* Green to bronze-green above. *Sides bronze-green mixed with pale cinnamon, with cinnamon patch on lower flank.* Breast and sides of neck whitish, creating partial collar connecting with pale eye line. *Tail deeply forked,* outer feathers very narrow, blackish, held closed or nearly so when perched.

ADULT FEMALE. Bronze-green to golden green above. Underparts warm white to cream, sides and flanks strongly washed cinnamon-rufous. Throat plain creamy white, washed with cinnamon; may show distinct bulge in side view. *Broad creamy white to pale cinnamon eye line bordered below by dusky cheek stripe. Tail long, forked, feathers narrow.* Central tail feathers (R1–2) green to bronze-green, outer pairs (R3–5) banded in bright rufous, green, and black with white tips.

IMMATURE MALE. (Not illustrated) Similar to adult female but with pale feather edges on upperparts when fresh. Usually shows first metallic gorget feathers within a few weeks of fledging.

IMMATURE FEMALE. (Not illustrated) Shows more extensive white in tail than adult female or immature male.

BAHAMA WOODSTAR   P. 181
Calliphlox evelynae

3.5–3.75" (9–9.5 cm). Extremely rare visitor to southeastern Florida. *Slim, long-tailed,* with extensive cinnamon-rufous in plumage.

ADULT MALE. *Gorget metallic rose-purple with violet highlights.* Grass green to golden green above. *Underparts cinnamon-rufous mottled with bright green, indistinct paler midline stripe. Long, deeply forked tail extends well past wingtips. Outer rectrices narrow, blackish, with broad cinnamon-rufous border on inner web.*

ADULT FEMALE. Grass green to golden green above. Throat and upper breast pale gray to whitish, washed pale rufous, faint green spangling at sides. *Dark cheek crescent, narrow pale eye-stripe.* Rich cinnamon-rufous underparts, indistinct paler midline stripe. *Long narrow tail* slightly rounded to double rounded, extends past wingtips. Outer rectrices banded in grayish rufous, green, and blackish with *rufous tips on R3–5*.

IMMATURES. Not illustrated. See text, p. 181.

adult male Lucifer

adult female Lucifer

adult male Lucifer

adult female Lucifer

adult male Lucifer × Black-chinned hybrid

adult male Lucifer × Black-chinned hybrid

adult male Bahama Woodstar

adult female Bahama Woodstar

PLATE 10

MAGNIFICENT HUMMINGBIRD
Eugenes fulgens

P. 174, PLS. 23, 2

4.5–5.25" (11–13.5 cm). Uncommon to fairly common in "sky island" mountains near Mexican border. Very large, slim, with *long black bill* Largely nonterritorial. Calls include hoarse *tschip* or *tcheep* notes.

ADULT MALE. *Brilliant apple green to turquoise green gorget, metallic violet to purple crown. Triangular white postocular spot* contrasts strongly with blackish face. Dark emerald to bronze-green above. *Breast velvety black with bronze-green highlights,* becoming dull medium to dark gray on shoulders and lower belly. Undertail coverts pale to medium bronze-gray centrally with broad whitish borders.

ADULT FEMALE. *Face dark with distinct white postocular triangle and ragged whitish postocular stripe.* Dark emerald to bronze-green above. Underparts medium ash gray washed green on sides and flanks, often with mottled or scaly appearance. Undertail coverts bronze-gray centrally with broad whitish borders. *Tail long, square to slightly notched, dark bronze-green with blackish band across corners and small dull whitish tips on R3–5. Bill very long.*

IMMATURE MALE. Darker than adult female, with strongly scaly appearance to underparts. Gorget dull, blotchy, with patch or disk of bright green small patch of metallic violet feathers over each eye. *Slightly notched tail bronze-green to bronze,* usually with broad blackish band across corners; *diffuse whitish edges on outer tail feathers.*

SECOND SPRING MALE. (Not illustrated) Crown and gorget often incomplete. Tail feathers retained until molt in second fall; pale tips may wear off outer pairs.

IMMATURE FEMALE. Resembles adult female but with distinct pale edges on feathers, particularly noticeable on upperparts, more extensive dull whitish in tail (tips of R2–5).

BERYLLINE × MAGNIFICENT HYBRID. See Plate 14.

adult male Magnificent

adult female Magnificent

adult male Magnificent

adult female Magnificent

immature male Magnificent

immature female Magnificent

immature male Magnificent

immature female Magnificent

PLATE 11

BLUE-THROATED HUMMINGBIRD   P. 169, PLS. 23,
Lampornis clemenciae

4.75–5.25" (12–13.5 cm). Uncommon and local in "sky islan
mountains of Southwest. Very large, proportionally long-tailed ar
short-billed. *Prominent white eye-stripe,* narrow pale malar stripe, da
gray cheek. *Back grass green becoming dull green to bronze on rum
blackish on uppertail coverts. Broad rounded blue-black tail has co
spicuous pure white tips on outer 2–3 pairs of feathers.* Underparts a:
gray, washed green on sides and flanks. Call a shrill *seep* or *tsee*
Sexes similar.

ADULT MALE. Very large, with *cerulean to cobalt blue gorget* (difficult to see).

ADULT FEMALE. Large; underparts, including gorget, entirely gray, often slight
mottled.

IMMATURE MALE. Similar to adult male but with iridescent blue typically co
fined to center of gorget, pale edges on feathers of upperparts whe
fresh.

IMMATURE FEMALE. Similar to adult female, with pale edges on feathers of u
perparts when fresh.

AMETHYST-THROATED HUMMINGBIRD   P. 1
Lampornis amethystinus

4.5–5" (11.5–12.5 cm). Potential vagrant to southern Texas from eas
ern Mexico. Similar to Blue-throated Hummingbird but with blu
black tail *narrowly tipped with gray on R3–5.* Calls include sharp, ha
chips, buzzy trills.

ADULT MALE. (Not illustrated.) Very large; dark gray below with *bright pinkis
purple gorget. Gray tips on outer tail feathers blend into black of ta
Song is similar to "peep song" of Blue-throated Hummingbird.

ADULT FEMALE. (Not illustrated) Large, with medium gray underparts, *stron
tawny wash to gorget. Gray tips on outer tail feathers* crisply defined.

IMMATURE MALE. Similar to adult female but larger, with dull gray throat, le
distinct gray tips on outer tail feathers.

IMMATURE FEMALE. (Not illustrated) Similar to adult female, with pale edges c
feathers of upperparts when fresh.

WEDGE-TAILED SABREWING   P. 1
Campylopterus curvipennis

4.75–5.25" (12–13.5 cm). Potential stray to southern Texas. *Larg
with very long wedge-shaped tail. Violet-blue crown.* White postocula
spot, dark gray cheek. Underparts pale gray to whitish, often slight
darker laterally. *Bill long, straight to slightly decurved; lower mandib
pinkish at base.* Sexes similar. See text, p. 115.

adult male Blue-throated

adult female Blue-throated

adult male Blue-throated

immature male Blue-throated

immature male Amethyst-throated

immature male Amethyst-throated

male Wedge-tailed Sabrewing

male Wedge-tailed Sabrewing

PLATE 12

PLAIN-CAPPED STARTHROAT
Heliomaster constantii

P. 178, PLS. 23,

4.5–5.25" (11.5–13.5 cm). Rare post-breeding visitor to the sout western United States. Large, dull, with *very long bill. Narrow gorg bordered by broad whitish malar stripes* contrasting with dusky gr cheeks. Upperparts dull green to olive bronze with *narrow patch white on lower back and rump* (not always conspicuous). Underpar medium gray with *broad pale midline stripe. Silky white flank tu* more conspicuous than in other species; usually concealed at re *Wings extend to or slightly beyond tip of tail.* R2–4 banded bronze ar blackish with *white spot at tip on inner web;* R5 broadly tipped whit *usually smudged with black on outer web.* Flight graceful, swiftlik Wags and fans tail in flight. Sexes virtually identical.

ADULT. Gorget feathers dark gray at chin, becoming red on lower third half, all edged in pale grayish buff.

IMMATURE. Gorget entirely or mostly blackish with pale edges on ea feather; pale feather edges on upperparts when fresh.

VIOLET-CROWNED HUMMINGBIRD
Amazilia violiceps

P. 163, PLS. 22,

4–4.5" (10–11.5 cm). Uncommon and local along streams in sout eastern Arizona, southwestern New Mexico; accidental in Texas, Ca fornia. Medium-large, with *snow-white underparts, blue to violet-bl crown, dull bronze-green to grayish bronze back, gray-green rump ar tail.* Bill coral red with variable black at tip. Sexes very similar; fema may show less intense iridescence on crown, slightly more black o bill. Immatures show narrow grayish buff feather edges on the uppe parts when fresh; bill may show more extensive black.

AZURE-CROWNED HUMMINGBIRD
Amazilia cyanocephala

P. 1

4–4.5" (10–11.5 cm). Potential vagrant to southern Texas from nort eastern Mexico. Resembles Violet-crowned but with mostly white u derparts *heavily mottled with olive green to bronze from sides of ne down sides to flanks;* may nearly meet across breast. *Undertail cove olive-gray with broad pale borders.* Crown deep metallic turquoise bright violet-blue. Bill thin, *blackish above, orange to coral red belo with narrow black tip on lower mandible.* Both sexes and all ages ve similar.

adult Plain-capped Starthroat

adult Plain-capped Starthroat

adult Plain-capped Starthroat

adult Plain-capped Starthroat

adult Violet-crowned

adult Violet-crowned

immature Violet-crowned

adult Azure-crowned

PLATE 13

BUFF-BELLIED HUMMINGBIRD
Amazilia yucatanensis

P. 154, PL.

3.75–4.25" (9.5–10.5 cm). Breeds in southeastern Texas, wint
north to northwestern Florida. Large with *glittering metallic app
green to turquoise green "bib" covering throat and breast*. Belly pale
medium grayish buff to cinnamon-buff. *Tail moderately to dee
notched, with dark rufous feathers variably bordered or washed gold
green to bronze. Undertail coverts pale to medium cinnamon-buff wi
broad whitish borders;* uppertail coverts mixed green and cinnamo
rufous. *Bill coral red with blackish tip.* Pale buff spot in front of e
narrow whitish crescent behind eye. Sexes very similar.

ADULT MALE. Iridescence of bib typically more brilliant, belly darker. T
deeply notched. Bill red with blackish tip, often with narrow black b
der on upper mandible extending to base. Aggressive and territorial.

ADULT FEMALE. Iridescence of bib muted by pale feather edges, most conspic
ous on chin; belly pale. *Tail square to shallowly notched.* Blood red b
more extensively blackish on upper mandible.

IMMATURES. Resemble duller adults, with dull cinnamon-rufous feather edg
on upperparts, mottled appearance to bib, more extensive black
bill. R1 mostly or entirely greenish bronze.

IMMATURE MALE. Slightly brighter iridescence in bib, deeply notched tail.

IMMATURE FEMALE. Very dull underparts, square to moderately notched tail.

RUFOUS-TAILED HUMMINGBIRD
Amazilia tzacatl

P. 1

4–4.25" (10–11 cm). Reported but poorly documented vagrant
southern Texas. Large, dark, with *glittering metallic grass green
turquoise green "bib" extending to upper belly.* Lower sides, flanks d
bronze-green to golden green; center of belly dull brownish gray. *T
square to slightly notched,* feathers dark rufous-brown moderately bo
dered in bronze-green to golden green. *Undertail coverts rich cinn
mon-rufous,* contrasting with whitish femoral tufts. Uppertail cove
mostly dark rufous. Bill coral red with blackish tip. Pale cinnamo
spots in front of and behind eye. Sexes similar.

ADULT MALE. Typically shows more brilliant iridescence on slightly more e
tensive bib; belly darker gray. Bill red with blackish tip.

ADULT FEMALE. Typically has iridescence of bib muted by pale feather edge
most conspicuous on chin; belly slightly paler gray. Bill more exte
sively blackish on upper mandible, often extending to base of bill.

IMMATURES. Similar to adults but duller, with cinnamon-rufous feather edg
on upperparts, mottled appearance to green bib, more extensive bla
on bill.

adult male Buff-bellied

adult female Buff-bellied

adult male Buff-bellied

adult female Buff-bellied at nest

immature male Buff-bellied

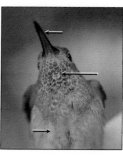

immature female Buff-bellied

adult male Rufous-tailed

adult female Rufous-tailed

PLATE 14

BERYLLINE HUMMINGBIRD
P.

Amazilia beryllina

3.75–4″ (9.5–10 cm). Very rare summer resident of "sky islar mountains of southeastern Arizona; accidental in southwestern N Mexico, western Texas. Medium-large, dark, with *glittering app green to turquoise green throat and breast, broad band of bright cinn mon-rufous at base of primaries and secondaries.* Belly and undert coverts dull fawn to brownish gray. Back bright green to golden gre becoming dull purplish bronze on rump. *Square to slightly notched t dark rufous-brown with strong violet-purple sheen; uppertail cove dark violet-purple.* Bill bicolored; *upper mandible blackish, lower re dish or dull orange at base with blackish tip.* Sexes similar.

ADULT MALE. Brilliant metallic "bib" extends across entire throat, breast, a upper belly. Belly dull brownish gray to cinnamon-gray. Tail square slightly notched.

ADULT FEMALE. Like adult male but whitish chin, iridescence of less extensi "bib" muted by pale feather edges, dull grayish fawn belly; tail squar

IMMATURE MALE. Extensive green to bronze-green mottling from sides of ne to flanks. More intense iridescence at center of throat than adult male. Ragged lower border to bib, broad cinnamon-buff edges on u perparts. May show metallic green feathers individually or in patch on throat and breast.

IMMATURE FEMALE. Resembles adult female but duller, with less intense irid cence. Broader pale margins on throat and breast feathers. Ragg lower border to bib, broad cinnamon-buff edges on upperparts.

BERYLLINE × MAGNIFICENT HYBRID, ADULT MALE. Iridescent coppery bronze tail. G get poorly defined, aqua blue blending to bright green.

CINNAMON HUMMINGBIRD
P.

Amazilia rutila

4–4.5″ (10–11.5 cm). A striking tropical species accidental in sout eastern Arizona, southern New Mexico. Large with distinctive *brig cinnamon-buff to cinnamon-rufous underparts,* coral red bill wi black tip. Sexes virtually identical.

ADULT. Crown, nape, and upper back bright green, becoming bronze-gre to bronze mixed with rufous on lower back and rump; uppert coverts bronze-green broadly bordered in bright rufous. Tail slightly moderately notched, with bright cinnamon-rufous feathers variabl bordered at tips in dark bronze-green. Bill coral red with blackish t Lores same color as throat; pale buff crescent behind eye.

IMMATURE. More extensive black on bill, pale feather edges on upperpar duller underparts.

adult male Berylline

adult female Berylline

immature male Berylline

adult female Berylline

adult male Berylline × Magnificent hybrid

adult male Berylline × Magnificent hybrid

adult Cinnamon

adult Cinnamon

PLATE 15

WHITE-EARED HUMMINGBIRD
Hylocharis leucotis

P. 141, PLS. 22,

3.5–4" (9–10 cm). Rare, local, and irregular in "sky island" mountai of southeastern Arizona, southwestern New Mexico, western Tex. Medium-small, with *large head, short straight bill, bold white ey stripe, blackish cheek, whitish underparts heavily spangled with gree* Upperparts golden green to bronze-green, rump and uppertail cove broadly edged cinnamon-rufous when fresh. Tail long, square slightly notched, central feathers deep bronze-green. Call a sha metallic *tchik* or *tink*, richer than that of Anna's Hummingbir Adults molt May–August, immatures August–October.

ADULT MALE. *Broad bright white eye-stripe arches over top of eye, contrasts w blackish cheek. Forecrown and chin blue-violet.* Solid metall turquoise green of gorget extends onto sides and flanks, becomi green spangles broadly edged in whitish. Belly white centrally. B coral red with black tip.

ADULT FEMALE. *Broad white postocular stripe extends from above eye to should contrasting with blackish cheek.* Underparts ivory to creamy whi with *spangles of bronze-green to turquoise green on throat continui down sides.* Outer tail feathers banded in green and blue-black, d white tips on R3–5. Bill mostly dusky to blackish above, dull orang red with black tip below.

IMMATURE MALE. Resembles adult female except for patch of bright green i descence at center of gorget, smaller white tips on outer tail feathe slightly more red at base of upper mandible, more conspicuous cinn mon-rufous edges on upperparts. **SECOND-YEAR MALE** may have full gre gorget with little or no violet on chin and forecrown.

IMMATURE FEMALE. Similar to adult female; may show more distinct dull cinn mon-rufous edges on upperparts, duller orange and more extensi blackish on bill, more extensive white tips on outer tail feathers, pa ticularly R3.

XANTUS'S HUMMINGBIRD
Hylocharis xantusii

P. 1

3.25–3.75" (8.5–9.5 cm). Endemic to Baja California, two records f southern California, one for southern British Columbia. Very simi to White-eared; distinguished by *cinnamon underparts and dark rufo brown in tail.* Calls include dry rattle similar to that of Broad-bill Hummingbird, metallic *tik* or *tink* notes similar to calls of Whit eared. See text, p. 145.

adult male White-eared

adult female White-eared

adult male White-eared

immature female White-eared

second-year male White-eared

immature female White-eared

immature male White-eared

adult male Xantus's

PLATE 16

BROAD-BILLED HUMMINGBIRD   P. 136, PLS. 22,
Cynanthus latirostris

3.5–4" (9–10 cm). Locally common in southeastern Arizona, extren
southwestern New Mexico. Small, slender, with *long mobile tail*
nearly constant motion. Bill long, broad-based, red or orange and blac
Call is a raspy *chit* or *ji-dit*, often run into long chatter.

ADULT MALE. *Glittering sapphire blue gorget* blends into emerald green breas
sides, belly. Whitish to pale gray undertail coverts contrast with da
underparts. *Tail long, deeply notched, dark steel blue with dark gr*
edges broadest on central feathers. Small white postocular spot.

ADULT FEMALE. Entirely green to bronze-green above, pale to medium gray b
low with plain throat and some green spangling on sides. *Dull wh*
postocular stripe widest behind eye, cheek sooty gray. Tail long, doubl
rounded, outer feathers banded in green and steel blue, dull white ti
on outer 2–3 pairs. Bill mostly blackish, dull orange confined to low
mandible, base of upper mandible.

IMMATURE MALE. Resembles adult female but with a small patch, stripe,
scattering of blue feathers on throat, broad pale edges to feathers
upperparts, more orange at base of bill. Tail mostly steel blue, wi
small white tips on R4–5, indistinct gray edges on R1–3.

IMMATURE FEMALE. Duller in color than adult female, with broad pale edges
feathers of upperparts. Bill entirely blackish above.

CUBAN EMERALD   P. 1
Chlorostilbon ricordii

3.5–4" (9–10 cm). Very rare, irregular stray to Florida, poorly doc
mented in the United States. Small, with *long forked tail*. Bill short
medium-length, blackish above, orange to coral red below.

ADULT MALE. *Underparts glittering bright green to golden green,* becomin
bronze-green on flanks, belly. Gorget *golden green* to deep blue. Conspi
uous white postocular spot. *Tail long, forked;* central feathers *dark gree*
ish bronze, outer pairs greenish black to black. Undertail coverts whitis

ADULT FEMALE. Upperparts grass green to bronze-green, underparts pale gr
to whitish becoming green laterally. *Diffuse band of green across low*
breast. Short white eye line, dark gray cheek. Forked tail extends far pe
wingtips; small white tips on R4–5.

IMMATURES. See text, p. 132.

GOLDEN-CROWNED EMERALD   P. 1
Chlorostilbon auriceps

(Not illustrated.) Potential stray to Arizona, New Mexico. See text, p. 128

CANIVET'S EMERALD   P. 1
Chlorostilbon canivetii

(Not illustrated.) Potential stray to southern Texas. See text, p. 130.

adult male Broad-billed

adult female Broad-billed

adult male Broad-billed

immature female Broad-billed

immature male Broad-billed

immature female Broad-billed

adult male Cuban Emerald

adult female Cuban Emerald

PLATE 17

GREEN VIOLET-EAR   P. 118, PLS. 23, 2
Colibri thalassinus

4.25–4.5" (11–11.5 cm). Rare and irregular visitor from tropic
mountain forests. *Large, dark, with slightly to moderately decurved bil*
Fast-moving, wary, often keeping to shadows. Frequently flicks an
fans tail in flight. Calls include dry rattle while feeding, loud 2-syllab
chip-tsirr while perched. Sexes nearly identical.

ADULT. *Satiny emerald to grass green below, with large deep violet-blue centr*
breast spot, metallic violet to violet-blue "ear," violet-blue band alon
chin. Belly duller, paler. *Tail blue-green above, deep blue below wit*
broad dark blue subterminal band. Bill black, slender. Female averag
smaller, slightly duller than male, with narrower violet-blue ch
band.

IMMATURE. Much duller, paler version of adult. Satiny grass green to oli
green overall, underparts washed dull grayish. *Violet-blue ear, brea*
spot indistinct, incomplete, or absent. Tail (specimen) similar
adult's. May show patches of bright metallic color on throat, breast.

GREEN-BREASTED MANGO   P. 1
Anthracothorax prevostii

4.5–5" (11.5–12.5 cm). Very rare vagrant from Mexico to souther
Texas (one record for North Carolina). Females and immature mal
distinctive; adult male superficially similar to other large dark hun
mingbirds.

ADULT MALE. (Costa Rica) *Throat dark emerald green with broad velvety blac*
central stripe extending onto breast. Breast dark blue to blue-gree
centrally, blending to dark leaf green and golden green on belly, side
Dark green to golden green above. Tail square to slightly notche
outer 3–4 pairs bright purple to violet above and below, edged in du
black. Undertail coverts dark green.

ADULT FEMALE. (Costa Rica) *Underparts white with broad dark vertical stripe*
midline, blackish on chin becoming dark emerald green to blue-gree
at base of throat. Narrow band of cinnamon brown may be present o
chin. Sides, flanks bright green to golden green. Tail square to sligh
rounded, *banded in purple, blue-black, and white on outer 3–4 pairs.*

IMMATURE MALE. (North Carolina, *left*; Texas, *right*) Similar to adult female b
with ventral stripe *broken or absent on chin, heavy rust brown mottli*
along edges of white underparts. Outer tail feathers banded purple an
blue-black, white tips on R3–5. May show black and dark blue-gree
feathers coming in through white and dull green of underparts.

IMMATURE FEMALE. (Not illustrated.) Similar to immature male but *tail most*
blue-black with white tips on R2–5.

adult Green Violet-ear

immature Green Violet-ear

adult Green Violet-ear

immature Green Violet-ear tail (specimen)

adult male Green-breasted Mango

adult female Green-breasted Mango

immature male Green-breasted Mango

immature male Green-breasted Mango

PLATE 18

HEADS I: ADULT *SELASPHORUS* AND *STELLULA*

These members of the genera *Selasphorus* and *Stellula* share brig
green crowns, white underparts washed with rufous. Most also ha
extensive rufous in the tail. Straight to slightly decurved bills ran
from very short to medium length.

ADULT MALES. Gorgets are shades of red or orange, appearing blackish fro
many angles.

ALLEN'S AND RUFOUS. *Heads of these two species are virtually indistinguis*
able. Gorget red-orange to coppery or golden. Bills medium-short
medium (averaging slightly longer in *sedentarius* race of Allen's).

BROAD-TAILED. *Solid rose red gorget* contrasts with white upper breas
cheeks, lores dull gray-green. Bill medium-long.

CALLIOPE. Gorget consists of *wine red streaks over white backgroun*
elongate at corners. *Bill very short*, approximately equal to rest
head.

ADULT FEMALES. Throat markings range from small, sparse stipples and spa
gles to large ragged patches of malelike iridescence at center of go
get.

ALLEN'S AND RUFOUS. Heads of these two species are virtually indisti
guishable. Both show *strong rufous wash to face and gorget, iridesce*
patch of variable size and shape at center of gorget.

BROAD-TAILED. *Face grayish, gorget usually evenly stippled and spangl*
with dusky to dull bronze-green with little or no rufous wash. M
show small patch of enlarged red-bronze to rose red spangles at low
center of gorget. Bill medium-long.

CALLIOPE. *Face grayish, gorget usually evenly spangled with dull bronz*
green with little or no rufous wash. May show small patch of enlarge
red-bronze to wine red spangles at lower center of gorget. *Bill sho*
slightly longer than rest of head.

adult male Rufous

adult female Rufous

adult male Rufous gorget

adult female Rufous gorget

adult male Broad-tailed

adult female Broad-tailed

adult male Calliope

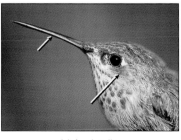

adult female Calliope

PLATE 19

HEADS II: IMMATURE *SELASPHORUS* AND *STELLULA*

Immatures typically show pale feather edges on crown, less obvious Allen's and Rufous.

IMMATURE MALES. Gorget markings are typically heavier ("five o'clock shadow") than in females, often showing metallic feathers scattered througho or concentrated along lower margin rather than in a discrete centr patch.

ALLEN'S AND RUFOUS. Heads of these two species are virtually indisti guishable. *Faces and gorgets washed with rufous over bronze-gre markings.* Bills medium-short to medium (average slightly longer *sedentarius* race of Allen's).

BROAD-TAILED. *Face grayish,* gorget usually evenly spangled with bronz green with *little or no rufous wash.* Bill medium-long.

CALLIOPE. *Face grayish,* gorget usually evenly spangled with dull bronz green with *little or no rufous wash.* May show scattered round or elo gate iridescent feathers in gorget. *Bill very short,* approximately equ to rest of head.

IMMATURE FEMALES. Throat markings range from nearly immaculate white ce trally in some Rufous and Allen's to evenly spangled with dull bronz green or dusky.

ALLEN'S AND RUFOUS. Heads of these two species are virtually indisti guishable. Both show *dull rufous wash to face, cinnamon edges feathers of crown and cheeks.* Gorget markings variable, from immac late white at center with large bronze spangles at corners to dense spangled with dull bronze-green. Bills medium to medium-long (ave age slightly longer in Allen's).

BROAD-TAILED. *Face grayish,* gorget usually evenly stippled to spangle with dull bronze-green or dusky with *little or no rufous wash.* Feathe of crown edged in dull grayish buff. Bill medium-long.

CALLIOPE. *Face grayish,* gorget usually evenly spangled with dull bronz green or dusky with *little or no rufous wash.* Feathers of crown edge in dull grayish buff. *Bill short,* slightly longer than rest of head.

immature male Allen's

immature female Allen's

immature male Rufous

immature female Rufous

immature male Broad-tailed

immature female Broad-tailed

immature male Calliope

immature female Calliope

PLATE 20

HEADS III: ADULT *ARCHILOCHUS* AND *CALYPTE*

These members of the genera *Archilochus* and *Calypte* share gre
crowns and backs, whitish to medium gray underparts, tails witho
significant rufous coloration.

ADULT MALES. Gorgets appear blackish from many angles. *Archilochus* ma
have bands of noniridescent black at the top border of the gorget. C
lypte males have gorgets with elongate corners, crowns the same co
as the gorget.

BLACK-CHINNED. *Velvety black chin bordered below by broad band of met
lic violet.* Head often appears all black, contrasting strongly with wh
upper breast. Bill medium-long to long, straight to slightly decurved

RUBY-THROATED. *Gorget ruby red (fresh) to coppery red (worn) border
above by narrow black chin strap.* Face blackish; entire head may a
pear dark from some angles, contrasting strongly with white up
breast. Bill medium length, straight or nearly so.

ANNA'S. *Gorget, crown brilliant rose red (fresh) to dull coppery r
(worn).* Elongated corners of gorget are erected during displa
longer in mature males. *Eyebrow grayish; breast dull medium to p
gray, slightly scaly.* Bill medium length, straight or nearly so.

COSTA'S. *Gorget, crown brilliant purple to violet. Extremely long m
tachelike extensions* may droop, sweep back across shoulders, or e
tend straight out during displays. Eyebrow grayish; *white "collar" e
tends from breast laterally under corners of gorget to connect wi
diffuse pale eye-stripe. Bill short, thin, slightly decurved.*

ADULT FEMALES. Throat may be immaculate whitish to pale gray, mottled d
gray, or marked with dull dusky streaks or spots concentrated centra
or patch of malelike iridescence. Throat often shows yellow pollen d
posits, brownish stains from feeding young.

BLACK-CHINNED. *Forecrown dull grayish* becoming green on nape, che
dull medium to dark gray, lores dark. Throat varies from immacula
pale gray to heavily spangled with dusky spots centrally. *Bill lor
slightly to moderately decurved.*

RUBY-THROATED. *Crown deep green,* cheek medium to dark gray, lor
dark. Throat pale gray or whitish, immaculate to heavily spangled wi
dusky streaking. *Bill medium-long,* straight to slightly decurved.

ANNA'S. Crown green, cheek medium to dark gray, lores dull gray
dusky. *Gorget usually marked with ragged patch of rose red (fresh)
coppery (worn) iridescence on dull gray, faintly mottled backgroun
Bill medium length, straight.

COSTA'S. Crown green, cheek medium to dark gray, lores dull gray
dusky. *Gorget unmarked pale gray to whitish or with variable iride
cence.* Rare mature females *(bottom right)* show malelike gorget b
no iridescence in crown. *Bill short, slightly longer than rest of hea
thin, slightly decurved.* Crown and throat may become very dull
dirty prior to beginning of molt in summer.

adult male Black-chinned

adult female Black-chinned

adult male Ruby-throated

adult female Ruby-throated

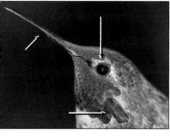

adult male Anna's

adult female Anna's

adult male Costa's

adult female Costa's (unusual gorget)

PLATE 21

HEADS IV: IMMATURE *ARCHILOCHUS* AND *CALYPTE*

Immatures of both sexes typically show conspicuous pale feather edges on crown and nape that wear off over time.

IMMATURE MALES. Gorget markings are typically heavier ("five o'clock shadow") than in females, often showing metallic feathers scattered throughout or concentrated along lower margin. Shape of gorget markings similar to adult male gorget.

BLACK-CHINNED. *Crown dull grayish tan* becoming dull green with pale edges on nape. Cheek dull medium to dark gray, lores dusky. *Gorget usually heavily patterned with dusky spangles, lower margin straight to slightly convex. Bill medium-long to long, straight to slightly decurved.*

RUBY-THROATED. *Crown dull green,* cheek dull medium to dark gray, lores dark. Gorget usually evenly spangled with dusky streaking, *lower margin straight to slightly convex.* Bill medium length, straight or nearly so.

ANNA'S. Crown dull green, *often with scattered rose red feathers, eyebrow grayish. Gorget background dull scaly or mottled gray, slightly concave at lower margin.* Breast dull medium to pale gray, scaly. *Bill medium length, straight or nearly so.*

COSTA'S. Crown dull green, *often with scattered purple to violet feathers, eyebrow grayish.* Gorget usually shows strong dusky markings, *lower margin strongly concave.* Whitish "collar" extends from breast laterally around corners of gorget to behind eye. *Bill short, thin, slightly decurved.*

IMMATURE FEMALES. Throat may be immaculate whitish to pale gray, mottled dull gray, or marked with dull dusky bronze to blackish markings concentrated centrally or patch of malelike iridescence. Normally pale gray to whitish throats often show yellow pollen deposits.

BLACK-CHINNED. *Crown dull grayish tan* becoming dull green with pale edges on nape. Cheek dull medium to dark gray, lores dusky. Throat varies from immaculate pale gray to heavily spangled with dusky streaking centrally. *Bill long, slightly to moderately decurved.*

RUBY-THROATED. *Crown dull green,* cheek medium to dark gray, lores dark. Throat varies from immaculate pale gray or whitish to heavily spangled with dusky streaking centrally. Bill medium-long, straight to slightly decurved.

ANNA'S. Crown dull green, cheek medium gray, lores dull gray to dusky. *Gorget usually mottled gray, often with a few small spangles of rose red (fresh) to coppery or bronze (worn) iridescence. Bill medium length, straight.*

COSTA'S. Crown dull green to grayish, cheek medium gray, lores dull gray to dusky. *Gorget usually unmarked pale gray to whitish. Bill short, slightly longer than rest of head, thin, slightly decurved.* Crown and throat may become very dull or dirty prior to beginning of molt in fall.

immature male Black-chinned

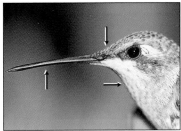

immature female Black-chinned

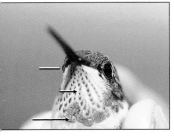

immature male Ruby-throated

immature female Ruby-throated

immature male Anna's

immature female Anna's

immature male Costa's

immature female Costa's

PLATE 22

HEADS V: SOUTHWESTERN SPECIES

BROAD-BILLED. Slim, long-necked, head proportionally small. *Long, robust bi* is broad-based, slightly decurved, with red or orange at base varying b age and sex.

ADULT MALE. *Sapphire blue gorget blending into emerald green of breas* Small white postocular spot (faint pale eye line usually absent in olde males). Bill blackish with variable red at base.

ADULT FEMALE. Bright grass green iridescence on crown, nape, sides o neck, with narrow grayish edges when fresh (late summer–early fall) *Whitish eye line becomes narrower toward shoulder; cheek dull gra* Throat unmarked or faintly mottled pale gray. Upper mandible most blackish with red-orange at base.

IMMATURE MALE. Patches of blue and green iridescence coming throug pale gray of underparts, bill mostly blackish above.

IMMATURE FEMALE. Dull grass green to golden green iridescence on crown nape, sides of neck. *Narrow whitish eye line, gray cheek.* Broad ta feather edges, especially prominent on crown, nape, cheeks. *Bi mostly blackish with dull orange at base of lower mandible.*

WHITE-EARED. Proportionally large chunky head; *bold white eye-stripe an blackish cheek. Short to medium-length bill is thin, straight to slightl decurved,* with red or orange at base.

SECOND-YEAR MALE. *Bold white eye-stripe becomes broader toward shoulde contrasts strongly with blackish cheek. Broad cinnamon-buff edges o* feathers of crown, nape. *Turquoise green gorget feathers* edged whitish Few or no violet feathers on forecrown, chin. Upper mandible les than half red. Immature (hatch-year) male shows central patch o green in gorget, mostly black upper mandible.

FEMALES similar but with *small turquoise green spangles on throat, breast sides;* mostly to completely black upper mandible.

ADULT (AFTER-SECOND-YEAR) MALE has *violet band on forecrown and chin* more extensive red at base of bill.

LUCIFER

IMMATURE FEMALE. *Strong cinnamon wash to face and underparts, un* marked throat, *curving pale eye line, dark cheek crescent, long, de curved bill.*

ADULT FEMALE, IMMATURE MALE similar.

VIOLET-CROWNED

ADULT. *Immaculate white underparts, violet-blue iridescence from crow extending onto cheeks, nape.* Bill bright coral red with narrow black tip

ADULT FEMALE may have slightly duller crown, more extensive black o bill; chin may become stained from feeding young.

IMMATURE. Underparts dull white without dark markings. Crown du violet-blue with broad pale edges; bill with more extensive blackis at tip.

second-year male Broad-billed

adult female Broad-billed

immature male Broad-billed

immature female Broad-billed

second-year male White-eared

immature female Lucifer

adult Violet-crowned

immature Violet-crowned

PLATE 23

HEADS VI: LARGE HUMMINGBIRDS

MAGNIFICENT

ADULT MALE. *Brilliant apple green to turquoise green gorget, violet to purple crown.* Entire head may appear black in poor light except for *triangular white postocular spot. Bill long,* all black.

ADULT FEMALE. *Crown deep emerald green,* cheek dark gray. Distinct postocular spot followed by *ragged, often indistinct eye line.* Throat pale to medium gray, mottled. *Bill long,* straight to slightly decurved.

IMMATURE MALE. *Feathers of head distinctly edged in pale grayish buff. Crown deep emerald green with spots of violet over eyes.* Cheek dark gray, contrasting with pale postocular spot and variable eye line. *Gorget feathers dark gray with broad whitish edges, central patch of metallic apple to turquoise green. Bill long,* straight to slightly decurved.

IMMATURE FEMALE. *Crown deep emerald green edged in pale grayish buff.* Cheek dark gray. Distinct postocular spot followed by ragged, indistinct eye line. Throat pale to medium gray, mottled and scaly. *Bill long,* straight to slightly decurved.

PLAIN-CAPPED STARTHROAT

Very long bill, bold whitish malar stripe. Gorget entirely dark gray to blackish (immature) or with dull metallic red on lower third to half (adult), feathers narrowly edged whitish.

BLUE-THROATED

IMMATURE MALE. *Feathers distinctly edged in pale grayish buff. Gorget feathers medium gray with pale edges, central patch of metallic blue* (seldom visible). Cheek dark gray, contrasting with whitish eye line. *Bill medium-short,* straight, may show pale pink or yellow at gape, base of lower mandible.

ADULT MALE similar but *gorget entirely brilliant cerulean to cobalt blue* (seldom visible), bill all black, narrow pale feather edges most conspicuous in spring.

IMMATURE FEMALE. *Crown emerald green edged in pale grayish buff.* Cheek dark gray. Distinct postocular spot followed by ragged, indistinct eye line. Throat pale to medium gray, mottled. *Bill medium length,* straight, may show pale pink or yellow at gape, base of lower mandible.

ADULT FEMALE narrow pale feather edges most conspicuous in spring, bill all black.

GREEN VIOLET-EAR

IMMATURE. Lacks pale eye line and strongly contrasting markings of other large hummingbirds. Violet to violet-blue "ear" may be incomplete or absent.

ADULT Virtually unmistakable, with emerald green head, metallic "ear."

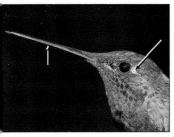

adult male Magnificent

adult female Magnificent

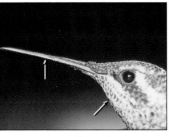

immature male Magnificent

Plain-capped Starthroat

immature male Blue-throated

immature female Blue-throated

adult male Blue-throated

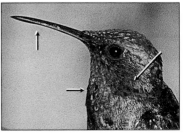

immature Green Violet-ear

PLATE 24

TAILS I: ADULT *SELASPHORUS* AND *STELLULA*

Most show rufous in tail, underparts.

ADULT MALES

ALLEN'S. Tail medium-long, rectrices narrower than in Rufous, R_2 *ta pers smoothly to sharp point*, R_5 *stiletto-like.*

RUFOUS. Tail long, rectrices broad (inner) to narrow (outer), R_2 *notche on inner web*, R_5 knifelike.

BROAD-TAILED. *Tail long, mostly blackish with violet sheen, outer pairs nar rowly edged rufous.* Smudgy white at tip of R_{4-5} variable, often ab sent.

CALLIOPE. *Tail very short, mostly dull gray, narrowly edged rufous nea base. R_1 angles to spade-shaped tip.*

ADULT FEMALES

ALLEN'S AND RUFOUS. Tails of these two species are virtually indistinguish able. Both show bright rufous at base of R_{2-5}, often on R_1 also, R pointed. Rufous usually shows *shallow indentation near tip of R_2; Al len's R_5 very narrow, no indentation in R_2 (immature male similar).*

BROAD-TAILED. Tail long, with rufous across bases of R_{1-3}, often mixe with black or green; *R_4 all green or with rufous on basal edges onl R_{3-5} rounded, with broad white tips.*

CALLIOPE. *Tail very short,* banded dull gray-green and black with whit tips on R_{3-5}, *variably edged rufous at base* (when present, extent of ru fous less than in Rufous, Broad-tailed, Bumblebee). R_{2-5} variabl tipped white (absent or indistinct on R_2). R_1 *vaguely spade-shaped a tip.*

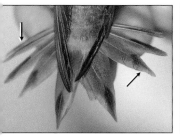

adult male Allen's

immature male Allen's (adult female similar)

adult male Rufous

adult female Rufous

adult male Broad-tailed

adult female Broad-tailed

adult male Calliope

adult female Calliope

PLATE 25

TAILS II: IMMATURE *SELASPHORUS* AND *STELLULA*

IMMATURE MALES. Rectrix shape, pattern usually similar to adult female.

ALLEN'S AND RUFOUS. Tails of these two species are virtually indistinguishable. Both show bright rufous at base of R_1-5, R_2 pointed, rufous and black. Rufous usually shows *shallow indentation near tip of R_2*; Allen R_5 *very narrow, no notch in R_2*.

BROAD-TAILED. *Tail long*, with rufous at bases of R_1-3 concentrated at edges or heavily mottled with black, or green rufous edge on outer web of R_4. R_2 pointed, R_3-5 tipped white (narrow on R_3).

CALLIOPE. *Tail very short*, banded dull gray-green and black, *variably edged rufous at base*. R_2-5 tipped white (narrow to indistinct on R_2). R_1 *vaguely spade-shaped at tip*.

IMMATURE FEMALES. Rectrix shape, pattern usually less distinctive than in adult female, immature male. Typically show more white in tail, especially R_2-3.

ALLEN'S AND RUFOUS. Virtually indistinguishable. Rufous may show *faint indentation near tip of R_2*; Allen's R_5 *averages narrower*.

BROAD-TAILED. Tail long, with rufous across bases of R_1-3, *basal edge only of R_4 (if present)*. R_2-5 rounded, tipped white (narrow on R_2).

CALLIOPE. *Tail very short*, banded dull gray-green and black, often with tawny or cinnamon wash at base of R_3-5 (no rufous edges). R_2-5 tipped white (narrow to indistinct on R_2). R_1 *vaguely spade-shaped at tip*.

immature male Allen's

immature female Allen's

immature male Rufous

immature female Rufous

immature male Broad-tailed

immature female Broad-tailed

immature male Calliope

immature female Calliope

PLATE 26

TAILS III: ADULT *ARCHILOCHUS* AND *CALYPTE*

Members of the genera *Archilochus* and *Calypte* have tails without significant rufous coloration.

ADULT MALES. Outer rectrices lack white.

BLACK-CHINNED. *Tail deeply notched*, extends slightly beyond wingtip. *Outer feathers pointed, blackish washed bronze-green at tips.*

RUBY-THROATED. Tail long, *deeply notched to forked*, outer feather pointed, blackish.

ANNA'S. Tail feathers gray, darker at edges bordering paler translucent areas; R5 narrow, rounded at tip.

COSTA'S. Tail feathers gray, darker at edges; R5 very narrow, curved inward, tapering to point.

ADULT FEMALES. All have tail feathers (R1) green or gray-green at base, blackish near tip (often indistinct or absent on R1–2), variable white tip on outer feathers (R3–5).

BLACK-CHINNED. *Tail square to slightly notched or double-rounded, extends slightly beyond wingtips.* R3–5 tipped white, *R4–5 pointed.*

RUBY-THROATED. *Tail moderately notched, extends well beyond wingtips.* R3–5 tipped white, R5 tapers to dull point.

ANNA'S. *Tail feathers broad, rounded.* R2–5 banded in *dull gray-green* and blackish, R3–5 tipped white (narrow or indistinct on R3).

COSTA'S. *Tail short, feathers rounded.* R2–5 banded in *dull gray-green* and blackish, R3–5 tipped white.

adult male Black-chinned

adult female Black-chinned

adult male Ruby-throated

adult female Ruby-throated

adult male Anna's

adult female Anna's

adult male Costa's

adultfemale Costa's

PLATE 27

TAILS IV: IMMATURE *ARCHILOCHUS* AND *CALYPTE*

All have tail feathers (R_1) green or gray-green at base, blackish ne
tip (often indistinct or absent on R_{1-2}), variable white tips on out
feathers (R_{2-5}).

IMMATURE MALES

BLACK-CHINNED. *Tail square to slightly notched or double-rounded, exten*
slightly beyond wingtips. R_{3-5} tipped white (narrow on R_3), R_4-
pointed.

RUBY-THROATED. *Tail notched, extends slightly beyond wingtips.* R_3-
tipped white (narrow on R_3), R_5 tapers to dull point.

ANNA'S. *Tail feathers broad, rounded.* R_{3-5} tipped white (indistinct
absent on R_3), *thin line of black extends into white tip along shaft*
R_5.

COSTA'S. *Tail short, feathers rounded.* R_{3-5} tipped white (indistinct
absent on R_3), *thin line of black extends into white tip along shaft*
R_5. R_5 narrow.

IMMATURE FEMALES

BLACK-CHINNED. *Tail square to slightly notched or double-rounded, exten*
slightly beyond wingtips. R_{2-5} tipped white (narrow on R_2), R_4-
rounded.

RUBY-THROATED. *Tail notched, extends slightly beyond wingtips.* R_3-
tipped white (narrow on R_2), R_5 rounded.

ANNA'S. *Tail feathers broad, rounded.* R_{3-5} banded in *dull gray-gree*
and blackish, R_{3-5} tipped white.

COSTA'S. *Tail short.* R_{3-5} banded in *dull gray-green* and blackish, R_3-
tipped white. R_5 narrow.

immature male Black-chinned

immature female Black-chinned

immature male Ruby-throated

immature female Ruby-throated

immature male Anna's

immature female Anna's

immature male Costa's

immature female Costa's

PLATE 28

TAILS V: SOUTHWESTERN SPECIES

BROAD-BILLED

> **ADULT MALE.** *Tail long, deeply notched, dark steel blue with dark gray edg* broadest on central pair of feathers.
>
> **ADULT FEMALE.** *Tail long, double-rounded*, outer feathers banded in gra green and steel blue, dull white tips on R_3-5 (narrow on R_3-4).
>
> **IMMATURE MALE.** Tail mostly steel blue, with narrow white tips on R_4- indistinct dark gray edges on R_1-3.
>
> **IMMATURE FEMALE.** *Tail long, double-rounded*, outer feathers banded green and steel blue, dull white tips on R_3-5 (narrow on R_3); bro pale edges on uppertail coverts.

WHITE-EARED

> **SECOND-YEAR MALE.** *Tail long, square to slightly notched*, R_2-5 bron green and blue-black, narrow white tips on R_3-5 (often indistinct absent on R_3).
>
> **FEMALES** similar but with broader white tips on R_3.
>
> **ADULT (AFTER SECOND YEAR) MALE** may lack white in R_3-5.

LUCIFER

> **IMMATURE FEMALE.** *Tail forked, feathers narrow.* R_1-2 green to bronz green, outer pairs banded in rufous, green, and black with white ti on R_3-5.
>
> **ADULT FEMALE, IMMATURE MALE** similar; less white in R_3.

VIOLET-CROWNED

> *Tail gray-green to grayish olive with diffuse white edges when fresh.*

AZURE-CROWNED

> (Not illustrated.) Similar to Violet-crowned.

adult male Broad-billed

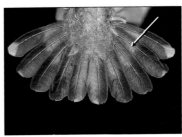

adult female Broad-billed

immature male Broad-billed

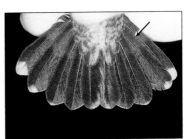

immature female Broad-billed

second-year White-eared

immature female Lucifer

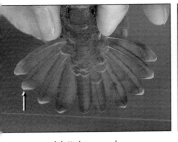

adult Violet-crowned

immature Violet-crowned

PLATE 29

TAILS VI: LARGE HUMMINGBIRDS

MAGNIFICENT

ADULT MALE. *Long, notched tail entirely dark bronze-green to bronze.*
ADULT FEMALE. *Long, notched tail banded green to bronze-green and blacish, with dull whitish tips on R_{2-5} (often narrow or indistinct on R_2*
IMMATURE MALE. *Long, notched tail dark bronze-green banded blackish R_{2-5}, diffuse whitish tips on R_{3-5}.*
IMMATURE FEMALE. Similar to adult female but with more white on R_2.

BLUE-THROATED

IMMATURE FEMALE. *Large rounded tail blue-black with conspicuous pu white tips on R_{3-5}, may have narrow white edge on R_2.*
IMMATURE MALE AND ADULTS similar; white area in R_3 may be small, ind tinct.

GREEN VIOLET-EAR

Tail blue-green above, deep blue below with broad dark blue subterm nal band. Adult and immature similar. (Specimen)

PLAIN-CAPPED STARTHROAT.

Tail short, bronze to bronze-green. R_{2-4} banded bronze and blacki with *white spot at tip on inner web*; R_5 broadly tipped white, *usual smudged with black on outer web.* Adult and immature similar. (Spec men)

BUFF-BELLIED

IMMATURE MALE. Tail moderately to deeply notched, R_1 rich rufous var ably tipped, bordered, or washed with golden green to bronze, R_2– similar but with iridescence confined to borders.
ADULT MALE (Not illustrated) Similar to immature male.
IMMATURE FEMALE. Similar to immature males but nearly square to mode ately notched.
ADULT FEMALE (Not illustrated) Similar to immature female.

adult male Magnificent

adult female Magnificent

immature male Magnificent

immature female Blue-throated

adult Green Violet-ear (specimen)

adult Plain-capped Starthroat (specimen)

immature male Buff-bellied

immature female Buff-bellied

PLATE 30

HYBRIDS

Hybridization between species is frequent and can explain some a[...]
biguous hummingbirds. Typical hybrids blend elements of the pare[...]
species, but results are not always predictable. Identification of [...]
brids is somewhat speculative. All birds shown are adult males.

COSTA'S × ANNA'S

Gorget rose purple with moderate extensions, upper breast whitis[...]
underparts with faint midline stripe. R3–5 intermediate in width b[...]
tween parent species.

RUFOUS × CALLIOPE

Gorget bright red with long spiky extensions; tail and underparts sh[...]
extensive rufous. R2 notched (not visible).

BROAD-TAILED × BLACK-CHINNED

Gorget dull reddish purple with narrow dark chin strap. Outer rect[...]
ces less pointed than Black-chinned's or Ruby-throated's. Outer p[...]
mary narrows abruptly at tip.

ANNA'S × BLACK-CHINNED

Gorget dull rose purple with slight extensions at corners, glints of p[...]
ple on otherwise dull dark green crown. R3–5 show grayish sem[...]
translucent edges. May sing a weak Anna's-like song.

ANNA'S × CALLIOPE

Gorget rose red with moderate, ragged extensions, forecrown sam[...]
color as gorget. R3–5 rounded, grayish, with narrow rufous edges [...]
inner web near base. May sing a weak Anna's-like song.

LUCIFER × BLACK-CHINNED

See Plate 9. Stockier than Lucifer, with darker gorget, shorter tail.

BERYLLINE × MAGNIFICENT

See Plate 14. Iridescent coppery bronze tail; gorget poorly define[...]
aqua blue blending to bright green.

adult male Costa's × Anna's

adult male Rufous × Calliope

adult male Broad-tailed × Black-chinned

adult male Broad-tailed × Black-chinned head

adult male Anna's × Black-chinned

adult male Anna's × Black-chinned

adult male Anna's × Calliope

adult male Anna's × Calliope tail

PLATE 31

ABNORMAL PLUMAGES

COMPLETE ALBINO RUBY-THROATED
Entirely white plumage, pink bill and feet, red eyes.

PARTIAL ALBINO RUBY-THROATED ADULT MALE
White feathers scattered among normally colored ones; bill, feet, r normal.

LEUCISTIC RUBY-THROATED IMMATURE
Whitish plumage suffused with brownish; bill, feet, eyes paler th normal.

LEUCISTIC ANNA'S ADULT MALE
Whitish plumage suffused with gray; bill, feet, eyes normal. Shape tail feathers identifies species, age, and sex.

SPHINX MOTHS

Several species of sphinx moths or hawk moths (family Sphingida are active in daylight and are regularly mistaken for hummingbirds; are shown. They are typically smaller than hummingbirds with d tinct markings on back and wings.

WHITE-LINED SPHINX (*Hyles lineata*)
Common and widespread throughout North America. Slightly smal than Calliope Hummingbird with distinct white markings on back a forewings, salmon pink band in hindwings, black-and-white chec ered pattern on long pointed abdomen.

HUMMINGBIRD CLEARWING (*Hemaris thysbe*)
Resembles a large bumblebeße with pale upper back, dark rump bar fluffy "tail," transparent wings broadly edged in rusty brown.

SNOWBERRY CLEARWING (*Hemaris diffinis*)
Resembles a large bumblebee with pale upper back, dark rump ban fluffy "tail," transparent wings narrowly edged in rusty brown.

CLAVIPES SPHINX (*Aellopos clavipes*)
One of several bumblebee-sized tropical sphinx moths with pale run bands. Markings resemble those of the tiny coquette hummingbir (*Lophornis*) found from Mexico to South America. A report of Blac crested Coquette (*Lophornis helenae*) from Big Bend National Park attributed to one of these moths.

complete albino Ruby-throated

leucistic immature Ruby-throated

partial albino adult male Ruby-throated

leucistic adult male Anna's

White-lined Sphinx

Hummingbird Clearwing

Clavipes Sphinx

Snowberry Clearwing

SPECIES
ACCOUNTS

WEDGE-TAILED SABREWING

Campylopterus curvipennis

4.75–5.25 in. (12–13.5 cm). Bill length: ♂ 26–31 mm, ♀ 23–28 mm; tail length: ♂ 43–50 mm, ♀ 38–44 mm.

This large hummingbird of eastern Mexico ranges north into southwestern Tamaulipas, the presumed origin of several other tropical species that have strayed into southern Texas; the potential exists for occurrence north of the Mexican border. The species gets its name from the modified shafts of its outer primaries, which are dramatically thickened and curved in adult males, less so in immature males and adult females. The function of this feature is unknown, though it may play a role in sound production or visual signaling during courtship displays.

DESCRIPTION

A large hummingbird with a long wedge-shaped or graduated tail, the central pair of feathers being much longer than the outer pair and extending well beyond the wingtips. Upperparts are bright green to emerald green, with blue to violet-blue crown blending with green of nape. White spot behind eye contrasts strongly with dark gray cheek. Underparts are pale gray to whitish, often slightly darker laterally; undertail coverts may show buffy wash. Bill is long, straight to slightly decurved; lower mandible is pinkish at base. Sexes are similar. **ADULT MALE:** Very large, with metallic deep blue to violet-blue crown blending with bright green on nape. Shafts of outer primaries extremely broad, flattened and curved near base. Tail green above with increasing dark suffusion toward tips of outer feathers. R4–5 mostly blackish, often with faint paler mottling at tip. **ADULT FEMALE:** Similar to male but smaller, with less extensive satiny deep blue to violet-blue on crown. Tail similar to male's, but usually with faint lighter mottling or well-defined light gray tips on R3–5. **IMMATURE MALE:** Similar to adult male but crown duller, usually some pale mottling in outer tail feathers. **IMMATURE FEMALE:** Similar to adult female but crown very dull blue, light gray tips on R3–5 usually large, well defined. Immatures of both sexes may show buffy wash on underparts as well as pale edges on feathers of upperparts.

SIMILAR SPECIES

Large size and distinctive tail shape distinguish it from most other hummingbirds. **BLUE-THROATED HUMMINGBIRD** has rounded blue-black tail with outer 2–3 pairs of feathers broadly tipped white, distinct white postocular line, proportionally short, straight bill. **MAGNIFICENT HUMMINGBIRD** has much shorter, slightly notched tail, darker gray underparts, straight all-black bill.

SOUNDS

CALLS include a steady, persistent chipping and a shrill, nasal *peek*. **SONG**, usually given from within dense vegetation, is complex and variable, beginning with hesitant insectlike chips, squeaks, and squeals followed by a series of excited warbled or gurgling notes. Males may sing year-round, sometimes in small loose groups. No distinctive flight sound is associated with the dramatically modified primaries of adult males.

BEHAVIOR

Often perches and forages along wall of vegetation at forest edge and on steep slopes. Flight style varies from rapid wingbeats typical of hummingbirds to slower wingbeats like those of swifts. Bold and curious, often approaching humans. Movements of wings and tail are associated with perched singing displays, suggesting that the modified primaries play a role in visual communication. **NEST** is a well-camouflaged cup attached to a horizontal branch. Breeds March to July.

HABITAT

Humid tropical forests, woodlands, and dense second growth, from near sea level to 4,500 ft. (1,400 m).

RESIDENT from within 250 mi. (400 km) of the U.S. border in southern Tamaulipas south to northern Oaxaca. A sedentary species not known to migrate; a stray north of resident range would most likely be a young bird dispersing in search of new breeding territory. Unrecorded north of Mexico.

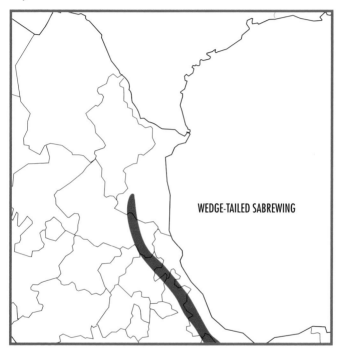

WEDGE-TAILED SABREWING

STATUS AND CONSERVATION

Fairly common to common within its range, even nesting in urban parks and residential gardens; subspecies *excellens* (Long-tailed Sabrewing) has a limited range in southern Veracruz and is considered vulnerable.

SUBSPECIES AND TAXONOMIC RELATIONSHIPS

The three recognized subspecies have completely separate ranges and may be distinct species. Subspecies *curvipennis*, which occurs closest to the U.S. border, has slightly longer bill than *pampa* of the Yucatán Peninsula. This species is sometimes split from *Campylopterus* into the genus *Pampa*.

 ## REFERENCES

Howell and Webb 1995
Peterson and Chalif 1973
Sutton 1972
Züchner 1999a

GREEN VIOLET-EAR PLS. 17, 23, 29

Colibri thalassinus

4.25–4.5 in. (11–11.5 cm). Bill length: 18–22 mm; tail length: 35–41 mm.

Normally found in mountain forests of southern Mexico and Central America, this large striking hummingbird makes surprisingly frequent appearances north of the tropics. Most U.S. records are from central and southern Texas, but individuals have strayed east to North Carolina and north to Ontario and Alberta. Though superficially similar to Magnificent and Blue-throated Hummingbirds, especially in immature plumage, it is far more likely to be seen east of the Great Plains than these species of the southwestern mountains. The species name means "sea green."

 ## DESCRIPTION

A large dark hummingbird with a slightly to moderately decurved bill. Sexes are similar. **ADULT** is grass green to golden green above, becoming more bronze on rump and uppertail coverts. Underparts satiny emerald to grass green, becoming duller and paler on belly. Glittering gorget feathers appear slightly convex. Undertail coverts pale tan or buff-gray glossed with dull green, or dull green to bronze-green broadly bordered in paler grayish buff. Tail is square to slightly notched, blue-green above, deep blue below with broad dark blue subterminal band; central feathers more green above, outer more blue. Bill black, slender. **ADULT MALE:** Large deep violet-blue central breast spot blends into green of throat and upper breast; violet-blue band along chin often connects with metallic violet to violet-blue "ear." **ADULT FEMALE:** Averages smaller and slightly duller than adult male, often with narrower violet-blue band on chin. **IMMATURES:** Much duller, paler versions of adults. Satiny grass green to olive green overall, with dull grayish wash to underparts. Violet-blue breast spot often indistinct, incomplete, or absent. Tail similar to adult's. May show dull grayish buff edges on upperparts. Molting immatures show some bright metallic color in patches, particularly noticeable on throat and breast.

SIMILAR SPECIES

Easily confused only with other large and/or dark hummingbirds. Adult male **MAGNIFICENT HUMMINGBIRD** has uniformly colored metallic apple to turquoise green throat, violet to purple crown, slightly notched bronze-green tail, distinct white spot behind eye. Adult male **BROAD-BILLED HUMMINGBIRD** is much smaller, with entire throat sapphire blue, undertail coverts whitish, bill red or orange-red basally. **BLUE-THROATED HUMMINGBIRD** has conspicuous white markings on face and tail. **SPARKLING VIOLET-EAR** (*Colibri coruscans*), in a South American species imported for zoo collections, is larger (5 in., 13 cm), with more extensive violet-blue on chin and breast.

SOUNDS

CALLS include a dry rattle given while feeding and a loud 2-syllable note, *chip-tsirr*, given while perched. **SONG** is a long, monotonous series of 1- to 3-syllable metallic notes, repeated frequently from dawn until dusk. Song is typically given from one of several exposed perches within the male's territory. **WING SOUND** is lower pitched than that of smaller species but not distinctive.

BEHAVIOR

A fast-moving, wary bird, seldom lingering long during visits to feeders. Often keeps to the shadows in dense vegetation, where color and other field marks may be difficult to discern. Frequently flicks, wags, and fans tail in flight. Differences in territorial behavior may relate to sex and age, with adult males most aggressively defending feeding territories. Like other large hummingbirds, it spends more time foraging for insects than taking nectar. Various species of *Salvia* with red or blue flowers are important nectar sources in Mexico, but Violet-ears visit a wide variety of flowers. **FLIGHT DISPLAY** is undulating, accompanied by singing; on alighting, male flutters open wings for several seconds. Courting pairs engage in undulating, side-by-side display flights, often accompanied by pigeonlike wing clapping. **NEST** is a soft, bulky cup built on a low branch of a tree or shrub; exterior is camouflaged with mosses, dried leaves, hanging grass blades. Northern populations have two breeding periods: early spring (March) and late summer to early fall (July to September). Nesting females are reportedly sensitive to intrusion and prone to abandoning nests because of disturbance.

Habitat

Humid to semiarid forest and woodland of oaks and conifers, shrubby second growth at forest edge, in canyons, and in overgrown clearings in mountains, 3,200–11,000 ft. (1,000–3,500 m). Often found in gardens and other intensely cultivated areas. Most U.S. sightings have been in areas with dense vegetation.

Distribution

BREEDS from central Jalisco and southern San Luis Potosí south to Peru and Bolivia. No breeding records north of Mexico. Resident or semiresident over much of breeding range. **MIGRATION** is poorly understood but appears to be primarily altitudinal. In Mexico, many females and immatures appear to move south or to lower el-

GREEN VIOLET-EAR
(all records)

evations by November, reportedly returning during summer rainy season. Males are apparently more sedentary but may move to higher or lower elevations in nonbreeding season. Unpredictable **VAGRANT** in U.S. More than 30 records for eastern half of Tex. since 1961 (up to 4 in one season), mostly in Rio Grande Valley, Gulf Coast, Edwards Plateau. All spring records are from Tex. Other accepted records from Ala., Ark., Colo., Ky., La., Mich., Miss., Mo., N.C., Ohio, Okla., Wisc., Alta., Ont. Two reports from Calif., both in August 1977, were rejected. Records in U.S. span period from mid-April through mid-December, most falling between early May and late July, with a minor peak late August to early September. This pattern may represent movements of adults and young birds following the spring breeding season or dispersal of young adults in advance of the summer breeding season. Many are "one-day wonders," but average sighting period is 2 weeks; longest sighting period at a single location is 18 weeks.

STATUS AND CONSERVATION

Common to fairly common over most of its range in Mexico. May actually benefit from deforestation; edges of clear-cuts and dense second growth provide ideal habitat. It is unclear whether the dramatic increase in sightings beginning in the late 1980s is attributable to greater northward movements, perhaps related to habitat and population changes, or to increased awareness of the species because of its inclusion in newer field guides. Careful documentation of all northern vagrants, both photographically and through banding, is vital to unraveling the mystery of this species' migratory behavior.

SUBSPECIES AND TAXONOMIC RELATIONSHIPS

The northern subspecies, *thalassinus,* has been treated as a separate species, Mexican Violet-ear; distinguished from three southern races by slimmer bill and more prominent violet-blue breast patch and chin band. One of at least four species of violet-ears, found from central Mexico to South America. Some of its relatives, including the Sparkling Violet-ear, have been imported for zoos and private collections.

PLUMAGE VARIATION AND MOLT

Sexes are so similar as to complicate understanding of behavior, particularly migration. Immatures are easily separated from adults by much duller plumage. Adults molt in spring, immatures late winter through summer.

◆ REFERENCES

Howell and Webb 1995
Johnsgard 1997
Meisenzahl 1998
Mlodinow and O'Brien 1996
Newfield 2001
Oberholser 1974
Stiles 1999a
Tarbutton and Clapp 1998
Wagner 1945

GREEN-BREASTED MANGO   PL. 17

Anthracothorax prevostii

4.5–5 in. (11.5–12.5 cm). Bill length: ♂ 24–29 mm, ♀ 25–31 mm; tail length: ♂ 35–37 mm, ♀ 34–36 mm.

Found over much of the humid tropical regions of Mexico and Central America, this striking species has been reported north of the border with increasing frequency since the first U.S. sighting in 1988. Most northern strays are immature males, whose combination of large size and striking plumage pattern makes them unlikely to be overlooked. However, strong similarities among the various mango species and the importation of hummingbirds for zoo collections complicate identification. Formerly known as Prevost's Mango.

 DESCRIPTION

A large colorful hummingbird with a long decurved bill and dramatic sexual dimorphism. **ADULT MALE:** Dark emerald green above becoming golden green on rump and uppertail coverts. Throat is dark emerald green with broad velvety black central stripe extending onto breast. Breast is dark blue to blue-green centrally, blending to dark leaf green and golden green on belly and sides. Tail is square to slightly notched, central feathers dark coppery bronze to bronze-green, outer 3–4 pairs bright purple to violet above and below with underlying reddish pigment, edged in dull black. Undertail coverts dark green, femoral tufts white. **ADULT FEMALE:** Similar to adult male in size but with paler, more bronze-green upperparts, boldly patterned underparts. Throat, breast, and belly white with broad dark vertical stripe at midline, blackish on chin becoming dark emerald green to blue-green at base of throat. Narrow band of cinnamon brown may be present on chin. Flanks and sides bright green to golden green. White of breast blends to grayish on lower belly. Tail square to slightly rounded, banded in purple, blue-black, and white on outer 3–4 pairs. Undertail coverts mostly grayish to dusky green with broad whitish border. A small proportion of adult females acquire male-like plumage. **IMMATURES:** Similar to adult female but with dark ventral stripe broken or absent on chin, heavy rust brown mottling along edges of white underparts. **IMMATURE MALE:** Outer tail feathers banded purple and blue-black, with white tips on R3–5. Undertail coverts dark green basally, broadly whitish at tips. May show black and dark blue-green feathers coming in through white and duller green of underparts. **IMMATURE FEMALE:** Tail mostly blue-black, with little purple or reddish; white tips on R2–5.

SIMILAR SPECIES

Adult male may be confused with other large dark hummingbirds. **MAGNIFICENT HUMMINGBIRD** has uniformly colored metallic apple to turquoise green gorget, violet to purple crown, bronze-green tail, distinct white spot behind eye, straight bill, pale crissum. **GREEN VIOLET-EAR** has blue-green tail with dark blue subterminal band, violet-blue "ears" and breast patch, paler undertail coverts. Adult females and immatures are easily confused only with similar mangos. In **BLACK-THROATED MANGO** (*A. nigricollis*), a South American species painted by John James Audubon from a specimen purportedly collected in Florida, females and immature males have green iridescence in dark belly stripe; similar **GREEN-THROATED MANGO** (*A. viridigula*) is also South American and unlikely to occur in the United States except as escape from captivity. Immature male **ANTILLEAN MANGO** (*A. dominicus*) of Hispaniola and Puerto Rico should be considered as a possibility for any Florida mango sightings; immature male resembles female Green-breasted but with no green in central stripe.

SOUNDS

CALLS include liquid *tseep* or *tschip* notes, an explosive buzzy note and a loud, high-pitched twittering during territorial interactions. **SONG** a buzzy, metallic *kazick-kazee,* usually given in a short series from high perch. **WING SOUND** is lower pitched than in smaller species but not distinctive.

BEHAVIOR

Highly insectivorous, often seen in extended fly-catching bouts high in the air. Males are more vocal than females and often defend feeding territories. Flicks tail open while feeding. **NEST** is a shallow cup of plant down sparsely camouflaged with lichen, bark, and other plant debris, usually placed in fairly open situation on leafless branch or forked twig. Nests March to June in northern Mexico.

HABITAT

Open savannahs, tree-dotted pastures, orchards, mangroves, tall second growth, edges of forest and dense woodland, sea level to 4,000 ft. (1,200 m).

DISTRIBUTION

BREEDS from southern Tamaulipas south to northern Oaxaca, resident Tabasco and Chiapas through Yucatán Peninsula and along Caribbean and Pacific slopes of Central America. Winter visitor to Pacific slope from Oaxaca to El Salvador. Northern subspecies is partially migratory; departs southern Tamaulipas and Veracruz by late September, returning in late February. Infrequent **VAGRANT** in southern and coastal Tex., beginning with a poorly documented

GREEN-BREASTED MANGO

sighting in September 1988 just ahead of Hurricane Gilbert. An immature male banded in N.C. (November 2000) is exceptional. Most sightings are August to September, during migration; winter records may represent individuals that arrived weeks earlier but went undetected until weather drove them to feeders. Sighting in May of an individual in immature plumage may represent migratory "overshoot" by an inexperienced bird or dispersal from an early nesting. An adult male in McAllen, Tex. (February 2000) is likely a returnee that first visited as an immature.

STATUS AND CONSERVATION

This species actually benefits from clearing of primary forest for agriculture and is common in gardens, parks, and plantations. Population expansion due to deforestation in eastern Mexico may be a significant factor in recent sightings in Texas.

SUBSPECIES AND TAXONOMIC RELATIONSHIPS

Northern subspecies, *prevostii*, extends south to Guatemala and Belize. Four other subspecies occur between Honduras and Peru; southern populations may constitute a separate species. Approximately 8 species of mangos are distributed through Mexico, Central and South America, and the Caribbean; the name comes from their attraction to flowering mango trees. Taxonomic relationships within this genus are poorly understood; this species is sometimes regarded as conspecific with Black-throated Mango. The oddest member of this group is the Fiery-tailed Awlbill, whose short bill turns up abruptly at the tip.

PLUMAGE VARIATION AND MOLT

Adult female may show narrow band of rust brown on chin, less extensive than cinnamon brown mottling at edge of throat and breast in immatures. Immatures may be sexed by extent of purple and white in tail—more purple in males, more white in females. Molt takes place in winter, though immature males may begin showing some adult body plumage by late summer.

REFERENCES

Howell and Webb 1995
Johnsgard 1997
Raffaele et al. 1998
Stiles 1999b
Stiles and Skutch 1989

ANTILLEAN CRESTED HUMMINGBIRD

Orthorhyncus cristatus

3.25–3.75 in. (8.5–9.5 cm). Bill length: ♂ 7.5–10 mm, ♀ 9–12 mm.

This small striking hummingbird of the eastern Caribbean is the subject of one of North America's most mind-boggling ornithological mysteries. A specimen salvaged in Galveston, Texas, almost 2,000 mi. (3,200 km) from the nearest known point of occurrence in eastern Puerto Rico, could not be attributed to storm, ship assist, or escape from captivity. Though a reappearance of this species in the United States is highly unlikely, a remote possibility exists for a stray to reach Florida.

 ## DESCRIPTION

A small stout-bodied hummingbird, similar in size to Ruby-throated but with a very short bill. **ADULT MALE:** Unmistakable, with flattened, pointed crest of brilliant metallic green to golden green, often faintly tipped in blue-green or blue, contrasting with dark green nape and face; upperparts dull metallic green to bronze-green, underparts sooty gray to blackish, paler on throat and upper breast, glossed with dark bronze-green on sides; tail rounded, central feathers dark green, outer feathers blackish washed with violet-purple iridescence below. **ADULT FEMALE:** Bright green above; underparts dull dark gray to dusky, paler on throat and breast; no white spot behind eye. Tail rounded, central feathers green, outer 3 pairs (R3–5) banded in dull green and blue-black, with pale ash gray to grayish white tips. May appear slightly crested. **IMMATURES:** Similar to adult female; immature male darker below with small spot or narrow crescent of white on R5.

 ## SIMILAR SPECIES

Female and immature male **RUBY-THROATED HUMMINGBIRD** are slimmer, with whitish to pale gray underparts and longer bill. Tail extends beyond wingtips. Female and immature male **BLACK-CHINNED HUMMINGBIRD** are slimmer, with pale grayish underparts, much longer bill.

 ## SOUNDS

CALLS include an emphatic *pit-chew*. **SONG** is apparently undescribed. Wing sound in normal flight not distinctive, but male makes clapping sound during courtship display.

Behavior

Feeds from near ground to tree canopy. Commonly used nectar plants in the Caribbean include hibiscus, citrus trees, lantana, porterweed, and legumes such as royal poinciana and orchid tree. Feeding territories are most often held by males. Residents of arid scrub feed more extensively on invertebrates during dry season. Courtship includes a slow descending FLIGHT DISPLAY from above female followed by a rapid SHUTTLE DISPLAY in front of her accompanied by clapping sounds. Male's crest is erected during display. NEST is a cup of plant fibers and spider silk camouflaged with lichens and plant debris, placed in tree, shrub, or vine 2–7 ft. (0.6–2 m) above ground. Breeds mostly January to August.

Habitat

Partial to arid habitats characterized by cacti and agaves but also found in forest openings and edges. Adapts readily to human environments, including gardens and plantations.

Distribution

RESIDENT from northeastern Puerto Rico through Virgin Islands and Lesser Antilles, most common below 1,600 ft. (500 m). Apparently sedentary. In early February 1967, the badly damaged carcass of an adult male was rescued from household trash on Galveston Island, Tex., where it had been discarded by two local boys who claimed to have captured the bird alive. No storms were associated with this record, and there are no subsequent records from anywhere in the U.S. The Texas Bird Records Committee does not include this species on its list.

Status and Conservation

Common throughout its range; adapts readily to human alteration of habitats. Expanding populations in Puerto Rico may slightly increase the remote likelihood of future occurrences in the United States as storm- or ship-assisted visitors to Florida.

Subspecies and Taxonomic Relationships

Texas specimen (now in American Museum of Natural History) was identified as subspecies *exilis,* found from eastern Puerto Rico south through the Lesser Antilles to St. Lucia. The sole member of its genus, the Antillean Crested has no close relatives in North America or elsewhere in the Caribbean.

REFERENCES

Bleiweiss et al. 1997
Johnsgard 1983
Pulich 1968
Raffaele et al. 1998
Schuchmann 1999

GOLDEN-CROWNED EMERALD

PL. 16

Chlorostilbon auriceps

3–3.75 in. (7.5–9.5 cm). Bill length: ♂ 13–14 mm; ♀ 13–16 mm; tail length: ♂ 40–47 mm, ♀ 29–36 mm.

Sometimes considered a subspecies of the Fork-tailed Emerald, this small hummingbird of coastal western Mexico occurs within 500 mi. (800 km) of the southwestern border of the United States. Though it has not yet been reported in the United States, female-plumaged individuals could easily be overlooked in southeastern Arizona because of their resemblance to the Broad-billed Hummingbird.

DESCRIPTION

A small short-billed hummingbird with a very long notched to deeply forked tail. **ADULT MALE:** Glittering emerald green to grass green below, golden green to bronze-green above, with pale undertail coverts and small inconspicuous whitish spot behind eye. Tail is very long, deeply forked, blackish to blue-black with broad dull gray tips on inner pairs of feathers becoming narrower and less distinct on outer pairs. Short straight bill is coral red with black tip. **ADULT FEMALE:** Grass green to golden green above, pale gray below, with whitish line behind eye, narrow dark gray stripe on cheek; tail forked, R3–5 banded gray-green, blackish, and white, outer web of R5 whitish basally. **IMMATURE FEMALE:** Similar to adult female but with pale feather edges on upperparts, more white on R3. **IMMATURE MALE:** Resembles adult female but with longer, more deeply forked tail with outer pairs of feathers blue-black, less distinct dull whitish to gray tips on R4 and R5, inner pairs washed green with gray tips, widest on R1. Often shows irregular patches of green on underparts.

SIMILAR SPECIES

CANIVET'S EMERALD, potential stray to southern Texas, is very similar. Adult male has shorter, less deeply forked tail with broader feathers. Females and immature male have deeply notched tail with small patches of whitish near base of R_5 bordered above and below by blackish. Adult male **BROAD-BILLED HUMMINGBIRD** is larger with sapphire blue on throat, longer bill. Shorter, notched tail is steel blue with broader feathers. Female has longer bill, square to slightly notched tail with no white at base of R_5.

Sounds

CALLS include dry chatter similar to that of Broad-billed Hummingbird.

Behavior

Wags fanned tail, much like Broad-billed Hummingbird. Often takes nectar from short-tubed flowers primarily pollinated by insects and seldom visited by other hummingbirds. Forages at low

CANIVET'S

GOLDEN-CROWNED

GOLDEN-CROWNED/CANIVET'S EMERALD

to middle height; primarily a trapliner or territory parasite. NEST is composed of plant down and strips of bark, often attached to hanging leaves or twigs near ground level. Nests February to July.

 HABITAT

Thickets, scrub, dense second growth in tropical deciduous forest and dry to humid woodland. Similar to Canivet's Emerald.

 DISTRIBUTION

RESIDENT southwestern Durango and southeastern Sinaloa south to southern Oaxaca. Seasonal movements primarily altitudinal but may wander in response to nectar availability. No records north of Mexico.

 STATUS AND CONSERVATION

Generally common, readily adapting to habitats modified by human activity.

 SUBSPECIES AND TAXONOMIC RELATIONSHIPS

Along with the closely related Canivet's Emerald, this species is often treated as a subspecies of the Fork-tailed Emerald, *Chlorostilbon forficatus,* or of the Blue-tailed Emerald, *C. mellisugus.* Its closest relative north of Mexico is the Broad-billed Hummingbird, which it resembles in plumage, voice, and behavior.

 PLUMAGE VARIATION AND MOLT

Adults molt February to July in southern Mexico.

 REFERENCES

Bündgen 1999a
Howell and Webb 1995
Johnsgard 1997

CANIVET'S EMERALD   PL. 16

Chlorostilbon canivetii

3–3.5 in. (7.5–9 cm). Bill length: ♂ 13–14 mm, ♀ 13–16 mm; tail length: ♂ 30–38 mm, ♀ 27–32 mm.

The northeastern representative of the Fork-tailed Emerald

complex ranges north into southwestern Tamaulipas, the presumed origin of several other Mexican species that have strayed into southern Texas. Not reported in the United States but should be considered as a possibility for sightings of presumed female-plumaged Broad-billed Hummingbird in the eastern half of Texas.

DESCRIPTION

A small short-billed hummingbird with a long notched to deeply forked tail. **ADULT MALE:** Glittering grass green to emerald green below, grass green to bronze-green above, with pale undertail coverts and small inconspicuous whitish spot behind eye. Tail long, forked, blackish to blue-black with broad dull gray tips on inner pairs of feathers becoming narrower and less distinct on outer pairs. Short straight bill is coral red with black tip. **ADULT FEMALE:** Grass green to bronze-green above, pale gray below, with whitish line behind eye, narrow dark gray stripe on cheek; tail deeply notched, R3–5 banded gray-green, blackish, and white, R5 with small patches of whitish near base bordered above and below by blackish. **IMMATURE FEMALE:** Similar to adult female but with pale feather edges on upperparts, more white on R3. **IMMATURE MALE:** Resembles adult female but with longer, more deeply forked tail, outer pairs of feathers blue-black with less distinct dull whitish to gray tips on R4 and R5, inner pairs washed green with gray tips, widest on R1. Often shows irregular patches of green on underparts.

SIMILAR SPECIES

GOLDEN-CROWNED EMERALD, potential stray to southwestern states, is very similar. Adult male has longer, more deeply forked tail with narrower feathers. Females and immature males have deeply notched tail with larger patches of whitish at base of R5. Adult male **CUBAN EMERALD** has entirely dark upper mandible; female has no white at base of R5. Probable rare stray to Florida. Adult male **BROAD-BILLED HUMMINGBIRD** is larger with sapphire blue on throat, longer bill, and shorter notched steel blue tail. Female has longer bill, square to slightly notched tail with no white at base of R5.

SOUNDS

CALLS include dry chatter similar to that of Broad-billed Hummingbird.

BEHAVIOR

See Golden-crowned Emerald. Nests February to May.

HABITAT

Thickets, scrub, dense second growth in tropical deciduous forest and dry to humid woodland.

DISTRIBUTION

RESIDENT southern Tamaulipas to Yucatán Peninsula, Belize, northern Guatemala, Bay Islands of Honduras. Seasonal movements primarily altitudinal, but may wander in response to nectar availability. No records north of Mexico. (See map under Golden-crowned Emerald, p. 129.)

STATUS AND CONSERVATION

Generally common, readily adapting to habitats modified by human activity.

SUBSPECIES AND TAXONOMIC RELATIONSHIPS

See Golden-crowned Emerald.

PLUMAGE VARIATION AND MOLT

Adults molt February to July in southern Mexico.

REFERENCES

Bündgen 1999a
Howell and Webb 1995
Johnsgard 1997

CUBAN EMERALD   PL. 16

Chlorostilbon ricordii

3.5–4 in. (9–10 cm). Bill length: ♂ 14–18 mm, ♀ 17–19 mm; tail length: ♂ 38–40 mm, ♀ 36–40 mm.

Apparently a rare and irregular stray to Florida, this common hummingbird of Cuba and the Bahamas has not been adequately documented in the United States. Despite more than a dozen sightings in Florida since 1943, no specimen or unequivocal photographs exist, relegating this species to hypothetical status as a U.S. visitor. The most compelling reports have described adult males, with details sufficient to eliminate Buff-bellied and Broad-billed Hummingbirds. The species name honors Alexandre Ricord, a Maryland-born surgeon-naturalist who collected specimens in the West Indies.

DESCRIPTION

A small hummingbird with a long forked tail, short to medium-length slightly decurved bill with orange to coral red at base of lower mandible. **ADULT MALE:** Grass green to bronze-green above, glittering bright green to golden green below, becoming bronze-green on flanks and belly. Throat and breast range from golden green to deep blue, depending on angle and light. Small white spot behind eye contrasts strongly with dark face. Tail is long, forked; central feathers dark greenish bronze, becoming greenish black to black on outer pairs, faintly glossed with bluish green above, violet-blue below; undertail coverts whitish, variably streaked with gray. Medium-length bill is straight to slightly decurved, blackish above, lower mandible orange-red at base with black tip. In poor light may appear all dark except for postocular spot and undertail coverts. **ADULT FEMALE:** Grass green to bronze-green above. Pale gray to whitish below becoming green from sides of neck to flanks, with diffuse band of green across lower breast, very narrow to broken at center. Short white eye line contrasts with dark gray cheek. Forked tail extends far past wingtips; R1 bronze-green, outer pairs darker, with small white tips on R4 and R5. Bill as in male but longer; lower mandible red orange basally with more extensive black at tip. **IMMATURE FEMALE:** Similar to adult female but with pale feather edges on upperparts, more white on R3. **IMMATURE MALE:** Resembles adult female but with longer, more deeply forked tail; outer pairs of feathers blue-black with less distinct dull whitish to gray tips on R4 and R5, inner pairs washed green with gray tips, widest on R1. Often shows irregular patches of green on underparts.

SIMILAR SPECIES

CANIVET'S EMERALD, potential stray to southern Texas, is similar in size, but adult male has blackish tail with gray tips, more extensive red on bill. Females and immature males have white patches at base of outer tail feathers. Adult male **BROAD-BILLED HUMMINGBIRD**, an unverified vagrant to Florida, is slightly larger with sapphire blue throat and much shorter, notched steel blue tail with gray tips on inner pairs; longer bill has more extensive red at base. Females and immature males have shorter square or slightly notched tail, outer pairs banded in grass green and blue-black with dull whitish tips. **BUFF-BELLIED HUMMINGBIRD**, rare winter resident in northwestern Florida, is much larger, with brighter green throat and breast, pale cinnamon-buff to grayish buff belly, dark rufous tail edged in bronze-green; red on bill usually more extensive. **GREEN VIOLET-EAR** is much larger, with all-black bill, square blue-green tail, patches of violet-blue on cheeks and breast.

♪ Sounds

CALLS include a high-pitched two-syllable squeak and a squeaky twitter, often given when taking flight. **SONG** is a high-pitched rapid series of *slee* notes. Males reportedly have particularly noisy flight.

Behavior

A tame, easily approached species. Highly territorial and aggressive, often attacking much larger birds. Visits a variety of flowers, including ornamentals such as bougainvillea, usually in low to middle tiers of vegetation. Feeds extensively on invertebrates, including spiders and prey plucked from their webs. Courtship displays are undescribed. **NEST** is a tiny cup of soft plant fibers, feathers, and animal hair, exterior camouflaged with lichen, plant debris, and long dangling strips of bark, placed 3–10 ft. (1–3 m) above ground in a shrub, vine, or spiny euphorbia. May refurbish nest for multiple broods. Aggregations of up to 6 occupied nests in a single shrub have been reported in Cuba. Breeds year-round.

Habitat

Widely distributed in lowlands to middle elevations, especially in woodlands, shrubby undergrowth of open pine forest, coastal scrub; readily adapts to habitats modified for human use, including gardens, parks, and plantations.

Distribution

RESIDENT throughout Cuba, including Isle of Pines, and on the islands of Grand Bahama, Andros, and Abaco in the Bahamas, including many neighboring keys. **VAGRANTS** have been reported sporadically in Florida since 1943. Most sightings have come from

CUBAN EMERALD

the central to southern Atlantic Coast, nearest the birds' presumed origin in the Bahamas. Few reports, even those of adult males, provide enough details to rule out similar species such as Broad-billed and Buff-bellied Hummingbirds. A bird in N.C. tentatively identified as a Cuban Emerald turned out to be a Green Violet-ear. Thorough documentation of future sightings, preferably with photographs, video, or banding, is necessary to verify this species' presence in the U.S.

STATUS AND CONSERVATION

Common to abundant within its range and not considered threatened. Brace's Emerald (*Chlorostilbon bracei*), a less fortunate relative known only from a single small island in the Bahamas, is the only hummingbird species so far verified to have become extinct in historic times.

SUBSPECIES AND TAXONOMIC RELATIONSHIPS

The only identified subspecies, *bracei*, was posthumously classified as a full species. The emeralds are closely related to the Broad-billed Hummingbird, a common species in parts of southeastern Arizona and a rare vagrant to the southeastern United States.

REFERENCES

Bündgen 1999b
Cruickshank 1964
Garrido and Kirkconnell 2000
Johnsgard 1997
Raffaele et al. 1998
Robertson and Woolfenden 1992
Sprunt 1954
Stevenson and Anderson 1994
Stimson 1944

BROAD-BILLED HUMMINGBIRD   PLS. 16, 22, 28

Cynanthus latirostris

3.5–4 in. (9–10 cm). Bill length: ♂ 20–22 mm, ♀ 20–23 mm; tail length: ♂ 28–35 mm, ♀ 27–31 mm.

This mild-mannered jewel is one of the most beautiful and exotic looking of northern hummingbirds. Its broad, expressive tail is in nearly constant motion as it flits about the desert scrub and riparian woodlands of its southwestern home. Its voice, consisting mostly of raspy, insectlike chittering, is very different from that of most North American hummingbirds. Locally common in southern Arizona and extreme southwestern New Mexico, it is the most common hummingbird in the lowlands of northwestern Mexico. Its uninspired common name comes from the species name, which translates as "broad bill."

DESCRIPTION

A small slender hummingbird with a rounded head, long neck, long broad-based bill, and long mobile tail. Sexes are similar in size and proportions, though the male's dark color and slightly longer tail may make him appear larger. **ADULT MALE:** Distinctive, with glittering sapphire blue gorget blending into emerald green of breast, sides, and belly. Whitish to pale gray undertail coverts and white femoral tufts contrast strongly with dark underparts.

Back deep green to bronze-green, becoming duller on rump and uppertail coverts. Tail long, deeply notched, dark steel blue with dark gray edges broadest on central pair of feathers. Face dark with small, often indistinct white postocular spot; faint whitish eyeline usually absent in mature males. Bill long, broad-based, red at base with variable and often extensive black at tip (more extensive in nonbreeding season). **ADULT FEMALE:** Entirely green to bronze-green above, pale to medium gray below with plain throat and some grass green spangling on sides. Dull white postocular stripe is widest behind eye, contrasts with sooty gray cheek. Tail long, double-rounded; broad, rounded outer feathers banded in emerald green and steel blue, with dull white tips on outer 2–3 pairs (often absent from R3). Bill blackish, broad at base, with dull pinkish orange confined to lower mandible, base of upper mandible. **IMMATURE FEMALE:** Duller in color than adult female, with broad pale edges to feathers of upperparts, white tips on R3–5 (often very small on R3). Bill entirely blackish above. **IMMATURE MALE:** Resembles female but with a small patch, stripe, or scattering of blue feathers on throat, broad pale edges to feathers of upperparts, more orange at base of bill; tail more blue, with small white tips on R4–5, indistinct dull gray edges on R1–3.

SIMILAR SPECIES

Female and immature male **WHITE-EARED HUMMINGBIRD** are similar in size but chunkier, with larger head in proportion to body. Broader white postocular stripe contrasts strongly with blackish cheek. Throat and sides of upper breast spangled with bronze-green to blue-green. Bill thinner, shorter. Call is a sharp, metallic *tchik* or *tink*. Emeralds are smaller, with shorter, thinner bills. Adult male **CANIVET'S EMERALD** has glittering green crown, throat, and underparts, forked blue-black tail. Female has deeply notched tail with small whitish patches at base of narrow outer feathers. Adult male **GOLDEN-CROWNED EMERALD** has glittering green crown, throat, and underparts, deeply forked blue-black tail. Female has forked tail with small whitish patches at base of narrow outer feathers. Much larger **MAGNIFICENT HUMMINGBIRD** has all-black bill. Adult male has metallic green gorget contrasting with blackish breast, flattened metallic purple crown, and distinct white postocular spot. Call is a mellow *tschip*. Much larger **BLUE- THROATED HUMMINGBIRD** has paler upperparts, large rounded blue-black tail with large pure white spots at corners, all-black bill. Call is a shrill *tseep*.

♪ SOUNDS

CALLS include harsh chatter consisting of *chit* or *ji-dit* notes, given singly or in series. Rapid repetition of chatter notes indicates alarm. Young birds have a more mellow twitter; may give a sweet *teep*, similar to fledgling's food-begging call, during aggressive encounters. **SONG** is a rapid, hoarse *jeejeejeejeejee* interspersed with single or double chipnotes; usually given from a prominent perch with throat feathers erected. Song appears to be highly variable and at least partly learned; males have been heard imitating songs of other species, including *whee-oo* of male Costa's. Male's wings "zing" during pendulum display; normal flight sound not distinctive.

✠ BEHAVIOR

One of the less combative hummingbirds. Aggressive interactions usually consist of calls and tail-fanning display. In both sexes the tail is in almost constant motion in flight, shuddering to a stop after the bird perches. Both sexes often sit with tail horizontal and feathers slightly fanned and separated vertically. Takes nectar from a variety of flowers, including agaves, chuparosa, desert honeysuckle, tree tobacco. Catches insects by hawking, gleaning. Bathes by fluttering on wet leaves or in shallow running water. During courtship and aggressive encounters, male performs **PENDULUM DISPLAY** accompanied by distinctive high-pitched zinging sound. **NEST** is made from plant fibers, shreds of bark, fine grasses bound together with spider web, sparsely camouflaged with small leaves, stem fragments, dried flowers, occasionally flat chips of lichen. Site is often low in a thick shrub or small tree, often near water or rock outcrops. Nests March to September; at least 2 broods per year.

HABITAT

In the United States, shrub thickets, washes, rocky slopes, and riparian woodlands in foothills and lower canyons of mountains to over 5,000 ft. (1,500 m); in northwestern Mexico, occurs in wider range of habitats from sea level to 7,200 ft. (2,200 m), including tropical deciduous forest. Rare in higher oak woodlands, mainly as post-breeding visitor.

DISTRIBUTION

BREEDS from southeastern Ariz., southwestern N. M., possibly western Tex. south to southern Mexico. Locally common in Ariz. in the drainage of the Santa Cruz R. and nearby mountain ranges

rare in winter within
U.S. breeding range

BROAD-BILLED
HUMMINGBIRD

(Santa Rita and Patagonia Mts.), and in extreme southwestern N.M. (Guadalupe Canyon); uncommon and local breeder north to Galiuro and Santa Catalina Mts., west to Baboquivari Mts., and east through southeastern Ariz. to southwestern N.M. (Peloncillo Mts.). Rare but apparently increasing during breeding season in far western Tex. (Big Bend National Park, Davis Mts); no recent nesting records. **RESIDENT** over most of its range, from southeastern Sonora and southwestern Chihuahua south. Migratory birds from northern populations are believed to winter near northern edge of resident range. A few individuals winter near feeders in southern and central Ariz., mostly at lower elevations. Migrants arrive on northern breeding grounds between early March and early April, depart by early October. May wander north or to higher elevations in late summer. Numerous fall and winter records from southern Calif. Apparently increasing fall and winter visitor to Gulf Coast; 4 individuals were banded in La. in one winter. Casual to accidental late summer through spring in southern Nev., N.M. (except Peloncillo Mts., Guadalupe Canyon), Tex., Ill., Ore., S.C., Utah, Wisc., N.B., Ont.

STATUS AND CONSERVATION

Locally common to abundant within its U.S. range. Habitat is vulnerable to grazing, residential and recreational development, and loss of riparian habitat because of groundwater pumping. Shift to dependence on feeders and gardens in areas of habitat destruction or degradation increases exposure to pesticides, predators (including domestic cats), windows, and chemical additives in artificial nectar. Accelerating conversion of natural desert to pasture for livestock in northwestern Mexico destroys nectar resources and may disrupt migratory pathways into the United States. May have benefited from introduction of nectar-rich tree tobacco from South America. Has reached at least 6 years of age in the wild.

 ## SUBSPECIES AND TAXONOMIC RELATIONSHIPS

Northwestern subspecies *magicus* nests in the United States; other subspecies confined to Mexico, though *latirostris* of northeastern and east-central Mexico, slightly larger with grayer undertail coverts and more green mottling on underparts of female, should be considered for sightings from southern Texas eastward. One of only two members of its genus, this species' closest relative is the Dusky Hummingbird, *Cynanthus sordidus*, of southwestern Mexico. However, it shows strong affinities to the emeralds of the genus *Chlorostilbon*. Hybrids have been reported with Violet-crowned and Magnificent Hummingbirds.

 ## PLUMAGE VARIATION AND MOLT

Second-year birds returning in spring are usually indistinguishable from older adults, but some younger males may show indistinct whitish line behind eye. Adults molt May to September, immatures July to November; molt is usually complete before northern adults depart breeding grounds. Young males typically show an irregular patch or stripe of metallic sapphire blue concentrated in the center of the gorget, which gradually fills in over the winter.

REFERENCES

Howell and Webb 1995
Oberholser 1974
Phillips et al. 1964
Powers and Wethington 1999
Russell and Monson 1998

ylocharis (Basilinna) leucotis
3.5–4 in. (9–10 cm). Bill length: ♂ 16–18 mm, ♀ 17–19 mm; tail length: ♂ 31–36 mm, ♀ 29–33 mm.

This strikingly marked, pugnacious hummingbird is common to abundant in the Sierra Madre of Mexico but rare, local, and irregular in the United States. Though this species was first collected in Arizona over a century ago, there were no reports in the United States between 1933 and 1961. In 1989 it established a presence in the Huachuca Mountains of southeastern Arizona, where it is currently a rare but regular summer resident. Males are highly vocal, singing from conspicuous perches and giving resonant call notes that Alexander Skutch likened to "the chiming of a small silver bell." Its species name translates as "white ear."

DESCRIPTION

A medium-small hummingbird of chunky proportions, with large head and short straight bill with red or orange at base. Distinguished in all plumages by combination of bold white eye-stripe combined with blackish cheek, heavily spangled with green. **ADULT MALE:** Distinctive, with broad bright white postocular stripe arching over top of eye and contrasting with blackish cheek. Forecrown and chin blue-violet; solid metallic turquoise green of gorget becoming separate large spangles of green broadly edged in whitish on sides and flanks. Belly dull white centrally. Upperparts deep green to bronze-green; uppertail coverts and rump edged in cinnamon-rufous. Tail long, slightly notched; central feathers bronze-green, R2–5 bronze-green and blackish, tips of R4–5 all dark or edged or tipped in dull whitish. Short straight bill is thin but broad-based, coral red and black. **ADULT FEMALE:** Entirely golden green to bronze-green above; uppertail coverts, rump, and forecrown edged in dull cinnamon-rufous. Dull ivory to creamy white below with spangles of bronze-green to turquoise green on throat becoming golden green on sides. Broad white postocular stripe extends from above eye to shoulder, contrasting with dusky to blackish cheek. Tail long, slightly notched, outer feathers banded in green and blue-black, with well-defined dull white tips on R4–5. Short straight bill is broad at base; upper mandible mostly blackish with some coral red or orange basally, lower mandible mostly orange or red with black tip. **IMMATURE MALE:** Resembles adult female except for irregular patch of bright metallic green feathers, smaller and less distinct whitish or pale gray tips on outer tail feathers. Upper mandible may be mostly blackish or with broad area of red at base. **SECOND-YEAR MALE:** Resembles adult male but

with blue-violet band on chin and forecrown reduced or absent.
IMMATURE FEMALE: Difficult to distinguish from adult female. Upper-parts slightly duller with broad dull cinnamon to tawny edges, buffy wash on underparts, duller orange and more extensive blackish on bill, more extensive white tips on outer tail feathers, particularly R3.

SIMILAR SPECIES

Female and immature male **BROAD-BILLED HUMMINGBIRD** are similar in size, but slimmer, with smaller head in proportion to body and longer, heavier bill. Narrower whitish postocular stripe shows less contrast with dark gray cheek. Throat and upper breast of females plain gray with no markings; immature male shows irregular splotches of dark blue to blue-green on throat and breast. Call consists of harsh *chit* or *ji-dit* notes, given singly or in series. Emeralds (genus *Chlorostilbon*) are smaller, slimmer, with longer, deeply notched or forked tails. **BLUE-THROATED HUMMINGBIRD** is much larger, with proportionally smaller head, plain gray underparts, large rounded blue-black tail with large pure white spots at corners, no red or orange in bill; call is a shrill *tseep*.

SOUNDS

CALL is a sharp metallic *tchik* or *tink*, similar to call note of Anna's Hummingbird but richer. **SONG** is a rapid staccato series of metallic chips interspersed with upslurred *zreek* or *zurr-eet* notes, either singly or in series. Males are typically more vocal than females.

BEHAVIOR

Assertive; males often guard nectar sources, driving off even larger species such as Magnificent Hummingbird. Takes nectar from a variety of red, blue, and yellow flowers with short to medium-length corolla tubes, including salvias and tree tobacco. Opportunistically takes nectar from longer flowers through holes chewed by insects. In Mexico, males congregate in singing assemblies, behavior not observed in the United States. Female active partner in courtship, enticing male into **DISPLAY FLIGHT** involving chasing and face-to-face hovering. **NEST** is a small cup of oak leaf wool and other plant fibers densely camouflaged with chips of lichen and bark fragments, usually built in shrub or low tree. A nest in the Huachuca Mountains, Arizona, was built in a New Mexican locust (also a nectar source) in a mixed grove of oaks and conifers at the edge of a burned area. Nests May to June in the United States, may raise 2 broods per season.

HABITAT

Pine-oak woodland and conifer forest in mountains, 4,500–10,000 ft. (1,400–3,100 m), lower in winter. In the United States it is rarely seen below oak belt of mountains; sightings in other habitats should be carefully documented to rule out Broad-billed Hummingbird.

DISTRIBUTION

BREEDS southeastern Ariz. (Huachuca and Chiricahua Mts.), extreme southwestern N.M. (Animas Mts.), south through Sierra Madre to southern Mexico, discontinuously in mountains south to Nicaragua. Arrives in Ariz. mid-April to May, departs August to October. **RESIDENT** or altitudinal migrant over most of its range, from southwestern Chihuahua, southeastern Coahuila south. **VAGRANT** or casual visitor June to October in southwestern and north-central N.M. (Peloncillo and Pinos Altos Mts.; Bernalillo, San

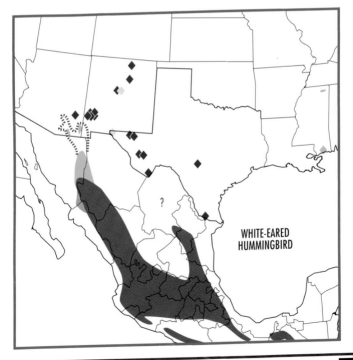

WHITE-EARED
HUMMINGBIRD

Miguel, and Taos Cos.), western and central Tex. (Davis, Guadalupe, and Chisos Mts., El Paso, Fredricksburg). Most records east and north of known breeding range are between late June and August, evidence of significant post-breeding movements. Migratory instinct apparently poorly developed, may limit northward expansion. Has attempted to winter in southeastern Ariz., evidently without success. A female wintering in coastal Miss. (November 1995 to January 1996) is exceptional.

STATUS AND CONSERVATION

Common to abundant in much of its range in Mexico, where it has managed to thrive despite droughts, heavy grazing by livestock, and accelerating timber harvest. Rare and local in the United States and likely to remain so.

SUBSPECIES AND TAXONOMIC RELATIONSHIPS

Northern subspecies *borealis* nests from Ariz. south to northern Sinaloa. Forms a superspecies with Xantus's Hummingbird, which is endemic to Baja California. Multiple hybrids with Broad-tailed Hummingbird have been observed in Arizona, where the two species share similar habitat in pine-oak woodland. A banded male hybrid apparently inherited its Broad-tailed parent's earlier migration schedule, arriving in Ramsey Canyon between late February and early March each year.

PLUMAGE VARIATION AND MOLT

Male plumage may take more than two years to develop full color. Younger males may show full green gorget but little or no violet on chin and forecrown and dull whitish tips on outer tail feathers. Some mature males also retain narrow pale tips on R4–5. In northern populations, adults molt May to August, immatures August to October; second-year males molt slightly later than older males.

REFERENCES

Howell and Webb 1995
Johnsgard 1997
Russell and Monson 1998
Skutch 1999
Züchner 1999b

llocharis (Basilinna) xantusii
3.25–3.75 in. (8.5–9.5 cm). Bill length: ♂ 17–19 mm, ♀ 17–19 mm.

The only hummingbird endemic to Baja California, this species has strayed to southern California and southern British Columbia. It is a sibling species of the White-eared Hummingbird, from which it is separated by the Gulf of California. The two species share a bold white eye-stripe, but rich cinnamon and rust tones present in all plumages set Xantus's apart. The species was named in honor of its eccentric collector, John Xántus. Formerly known as Black-fronted Hummingbird.

DESCRIPTION

A medium-small chunky hummingbird with a large head and short thin bill, distinguished by bold white eye-stripe and blackish cheek combined with cinnamon underparts and dark rufous brown in tail. **ADULT MALE:** Bright green to bronze-green above, with rufous edges on uppertail coverts. Forecrown and chin blackish with faint violet wash, becoming bright metallic green on lower gorget. Cinnamon-buff below, green of gorget becoming spangles on sides. Tail rusty brown above with golden green edges, broadest on R1, violet-purple wash below. Thin straight bill is red with blackish tip. **ADULT FEMALE:** Bright green to bronze-green above, with broad rufous edges on uppertail coverts. Forecrown dusky grayish to rufous. Cinnamon-buff below, sides of breast lightly spangled with green. Tail rusty brown with broad golden green margins; R1 mostly golden green, R3–5 marked with dusky subterminal band and pale tips. Thin straight bill mostly dusky to blackish above, dull orange-red below. **IMMATURE MALE:** Resembles adult female except for extensive green in gorget. **IMMATURE FEMALE:** Difficult to distinguish from adult female but may show more distinct rufous edges on feathers of upperparts, duller orange and more extensive blackish on bill.

SIMILAR SPECIES

Bold white eye-stripe contrasting with dark cheek distinguishes it from most hummingbirds of similar size. **WHITE-EARED HUMMINGBIRD** has white underparts heavily spangled with green, no cinnamon or rufous in tail.

♪ SOUNDS

Voice similar to that of White-eared Hummingbird but raspier. **CALLS** include a dry rattle similar to that of Broad-billed Hummingbird, metallic *tik* or *tink* notes given singly or in short series, and rapid chittering in combat. **SONG** is a series of raspy twitters and chips.

🦅 BEHAVIOR

Takes nectar from a variety of herbs, shrubs, and trees, including Mexican lobelia, Baja fairy-duster, Baja madrone. Hunts insects around oaks and pines. **NEST** is a substantial cup of oak leaf wool and other plant fibers densely camouflaged with chips of lichen, catkins, and plant debris, built low in an oak, willow, or cottonwood, often near flowing water. Nests February to April in north, July to September in south.

🏔 HABITAT

Desert scrub, thickets in washes and canyons, tropical deciduous woodland, oak woodland, and gardens at lower elevations, up to pine-oak woodland in the mountains, sea level to 5,000 ft. (1,500 m).

🐦 DISTRIBUTION

RESIDENT from southern end of Baja California along eastern slope to mid-peninsula. Sedentary or short-distance migrant; some northward movement has been detected outside the breeding season. **VAGRANTS** have wandered north of Mexico at least twice. In December 1986 a male was observed away from feeders in eastern San Diego Co., Calif. The following year, a female spent January to March in a yard in Ventura, Calif., where she nested unsuccessfully. From November 1997 to September 1998, a female took up residence near a feeder in Gibsons, B.C. No satisfactory explanation has been offered for this extraordinary record.

📊 STATUS AND CONSERVATION

Endemic to Baja California, this species has apparently not been harmed by limited human activities in this forbidding landscape. Continued recreational development should have few adverse effects on its populations unless its canyon oases are filled with resorts and vacation homes. It has a mutualistic relationship with an endemic tree, the Baja madrone. The tree depends on the hummingbird for pollination, in turn providing the birds with

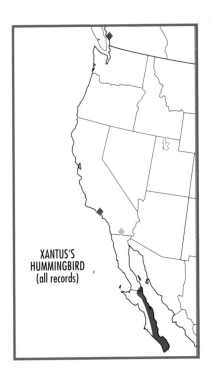

XANTUS'S
HUMMINGBIRD
(all records)

nectar in late winter and early spring when few other plants are in bloom.

Subspecies and Taxonomic Relationships

As expected for a species of such limited distribution, no subspecies have been described. Xantus's and White-eared Hummingbirds form a superspecies, separated by the Gulf of California. The two species may have diverged from a common ancestor beginning between 5 and 10 million years ago, when tectonic movements of the Pacific Plate split Baja California away from the mainland of Mexico.

Plumage Variation and Molt

Some females show faint spangling on chin and upper gorget like White-eared Hummingbird. Molt period similar to that of White-eared.

Arriaga et al. 1990
Hainebach 1992
Howell and Webb 1995
Johnsgard 1997
Peterson and Chalif 1973
Scott 1999

BERYLLINE HUMMINGBIRD

PL. 14

Amazilia (Saucerottia) beryllina

3.75–4 in. (9.5–10 cm). Bill length: ♂ 18–20 mm, ♀ 19–21 mm; tail length: ♂ 27–33 mm, ♀ 26–32 mm.

A handsome hummingbird of Mexico's Sierra Madre, this species has visited the "sky island" mountains of southeastern Arizona on a nearly annual basis since the mid-1970s. It has nested in the Huachuca and Chiricahua Mountains and may be expanding into similar sky island mountain ranges in the Big Bend region of Texas. The conspicuous "flash" at the base of its primaries and secondaries is unique among hummingbirds north of Mexico. Named for the green gemstone beryl.

 DESCRIPTION

A medium-large dark hummingbird with glittering apple green to turquoise green throat and breast. Wings dusky gray with band of bright cinnamon-rufous across bases of secondaries, inner primaries. Sides and flanks spangled with dull bronze-green. Belly dull fawn to brownish gray, undertail coverts washed cinnamon with broad pale buff to ivory margins, contrasting with white femoral tufts. Back bright green to golden green becoming dull purplish bronze on rump. Square to slightly notched tail dark rufous-brown with strong violet-purple sheen; uppertail coverts dark violet-purple. Bill bicolored; upper mandible blackish, lower reddish or dull orange at base with blackish tip. Sexes similar. **ADULT MALE:** Brilliant metallic "bib" extends across entire throat, breast, and upper belly. Narrow whitish postocular crescent, pale preocular spot. Belly dull brownish gray to cinnamon-gray. Tail square to slightly notched. **ADULT FEMALE:** Like adult male but chin whitish, iridescence of less extensive "bib" muted by whitish edges and bases of feathers. Belly paler dull grayish fawn; tail square. **IMMATURES** resemble adults but duller, with less intense iridescence on throat and breast, ragged lower border to "bib," broad cinnamon-buff edges on upperparts. **IMMATURE MALE:** May show extensive bronze-green mottling from sides of neck to flanks, more intense iridescence at center of throat than adult female. Older immature males show patches of metallic green on throat and breast. **IMMATURE FEMALE:** Less intense iridescence, broader pale margins on throat and breast feathers than adult female.

SIMILAR SPECIES

Other large dark hummingbirds lack cinnamon-rufous wing flash. **BUFF-BELLIED HUMMINGBIRD** has bright buff to pale grayish buff belly in both sexes, more restricted green "bib," bright rufous tail with broad green margins, R1 often entirely golden green or bronze-green. **RUFOUS-TAILED HUMMINGBIRD** has dark rufous-brown tail with green to bronze edges. **AMAZILIA HUMMINGBIRD** (*Amazilia a. amazilia*), a South American species that has escaped from captivity in the United States, has bright rufous lower breast and belly, rufous tail with bronze-green margins. Male **MAGNIFICENT HUMMINGBIRD** has black chest with subtle green wash, bronze tail, distinct white postocular spot on dark face.

SOUNDS

CALL is a throaty, querulous *dzr'eer* or *brr-'irr,* lower pitched and more mellow than harsh chips of Violet-crowned. **SONGS** include a loud *du-tu-deet'* and a long series of high-pitched hisses, twitters, and chips.

BEHAVIOR

Males are territorial, more so in absence of larger species such as Blue-throated. Takes nectar at a variety of flowers, including salvias and scarlet bouvardia; feeds extensively on insects. Frequents shady forest understory, where iridescent colors are difficult to see. Courtship behavior is poorly studied, but male sings from a conspicuous perch within his territory during early breeding season. **NEST** is a soft cup of whitish plant fibers or thin grass blades, exterior densely shingled with chips of lichen, often with thin strip of grass dangling from bottom; in Arizona usually built on high thin twig in subcanopy of Arizona sycamore. Northern populations nest May to September, mostly late June to August.

HABITAT

BREEDS in open tropical deciduous forest, oak, and pine-oak woodland, thickets in canyons, sycamore-maple riparian forest, 3,000–10,000 ft. (1,200–3,100 m). **RESIDENT** over most of range; may move to lower elevations in nonbreeding season.

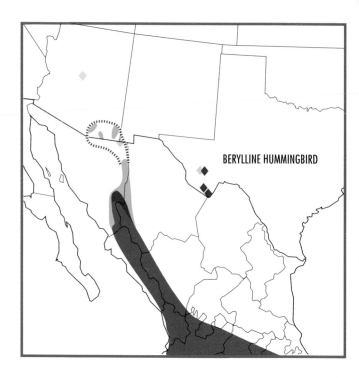

BERYLLINE HUMMINGBIRD

 DISTRIBUTION

BREEDS from southeastern Ariz. (rare), western Chihuahua, eastern Sonora through western and southern Mexico to El Salvador and Honduras. **RESIDENT** over most of breeding range, from far southern Sonora south; may move to lower elevations in winter. Temporarily abandons areas where nectar supplies are reduced by drought or frost. Migration begins as early as March in Mexico, where it is mostly altitudinal. Most U.S. records June to August. Typically arrives in Ariz. May to June, departs by mid-September. First recorded in the U.S. in 1967; now rare but regular in southeastern Ariz. Several nest records for Huachuca and Chiricahua Mts., sight records for Santa Rita Mts. **VAGRANT** in western Tex. (Big Bend National Park, Davis Mts.), southwestern N.M. (Guadalupe Canyon).

STATUS AND CONSERVATION

Common and apparently secure in Sierra Madre of Mexico. Gravitates toward feeding stations in the United States, which increases risk of contact with pesticides, cats, and windows.

SUBSPECIES AND TAXONOMIC RELATIONSHIPS

Northern subspecies *viola* is slightly duller on rump than *beryllina* of central Mexico. Some taxonomists propose dividing the 28 members of the genus *Amazilia* among 4 genera. Under this classification, the Berylline Hummingbird is the only U.S. species assigned to the genus *Saucerottia*, whose 9 members are characterized by purple to blue iridescence in the tail. An adult male hybrid with Magnificent Hummingbird in Arizona showed a narrow cinnamon-buff flash in the wings, aqua blue gorget, and coppery bronze tail.

PLUMAGE VARIATION AND MOLT

Pattern of white mottling on bib of females variable, may help in distinguishing between individuals. Northern adults molt spring to early summer, immatures fall to winter.

REFERENCES

Anderson and Monson 1981
Howell and Webb 1995
Johnsgard 1997
Mlodinow and O'Brien 1996
Russell and Monson 1998
Weller 1999e

UFOUS-TAILED HUMMINGBIRD   PL. 13

nazilia tzacatl
4–4.25 in. (10–11 cm). Bill length: ♂ 18–23 mm, ♀ 20–24 mm; tail length: 29–35 mm.

This common species of the humid tropics is similar enough to the Buff-bellied Hummingbird that a vagrant within the latter's range in southern Texas might be overlooked. Like the Buff-bellied, it is active and pugnacious, defending feeders where available as well as flowers such as firebush and sultan's-turban hibiscus. The species name means "grass" in Nahuatl, the language of the Aztecs, an apt description of the color. Formerly known as Reiffer's Hummingbird.

Description

A large dark hummingbird with glittering metallic grass green to turquoise green "bib" covering throat, breast, and upper belly; lower sides and flanks dull bronze-green to golden green; center of belly dull brownish gray. Tail is square to slightly notched, with dark rufous-brown feathers moderately bordered in bronze-green to golden green. Undertail coverts rich cinnamon-rufous, contrasting with whitish femoral tufts; uppertail coverts mostly dark rufous. Bill red and blackish, varying in proportion by age and sex. Pale cinnamon spots in front of and behind eye. Sexes very similar, not always readily distinguishable. **ADULT MALE:** Typically shows more brilliant metallic green on slightly more extensive bib, darker gray belly. Bill red with blackish tip. **ADULT FEMALE:** Typically has metallic green of less extensive bib muted by pale feather edges, most conspicuous on chin; slightly paler gray belly. Bill more extensively blackish on upper mandible, often extending to base of bill. **IMMATURES:** Similar to adults but duller, with cinnamon-rufous feather edges on upperparts, mottled appearance to less extensive green bib, more extensive black on bill.

Similar Species

BUFF-BELLIED HUMMINGBIRD has bright buff belly in both sexes, slightly to distinctly notched tail with broader green margins on individual feathers, R1 often entirely golden green or bronze-green, uppertail coverts mostly green. Undertail coverts pale to medium cinnamon-buff with broad pale borders. **BERYLLINE HUMMINGBIRD** has bright cinnamon band at base of secondaries and inner primaries, dark rufous-brown tail overlaid with violet-purple iridescence; female has paler ash gray to grayish buff belly. **AMAZILIA HUMMINGBIRD** (*Amazilia a. amazilia*), a South American species that has escaped from captivity in the United States, has bright rufous lower breast and belly.

Sounds

CALLS include hard metallic *chik* or *chink* notes and a hoarse low-pitched chatter; in aggressive interactions, a shrill accelerating *tsee tsee tsee-tsee-ee'u*, and *chup chup chrrrrup-chup*. **SONG** is a long varied series of thin, high-pitched squeaks and nasal chips.

Behavior

Mostly territorial, driving other birds and even insects away from nectar sources. May feed while clinging to petals of larger flowers. Takes nectar at sultan's-turban hibiscus, firebush, heliconias, powderpuff, and many other flowers. **NEST** is formed from a variety of materials, including animal hair, both fine and coarse plant fibers, densely covered with mosses and chips of lichen; attached to a slender horizontal branch or fork 3–25 ft. (1–7 m) above ground. Nests at least December to September, perhaps year-round.

HABITAT

Edges and clearings in humid tropical forest, second growth, semiarid scrub thickets, undergrowth in tropical pine forest, gardens, plantations.

DISTRIBUTION

RESIDENT from eastern Mexico south into northwestern South America. Some seasonal elevational movements recorded in Central America. Unconfirmed stray to southern Tex. Specimens re-

old U.S. records uncertain,
no recent records

RUFOUS-TAILED HUMMINGBIRD

portedly collected at Fort Brown (Brownsville) in the summer of 1876 have since been lost, and sight records (11–12 November 1969 at LaPorte, 20 August 1975 in Brownsville) are poorly documented.

 ## STATUS AND CONSERVATION

A common to abundant species, adaptable to human alteration of its habitat.

 ## SUBSPECIES AND TAXONOMIC RELATIONSHIPS

Subspecies *tzacatl* is resident from eastern Mexico through central Panama. See Buff-bellied Hummingbird. Has hybridized with Cinnamon Hummingbird.

PLUMAGE VARIATION AND MOLT

In northern population, adults molt September to December, after breeding season.

REFERENCES

Howell and Webb 1995
Johnsgard 1997
Weller 1999a

BUFF-BELLIED HUMMINGBIRD   PLS. 13, 29

Amazilia yucatanensis

3.75–4.25 in. (9.5–10.5 cm). Bill length: ♂ 18–23 mm, ♀ 20–24 mm; tail length: 30–35 mm.

The only large hummingbird regularly found east of the Great Plains, this is also the only tropical hummingbird that is a regular feature of the bird life of the lower Rio Grande Valley and southeastern Texas. Aggressive and territorial, it typically dominates smaller hummingbirds at gardens and feeding stations. It is unusual among North American hummingbirds in that in the fall some individuals migrate northward along the Gulf Coast to winter as far east as western Florida. Individual birds often show strong attachments to their wintering sites, returning to the same feeding station each fall. Formerly known as Fawn-breasted Hummingbird.

DESCRIPTION

A large hummingbird with apple green to turquoise green "bib" covering throat and breast. Belly pale to medium grayish buff to pale cinnamon-buff with some dull bronze-green spangling along sides and flanks. Tail shape varies by age and sex from nearly square to deeply nothced; R1 rich rufous variably tipped, bordered, or washed with golden green to bronze, R2–5 similar but with iridescence confined to borders. Undertail coverts pale to medium cinnamon-buff with broad whitish borders; uppertail coverts mixed green and cinnamon-rufous. Bill red at base with blackish tip varying in extent by age, sex, and season. Dull buff to cinnamon spot in front of eye, narrow whitish crescent behind eye. Sexes very similar. **ADULT MALE:** Bib brilliant metallic green, including chin, belly pale cinnamon-buff, tail moderately to deeply notched. Bill coral red with blackish tip, usually with narrow black edges on upper mandible extending to base; brighter with less extensive blackish in breeding season. **ADULT FEMALE:** Bib less intense metallic green muted by pale feather edges; narrow band of pale buff on chin. Belly medium buff to pale cinnamon-buff. Tail slightly to moderately notched. Bill blood red with moderate to extensive blackish on upper mandible, varying seasonally as in male; lower mandible red to orange-red with black tip. **IMMATURES:** Resemble duller adults, with dull cinnamon-rufous feather edge on upperpart, mottled appearance to green bib, more extensive black on bill. **IMMATURE MALE:** Slightly brighter iridescence in bib, tail moderately to deeply notched. **IMMATURE FEMALE:** Very dull green bib, tail nearly square to moderately notched.

SIMILAR SPECIES

RUFOUS-TAILED HUMMINGBIRD has dull brownish gray belly, tail squared, rufous-brown with green to bronze edges, R1 and uppertail coverts more extensively rufous, undertail coverts rich cinnamon-rufous. **BERYLLINE HUMMINGBIRD** has bright cinnamon band at base of secondaries and inner primaries, dark rufous-brown tail overlaid with violet-purple iridescence; male has dark grayish to brownish gray belly. **AMAZILIA HUMMINGBIRD** (*Amazilia a. amazilia*), a South American species that has escaped from captivity in the United States, has bright rufous lower breast and belly.

SOUNDS

CALLS include harsh *tchip* or *tchik* notes, a slurred *chrrik*, and a nasal gnatcatcher-like *mew*. In aggressive interactions, a low-pitched, rapid *see-see-see-see-siu-siu*, descending in pitch, and a sharp *siik*. Scolding call is series of chips run together in a staccato rattle. Territorial individuals also give a gnatcatcher-like *mew* or *tsi-we*. **SONG** is a series of cascading, bubbly notes, often given from dense cover. Dry whirr apparently made by wings or tail. Shrill whistle, probably mechanical, is heard during male's dive display and territorial or courtship chases.

BEHAVIOR

Aggressive and territorial. In breeding season, males selectively exclude other males while tolerating females. Highly vocal, especially territorial males. Feeds at a variety of flowers, including Turk's-cap hibiscus, sultan's-turban hibiscus, coral-bean, Texas sage, Mexican olive; nonnative shrimplant is important nectar source for wintering birds. Captures insects by fly-catching, gleaning. Feeds at sapsucker wells in winter. Flicks tail intermittently in flight. Male's dive display rarely observed, not well documented. **NEST** is a soft cup of whitish plant fibers and animal hair, exterior camouflaged with chips of lichen, bark fragments, dried flower petals, other plant debris; built in fork of horizontal branch in shrub or small tree such as Texas ebony (*Pithecellobium flexicaule*), hackberry (*Celtis* spp.), coastal live oak (*Quercus virginianus*), and yaupon (*Ilex vomitoria*). Nests mid-March to September.

HABITAT

Humid coastal thorn scrub, oak woodlands, and thickets of subtropical vegetation such as palmetto (*Sabal*); also residential areas with gardens and feeders, especially in winter. In Texas, breeds primarily in coastal oak mottes with Turk's-cap hibiscus in understory and subtropical riparian forest of lower Rio Grande Valley.

DISTRIBUTION

RESIDENT from central Gulf Coast of Tex. to Yucatán Peninsula, northern Belize, northern Guatemala. After breeding, small numbers move northward along Gulf Coast, **WINTERING** eastward to western Florida, October to March. The few winter records away from the coastal plain include central Tex., Ark.

STATUS AND CONSERVATION

Texas population is apparently expanding northward and inland despite widespread destruction of native woodlands for cattle pas-

BUFF-BELLIED HUMMINGBIRD

ture, farm fields, and residential development, perhaps because of the introduction of feeders and exotic flowers. Individuals wintering in the north are vulnerable to severe winter storms; species apparently lacks cold-hardiness of wintering Rufous. Individuals have reached at least 9 years of age.

SUBSPECIES AND TAXONOMIC RELATIONSHIPS

Subspecies *chalconota* is resident from southern Texas to northeastern Mexico. Forms a superspecies with Cinnamon Hummingbird; less closely related to the superficially similar Rufous-tailed Hummingbird. Some taxonomists propose dividing the large genus *Amazilia* into three genera; under this classification Buff-bellied, Rufous-tailed, and Cinnamon Hummingbirds remain in the genus *Amazilia*, whose six members are characterized by rufous in the tail.

PLUMAGE VARIATION AND MOLT

Variation in bill color and plumage, particularly depth of tail notch and extent of iridescence on R1, make aging and sexing very difficult in the field. In northern populations, adults reportedly molt April to October, immatures April to November; more study needed.

REFERENCES

Chavez-Ramirez and Moreno-Valdez 1999
Howell and Webb 1995
Johnsgard 1997
Oberholser 1974

CINNAMON HUMMINGBIRD PL. 14

Amazilia rutila

4–4.5 in. (10–11.5 cm). Bill length: ♂ 19–24 mm, ♀ 20–24 mm; tail length: 31–37 mm.

The first report from Arizona of this striking tropical species was met with much skepticism, but diagnostic photos and a second well-documented sighting in New Mexico the following year placed this species firmly on the list of U.S. hummingbirds. The species name means "red" or "ruddy."

DESCRIPTION

A large hummingbird with distinctive bright cinnamon-buff to cinnamon-rufous underparts. Crown, nape, and upper back bright green, becoming bronze-green to bronze mixed with rufous on lower back and rump; uppertail coverts bronze-green broadly bordered in bright rufous. Tail is slightly to moderately notched, with bright cinnamon-rufous feathers variably bordered at tips in dark bronze-green. Bill coral red with blackish tip. Lores same color as throat; pale buff crescent behind eye. Sexes similar in both plumage and behavior; differences in bill color, depth of tail notch seen in closely related Buff-bellied Hummingbird not recorded for this species. **IMMATURES:** More extensive black on bill, pale feather edges on upperparts, duller underparts.

SIMILAR SPECIES

Virtually unmistakable. From behind it resembles **BUFF-BELLIED HUMMINGBIRD** but with green of R1 reduced to narrow margins near tip.

SOUNDS

Highly vocal during foraging and territorial interactions. CALLS and SONG similar to those of other *Amazilia*, especially Buff-bellied.

BEHAVIOR

Aggressive and territorial, with both sexes defending nectar sources from other hummingbirds and large insects. Peak foraging time shortly after dawn, followed by increase in territorial behavior. Courtship behavior is unstudied. NEST similar to that of Buff-bellied Hummingbird. Nests November to February, June to July, September in western Mexico.

HABITAT

In western Mexico, mainly dry tropical scrub and tropical deciduous forest, sea level to 5,200 ft. (1,600 m). In Belize and Yucatán

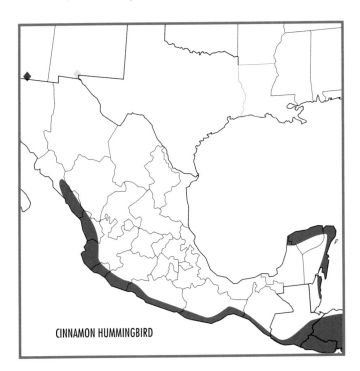

CINNAMON HUMMINGBIRD

Peninsula, occurs in coastal scrub, edges of fields and pastures, dry forest, and gardens near coast and on nearby islands.

 DISTRIBUTION

RESIDENT along Pacific slope from northwestern Mexico (northeastern Sinaloa) south to Costa Rica, on Caribbean slope from northeastern Belize to northern coast of Yucatán Peninsula. All populations apparently sedentary; no regular pattern of seasonal movements is known. Two U.S. records: 21–23 July 1992, Patagonia, Ariz. (Santa Cruz Co.), and 18–21 September 1993, Santa Teresa, N.M. (Doña Ana Co.).

STATUS AND CONSERVATION

Common to abundant within range and habitat; adaptable to human modification of habitats.

SUBSPECIES AND TAXONOMIC RELATIONSHIPS

Subspecies *diluta* of northwestern Mexico slightly paler below than *rutila* of southwestern Mexico. See Buff-bellied Hummingbird.

REFERENCES

Howell and Webb 1995
Johnsgard 1997
Weller 1999b

AZURE-CROWNED HUMMINGBIRD   PLS. 12, 28

Amazilia (Agyrtria) cyanocephala
4–4.5 in. (10–11.5 cm). Bill length: ♂ 19–23 mm; tail length: ♂ 28–35 mm.

A common hummingbird of the northern tropics, this species is found as far north as southern Tamaulipas, presumed origin of many other Mexican vagrants seen in southern Texas. It should be considered as a possibility for sightings of presumed Violet-crowned Hummingbird in southern and eastern Texas. Though it is fairly common, little is known of its natural history and behavior. Formerly known as Red-billed Azurecrown.

DESCRIPTION

A medium-large hummingbird with mostly white underparts, golden green to bronze-green back becoming dull bronze on rump. Crown deep metallic turquoise to bright violet-blue, blending to aquamarine on hindcrown, emerald green on cheeks, bright green on nape and sides of neck. Heavily mottled with olive green to bronze from sides of neck down sides to flanks; mottling visible at sides of breast and belly when perched, may nearly meet across breast in some individuals. Tail square to moderately notched, gray-green with narrow diffuse whitish edges when fresh; undertail coverts olive-gray with broad pale borders. Bill thin, blackish above, orange to coral red below with narrow black tip on lower mandible. Both sexes and all ages are very similar in color of plumage and bill. **ADULT FEMALE:** May have more azure to turquoise iridescence in crown, nape, sides of neck; averages slightly smaller than male, with slightly longer bill. **IMMATURES:** Resemble duller versions of adults with more dark mottling on underparts, conspicuous pale feather edges on upperparts.

SIMILAR SPECIES

VIOLET-CROWNED HUMMINGBIRD has mostly red upper mandible (except for some immatures), white undertail coverts, greenish bronze mottling on sides restricted to narrow band along sides of neck, under wings (invisible when perched).

SOUNDS

CALLS include hard, dry chips and rattles, similar to those of other *Amazilia*. **SONG** is a series of squeaks and chips, often doubled or tripled.

BEHAVIOR

Little studied. Sometimes gathers in large numbers around flowering trees; takes nectar from white mimosa-like blossoms of ice cream bean tree, elongate red-orange flowers of tropical mistletoe. Courtship and nesting little known. **NEST** may have a streamer of plant material attached to bottom. Nests March to August in eastern Mexico.

HABITAT

Humid oak and pine-oak woodland, forest edges and clearings, coffee plantations, mostly 2,000–8,000 ft. (600-2,400 m).

AZURE-CROWNED HUMMINGBIRD

 DISTRIBUTION

RESIDENT from southwestern Tamaulipas south to western Nicaragua. Northern populations apparently sedentary. Seasonal movements mostly altitudinal; nonbreeding birds often found at lower elevations. No records from U.S. but has wandered to southern Yucatán Peninsula in March, July.

STATUS AND CONSERVATION

A common to fairly common species over much of its range, yet little is known of its biology, ecology, and behavior.

SUBSPECIES AND TAXONOMIC RELATIONSHIPS

Subspecies *cyanocephala* is found throughout Mexico, intergrades with more green-crowned *chlorostephana* in northern Central America. See Violet-crowned Hummingbird.

PLUMAGE VARIATION AND MOLT

Variation in depth of tail notch and amount of bronze mottling on underparts may be linked to age or sex; needs further study. Molt cycle undocumented; apparently occurs in late spring, early summer.

REFERENCES

Howell and Webb 1995
Johnsgard 1997
Peterson and Chalif 1973
Weller 1999c

VIOLET-CROWNED HUMMINGBIRD   PLS. 12, 22, 28

Amazilia (Agyrtria) violiceps

4–4.5 in. (10–11.5 cm). Bill length: 21–24 mm; tail length: 27–32 mm.

A handsome, aggressive hummingbird that is very local in the United States. In southeastern Arizona, it nests along stream courses with sycamores in lower to middle elevations, though it may winter at feeders away from breeding habitat. Its brilliant coral red bill and immaculate white underparts make it one of the most distinctive of all North American hummingbirds.

DESCRIPTION

A medium-large hummingbird with snow-white underparts, dull bronze-green to grayish bronze back, and blue to violet-blue crown. Bill coral red with black tip. Tail gray-green to grayish olive with narrow diffuse white edges. Both sexes and all ages are very similar in color of plumage and bill, though females and immatures may show less dramatic metallic iridescence in the crown, more black on bill. **ADULT MALE:** Averages slightly larger than female, with slightly brighter iridescence on crown. **ADULT FEMALE:** Typically has more satiny iridescence on crown. During nesting season, may show a band of worn or stained feathers across breast ("nest mark") or dark staining on chin from feeding young. **IMMATURES:** Distinguished from adults primarily by narrow grayish buff feather edges on the upperparts and satiny iridescence of the crown, though the bill may show more extensive black.

Similar Species

AZURE-CROWNED HUMMINGBIRD, potential stray to southeastern Texas, has heavy bronze-green mottling on sides and flanks, entirely dark upper mandible, grayish undertail coverts.

Sounds

CALLS are hard chips typical of *Amazilia*: *chit, tchit-it, thik, tchiup.* In territorial interactions, a peevish *weep*, shrill *zeek*, drawn-out *tee-eep* repeated 3 to 5 times, or repeated *tship* or *teek* notes in rapid series, accelerating and descending in pitch. **SONGS** include a series of 4 to 6 plaintive *chew* or *teep* notes slightly descending in pitch, more like a songbird than the songs of most hummingbirds, and a sputtery series of squeaks, chips, gurgles, and hisses.

Behavior

An aggressive, energetic species, frequently seen chasing other hummingbirds. Takes nectar from century plants, ocotillo, penstemons, desert honeysuckle, Arizona thistle. Hunts insects in short aerial fly-catching sallies. Bathes by "slam-dunking," diving from a height and striking water's surface with force. Males sing from exposed perches, especially in early morning. Pre-copulatory displays are unrecorded. Mating has been observed in flight. **NEST** is a soft cup of pale plant fibers, exterior densely camouflaged with lichen, usually placed high in a sycamore tree. Nests at least as early as March in Mexico, mostly July to September in the United States.

Habitat

In the United States and northwestern Mexico, riparian woodland dominated by Arizona sycamore (*Platanus wrightii*), Fremont cottonwood (*Populus fremontii*), willows. Will forage in desert scrub and more open situations but stays close to areas of denser vegetation. Often winters at feeding stations with heavy shrub and tree cover away from breeding habitat.

Distribution

BREEDS from southeastern Ariz. (Sonoita Creek, Huachuca Mts., Chiricahua Mts., possibly Mule Mts.) and southwestern N.M. (Guadalupe Canyon) south to Chiapas. **RESIDENT** over most of breeding range, though most northern birds withdraw south in winter. **WINTERS** mostly from southern Sonora south. A few individ-

rare winter resident in southeast Arizona

VIOLET-CROWNED HUMMINGBIRD

uals winter near feeders in southeastern Ariz. Moves into Ariz. and N.M. in numbers in June, prior to onset of summer rains. **VA-GRANT** to central Ariz. (August, October), Calif. (July to December, March, May), western Tex. (March, July, December), southern Tex. (May, October), upper Tex. coast (March), northern N.M.

STATUS AND CONSERVATION

A common species over most of its range, adaptable to living in residential landscapes. Feeding stations in the United States probably help support breeding populations but increase exposure to hazards such as pesticides, cats, windows. Grazing and introduction of exotic grasses threaten the quality of its habitat in western Mexico, where feeding stations are rare.

SUBSPECIES AND TAXONOMIC RELATIONSHIPS

Northern subspecies *ellioti* has more uniformly green upperparts, bluer crown and cheeks than *violiceps* of southern Mexico. Some taxonomists propose dividing the 28 members of the genus *Amazilia* into 3 genera; under this classification Violet-crowned and Azure-crowned Hummingbirds are assigned to the genus *Agyrtria*, whose 9 members are characterized by white underparts. Has reportedly hybridized with Magnificent and Broad-billed Hummingbirds.

 PLUMAGE VARIATION AND MOLT

Additional study is needed to determine if subtle variations in plumage or bill color are useful in determining age and sex. Adults molt June to July, immatures August to October.

 REFERENCES

Baltosser 1989
Howell and Webb 1995
Johnsgard 1997
Mlodinow and O'Brien 1996
Weller 1999d

AMETHYST-THROATED HUMMINGBIRD   PL. 11

Lampornis amethystinus

4.5–5 in. (11.5–12.5 cm). Bill length: 20–23 mm; tail length: 29–32 mm.

A close relative of the Blue-throated Hummingbird, this species inhabits the higher elevations of Mexico's Sierra Madre Oriental south into northern Central America. A potential vagrant to the United States, it occurs as far north as southwestern Tamaulipas, a region that is the presumed origin of a number of Mexican species that have strayed to southern Texas. Size difference between the sexes is not as pronounced in this species as in the slightly larger Blue-throated Hummingbird.

 DESCRIPTION

A large dark hummingbird with a blackish tail and prominent white stripe behind the eye contrasting with a dusky cheek; faint pale buff malar stripe. Crown nape, and upper back dark green, becoming dull bronze on rump, blackish on uppertail coverts. Slightly notched tail blue-black narrowly tipped with medium to dark gray on R3–5. **ADULT MALE:** Large, with dark gray underparts, bright pinkish purple gorget feathers with narrow pale margins. Gray tips on outer tail feathers blend into black of tail. **ADULT FEMALE:**

Large, with medium gray underparts, tawny wash to gorget. Gray tips on outer tail feathers crisply defined. **IMMATURE MALE:** Similar to adult female but larger, with dull gray throat, diffuse gray tips on outer tail feathers. **IMMATURE FEMALE:** Resembles adult female but with conspicuous pale edges on feathers, particularly upperparts.

SIMILAR SPECIES

BLUE-THROATED HUMMINGBIRD has paler gray underparts, tail feathers with large white spots on tips of outer 2–3 pairs; call is a shrill *seep* or *tseep*.

SOUNDS

CALLS include sharp, hard chips and buzzy trills unlike typical calls of Blue-throated Hummingbird. **SONGS** include a series of mournful peeps, similar to "peep song" of Blue-throated Hummingbird. **WING SOUND** is lower pitched than in smaller species but not distinctive.

BEHAVIOR

Less aggressive and territorial than Blue-throated Hummingbird. Invades territories of smaller species to take nectar. Males sing from exposed perches. **NEST** is a large cup of plant down and spider silk, camouflaged with mosses, some lichens; often built hanging from a twig, vine, or root. Nests October to December, May to July in Mexico.

HABITAT

High montane forests of oaks and conifers, cloud forest, 300–10,000 ft. (900–3,000 m).

DISTRIBUTION

RESIDENT in Sierra Madre Oriental from southwestern Tamaulipas through to Oaxaca; range discontinuous through southwestern Mexico, Guatemala, Honduras. Probably migrates altitudinally like southern populations of Blue-throated Hummingbird. No records north of Mexico.

STATUS AND CONSERVATION

Still common within its range, but specialist in habitats under threat from unsustainable commercial logging.

AMETHYST-THROATED HUMMINGBIRD

Subspecies and Taxonomic Relationships

Subspecies *amethystinus* occurs in eastern Mexico. Closely related to Blue-throated Hummingbird, less so to other members of the genus *Lampornis* (mountain-gems).

Plumage Variation and Molt

Plumage differences between males and females are more pronounced in this species than in Blue-throated Hummingbird. Adults molt March to May in southern Mexico.

References

Howell and Webb 1995
Johnsgard 1997
Wagner 1957
Züchner 1999b

mpornis clemenciae
4.75–5.25 in. (12–13.5 cm). Bill length: ♂ 22–24 mm, ♀ 24–27 mm; tail length: ♂ 43–49 mm, ♀ 40–45 mm.

The Blue-throated is the largest hummingbird in the United States, up to three times heavier than the familiar Ruby-throated and Black-chinned. It ranges from southern Mexico to the sky island mountain ranges of western Texas, southern New Mexico, and southeastern Arizona. Its ecological needs are among the most specialized of any North American hummingbird. Though it shares the same mountain forests as the similarly sized Magnificent Hummingbird, the Blue-throated seldom strays far from canyon streams shaded by sycamores and maples. The male's shrill "peep song," audible even over the sound of rushing water, is the most conspicuous element of an unusually large vocal repertoire. The species was named by French ornithologist René Lesson in honor of his wife, Clémence.

DESCRIPTION

A very large, long-tailed hummingbird with contrasting white face markings and a large black and white tail. Proportionally small, rounded head with prominent white eye-stripe, less prominent white or pale buff malar stripe, and proportionally short, stout bill. Upperparts grass green on crown and nape becoming dull green to greenish bronze on rump, blackish on uppertail coverts. Underparts medium to dark ash gray, with wash of green on sides and flanks (amount varies geographically). Large rounded blue-black tail has conspicuous pure white tips on outer 2–3 pairs of feathers (R3–5); undertail coverts medium gray with broad whitish borders. Sexes similar. **ADULT MALE:** Very large, with cerulean blue to cobalt blue gorget that is often difficult to see. **ADULT FEMALE:** Large, with entirely gray underparts, including gorget. **IMMATURE MALE:** Similar to adult male but with gorget color typically confined to center of throat, pale buff edges on feathers of upperparts. **IMMATURE FEMALE:** Similar to adult female, with pale buff edges on feathers of upperparts; often with mottling on throat and/or breast.

SIMILAR SPECIES

Large size distinguishes it from most North American hummingbirds. Female **MAGNIFICENT HUMMINGBIRD** has longer bill, dark green upperparts contrasting strongly with gray underparts. Corners of notched dark green tail banded in bronze-green and blackish, with smaller dull whitish tips on outer 3–4 pairs of feathers. Call is a harsher *tchip*. PLAIN-CAPPED STARTHROAT has much longer bill, dark gray to blackish gorget with or without dull red band at bottom, broad whitish malar stripe, bronze back with white markings. Much shorter tail is banded in bronze to bronze-green and blackish with white spots on outer 4 pairs of feathers. AMETHYST-THROATED HUMMINGBIRD has smaller gray tips on black tail; male has bright pink-purple gorget. Female and immature male BROAD-BILLED HUMMINGBIRD are much smaller, with paler underparts; green central tail feathers; smaller, dingier white spots in tail; and some red or orange at base of bill. Call is a raspy insectlike chitter. WHITE-EARED HUMMINGBIRD is much smaller, with proportionally larger head, broader white eye-stripe contrasting with blacker cheek, thin short bill with red or orange at base. Call is a sharp, metallic *tchik* or *tink*.

Sounds

CALLS consist mainly of shrill *seep* or *tseek* notes, which may be given singly or in short series (*tsee-teek, tsee-tee-tseep*); different from adult calls of most species but superficially similar to begging calls of fledglings. A variety of peeps, squeals, chips, trills, and snarls are given during combat. SONGS of male are of two types: "peep song," consisting of long monotonous series of individual notes similar to the call note (typically 45–60 per minute), and "whisper song," a quiet but complex series of chips, gurgled phrases, and buzzy trills. Both songs are usually given while perched. Territorial males sing from perches under forest canopy, usually with bill pointed upward ("sea lion posture"); also call regularly during foraging and flights through territory. Female song, given in breeding season, is rarely heard. WING SOUND is lower pitched than in smaller species but not distinctive.

Behavior

Highly territorial, usually dominating at flower patches and feeding stations. Known for long chases and physical attacks on other hummingbirds. Also mobs predators such as hawks and owls. Boldly contrasting tail is spastically flicked open in hovering flight, fanned to maximum extent during aggressive and courtship displays. Dominant males call and flick tail frequently when foraging, may hang upside down from perch with tail fanned during confrontations. Takes nectar mostly from larger flowers, including mountain sage, canary columbine, bearded penstemon, Mexican lobelia, agaves; also exploits sapsucker sap wells. Largely insectivorous during dry season (late winter to early summer). Large size and mountain habitat make it among the most cold tolerant of all North American hummingbirds. A few individuals winter at feeding stations in mountains of Arizona, tolerating temperatures well below freezing for days at a time. Courtship displays consist primarily of singing and tail fanning. Female song attracts males. Unreceptive females often combative toward courting males, usually succeeding in driving them off with snarling attacks. NEST usually situated under an overhanging bank or cliff ledge, in a cave, under eaves of a building, or even inside an open shed or carport, but occasionally on a low tree branch; site is typically near a flowing stream, often directly over water. Interior of nest is lined with whitish to tan-buff oak and sycamore leaf wool and other plant fibers; exterior may be camouflaged with green mosses and/or finely branched lichens or left mostly bare if these are unavailable; flat chips of lichen favored by many other species are seldom used. Nests April to September in southwestern U.S., up to 3 broods per season. Nest site is usually reused both within and between seasons; female adds new material prior to each nesting.

🌲 Habitat

Moist mountain habitats from cool, shady canyons lined with sycamore and maple at northern edge of range to meadow edges in conifer forest in southern Mexico. Prefers middle to higher elevation riparian zones with perennial stream flow, but may forage in and migrate through drier habitats, including dry oak woodland and pine-oak forest. In arid Southwest, population density and distribution fluctuate with rainfall, expanding into drier canyons during wet years and concentrating in moist areas and around feeding stations during drought.

Distribution

BREEDS in U.S. primarily in sky island mountain ranges of western Tex. (Chisos and Guadalupe Mts.), southern N.M. (San Luis Mts.), and southeastern Ariz. (Chiricahua, Huachuca, and Santa Rita Mts.). A small breeding population exists on the Mogollon Rim in east-central Ariz.; regular sightings suggest breeding in Santa Catalina Mts. of Ariz., Peloncillo Mts. in extreme southeastern N.M., and mountains of west-central N.M. One nesting record from Tulare Co., Calif. Arrives on northern breeding grounds between mid-March and late April, departs by mid-October. RESIDENT from southern Chihuahua, Nuevo Leon, and south-

rare winter resident
in mountains of
southeastern Arizona

BLUE-THROATED HUMMINGBIRD

western Tamaulipas southward to southern Mexico. Migratory population is believed to winter near northern edge of resident range. A few individuals usually winter near feeding stations in the canyons of southeastern Ariz. Northern birds rarely found at lower elevations during migration, but migration in southern populations may be primarily elevational. **VAGRANT** to central Ariz., central N.M., Colo. (July to August); Edwards Plateau, Gulf Coast, lower Rio Grande Valley, and Panhandle of Tex. (mostly fall); La. (fall, spring), Calif. (summer), S.C. (August), N.D. (June), Utah (August).

STATUS AND CONSERVATION

Very local within its U.S. range; much less common than similar Magnificent Hummingbird. Habitat in the United States is largely protected within national parks and national forests but still vulnerable to land management policies such as suppression of natural forest fires that promote growth of nectar plants. Feeders help support populations in Huachuca and Chiricahua Mountains, especially when natural food is in short supply, but also increase exposure to predators, pesticides, windows, other hazards. Global warming may threaten fragile riparian habitat within U.S. range. Males outnumber females in Arizona populations. Has reached at least 8 years of age.

SUBSPECIES AND TAXONOMIC RELATIONSHIPS

Subspecies *phasmorus* of northeastern Mexico and far western Texas (Chisos and Guadalupe Mountains) has stronger green wash to underparts, slightly shorter bill, and brighter green upperparts than *bessophilus* of northwestern Mexico, southeastern Arizona, and southwestern New Mexico. Nominate race *clemenciae* is not found north of Mexico. Closest relatives are the Amethyst-throated Hummingbird of Mexico and northern Central America and the mountain-gems of Central America. DNA evidence suggests that its closest relative north of Mexico may be the Magnificent Hummingbird. Hybrids have been reported with Anna's, Black-chinned, Costa's, and Magnificent.

PLUMAGE VARIATION AND MOLT

Other than gorget color, few differences in plumage relate to age and sex. Young of both sexes have broad buffy edges on most feathers, most conspicuous on dark plumage of lower rump. Young males typically have a small area of bright metallic blue in the center of the gorget, which gradually fills in over the winter. Variations in amount and shape of white area at tip of R_3, from narrow streak to broad diamond, are not reliable indicators of age or sex. Both adults and immatures molt in winter, though molt may begin as early as late summer. Returning second-year birds are usually indistinguishable from older adults, though a few individuals may retain some wing and tail feathers and undergo partial molt in late summer.

REFERENCES

Bent 1940
Browning 1978
Oberholser 1974
Phillips et al. 1964
Williamson 2000

Eugenes fulgens

4.5–5.25 in. (11–13.5 cm). Bill length: ♂ 21–30 mm, ♀ 27–32 mm; tail length: ♂ 35–56 mm, ♀ 40–48 mm.

One of the most dramatic hummingbirds in the United States in both size and color. Adult males combine large size (second only to male Blue-throated) and overall dark color with brilliant metallic purple crown and green gorget. Females are less gaudy, resembling overgrown female Black-chinned. Normally associated with the sky island mountains near the Mexican border, it has strayed as far as Georgia, California, and Minnesota. Formerly known as Rivoli's Hummingbird in honor of Victor Masséna, Duke of Rivoli, whose wife, Anna, also had a hummingbird named in her honor.

DESCRIPTION

A large slim hummingbird with long bill, neck, and tail. **ADULT MALE:** Dark emerald to bronze-green above, with brilliant apple green to turquoise green gorget, metallic violet to purple crown. Triangular white spot behind eye contrasts strongly with blackish face. Breast velvety black with bronze-green highlights, becoming dull medium to dark gray on lower belly, contrasting with white femoral tufts; pale gray patches often visible at shoulders. Notched tail dark bronze-green. Undertail coverts pale to medium bronze-gray with distinct whitish borders. **ADULT FEMALE:** Dark emerald to bronze-green above, with distinct white triangle and ragged whitish stripe behind eye contrasting with dark cheek. Underparts medium ash gray, often appearing mottled or scaly because of slightly paler borders to feathers; undertail coverts bronze-gray centrally with broad whitish borders. Long square to slightly notched tail is dark bronze-green with blackish band across corners and small dull whitish tips on R3–5. **IMMATURE MALE:** Darker than adult female, with pale feather edges creating strongly scaly appearance to underparts. Gorget shows disk of bright green on dull, blotchy background; small patches of metallic violet feathers over each eye. Slightly notched tail is bronze-green to bronze, usually with broad blackish band across corners; diffuse whitish edges on outer tail feathers. **SECOND SPRING MALE:** Crown and gorget often incomplete. Tail feathers retained until molt in second fall; pale tips may wear off outer pairs. **IMMATURE FEMALE:** Resembles adult female but with distinct pale edges on feathers, particularly noticeable on upperparts, more extensive dull whitish in tail (tips of R2–5). Throat may appear mottled, scaly.

SIMILAR SPECIES

Large size distinguishes it from most North American hummingbirds. **GREEN VIOLET-EAR** has blue-green tail with dark blue subterminal band, no white spot behind eye. **BLUE-THROATED HUMMINGBIRD** has shorter bill, more prominent white eye-stripe, dull bronze-green lower back and rump, becoming blackish on uppertail coverts. Tail feathers blue-black with large white spots at tips of outer 2–3 pairs. Call is a shrill *seep* or *tseep*. **PLAIN-CAPPED STARTHROAT** has very long bill, broad whitish malar stripes bordering dark gray to blackish gorget with or without red band at bottom. Ragged white markings usually visible on bronze to bronze-green back. Much shorter tail shows smaller white spots on inner webs of outer 4 pairs of feathers. **BERYLLINE HUMMINGBIRD** is smaller, with little or no white behind eye. Shorter bill shows dull orange on lower mandible. **AMETHYST-THROATED HUMMINGBIRD** has more prominent facial markings, smaller dull gray tips on black tail. Male has dull green crown, bright pink-purple gorget.

SOUNDS

CALLS include hoarse *tschip* or *tcheep* notes, often doubled. Also chatters and squeals in combat; chase call is a rapid series of nasal chips, some drawn out into squeals. **SONG** is a series of hissing, gurgling, and sputtering phrases, interspersed with *tschip* and *tcheep* notes. Wing sound is lower pitched than in smaller species but not distinctive.

BEHAVIOR

Unlike most southern populations, Magnificents in the United States are largely nonterritorial, "trapline" foragers. Takes nectar less often than similar-sized Blue-throated Hummingbird. Depends largely on insects during spring dry season, may be substantially insectivorous year-round. Nectar sources include scarlet bouvardia, mountain sage, claret cup cactus, Arizona thistle, bearded penstemon, canary columbine, agaves. Little known about courtship and mating; displays undescribed. **NEST** is a large soft cup of whitish plant fibers, exterior camouflaged with chips of lichen and plant debris, placed on horizontal branch high in a tree. Nests April to August in the United States.

In the United States and northern Mexico, dry pine-oak woodland, mixed conifer forest, sycamore-maple riparian forest in mountains, 5,000–9,000 ft. (1,500–2,700 m).

 DISTRIBUTION

BREEDS in U.S. primarily in sky island mountain ranges of western Tex. (Chisos and Guadalupe Mts.), southeastern Ariz. (Chiricahua, Huachuca, Santa Rita, Santa Catalina, Pinaleño Mts.), southwestern and south-central N.M. (Animas, Peloncillo, Pinos Altos, Sacramento Mts.). Uncommon to rare in summer from Mogollon Rim north to White Mts., east into southwestern N.M. One nesting record from Colo. **RESIDENT** from southern Sonora and Chihuahua (rare in winter) south to southern Mexico, discontinuously through mountains of Central America to Costa Rica. Migrants arrive March to April, depart September to October. Young

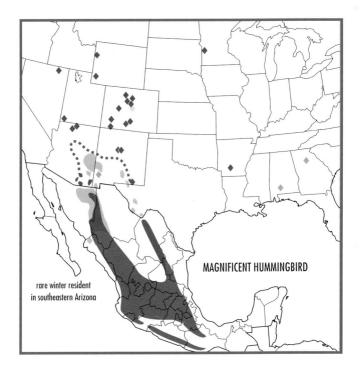

MAGNIFICENT HUMMINGBIRD

rare winter resident
in southeastern Arizona

males often highly nomadic; banded birds have traveled hundreds of miles between mountain ranges in a season. Often migrates through lower elevations, especially foothills, in spring and fall. Numerous reports from Colo. (May to October); also Ala. (September to February), Ark. (July), Calif. (April), Ga. (winter), Minn. (July), Nev. (June), Utah (July), Wyo. (June to July), southern Tex. (September).

STATUS AND CONSERVATION

Locally common within its U.S. range. Habitat in the United States largely protected within national parks and national forests but still vulnerable to land management policies such as suppression of natural forest fires. Feeders help support populations, especially when natural food is in short supply, but also increase exposure to predators, pesticides, windows, other hazards. Males greatly outnumber females in Arizona. Has reached at least 8 years of age.

SUBSPECIES AND TAXONOMIC RELATIONSHIPS

Subspecies *fulgens* occurs from the southwestern United States to southern Mexico. Southern subspecies *spectabilis* sometimes treated as separate species (Admirable Hummingbird). DNA studies suggest a relationship to the Blue-throated Hummingbird and its relatives. Hybrids have been reported with Violet-crowned, Berylline, Broad-billed, and Blue-throated Hummingbirds.

PLUMAGE VARIATION AND MOLT

Minor variations in amount of black in tail, color of shoulders of males (pale gray to dusky). Immature males highly variable in pattern of crown, gorget, breast. Adults molt late summer to early fall, immatures winter to early spring.

REFERENCES

Howell and Webb 1995
Powers 1996
Russell and Monson 1998

PLAIN-CAPPED STARTHROAT

Heliomaster constantii

4.5–5.25 in. (11.5–13.5 cm). Bill length: 31–37 mm; tail length: 27–34 mm.

This large hummingbird occasionally wanders into the southwestern United States from Mexico following the end of its nesting season. It is highly insectivorous, seldom visiting flowers or feeders but spending hours each day catching insects on the wing. Its extremely long bill distinguishes it from all other hummingbirds of the southwestern United States, but its facial markings, tail pattern, and white patch on back are also unique. Long tufts of silky white feathers on the flanks are visible mainly in flight, and smaller versions of these tufts may appear on other species. Believed to be named in honor of Charles Constant, a nineteenth-century physician, poet, and taxidermist.

 ## DESCRIPTION

A large dull hummingbird with a very long straight to slightly decurved bill, much longer than the rest of its head. Facial markings distinctive. Narrow gorget is dark sooty gray at chin, abruptly becoming dark cherry red to coppery red on lower third to half; feathers edged in pale grayish buff. Gorget bordered by broad whitish malar stripes contrasting with dusky gray cheeks. Upperparts dull green to olive-bronze; elongate vertical patch of white on lower back and rump is variable, not always conspicuous. Underparts medium mousy gray with faint bronze mottling; broad whitish midline stripe creates "vested" appearance. Long silky white flank tufts visible in flight, usually concealed at rest. Long wings extend to or slightly past tip of proportionally short tail. Tail pattern is unique: R1 bronzy, with or without dusky band at tip; R2–4 banded bronze and blackish with white spot at tip on inner web; R5 with broad white band at tip, usually smudged with black on outer web. Sexes are virtually identical in size, bill length, and coloration. **ADULT FEMALE:** May have band of metallic red in lower gorget continuous or divided into 2 lateral lobes; upper gorget and malar stripes may be stained brownish by feeding young. **IMMATURES:** Resemble adults except gorget entirely or mostly blackish with pale edges; pale feather edges on upperparts.

 ## SIMILAR SPECIES

Female and immature male **ANNA'S HUMMINGBIRD** can give appearance of narrow gorget with pale malar stripes but are much smaller, stouter, with proportionally shorter bill, less white in tail.

May show small white tufts on flanks. **BLUE-THROATED HUMMINGBIRD** has proportionally short bill, long blue-black tail with very large white corners, very narrow whitish or pale buff malar stripe. Female **MAGNIFICENT HUMMINGBIRD** is dark green above with slightly shorter bill; longer tail has dull whitish tips on R3–5 (R2–5 in immatures) not shifted toward inner web.

SOUNDS

Usually quiet. **CALLS** include mellow flycatcher-like *tsip* and *teep* notes. Chase call in aggressive encounters is a rolled series of chips, *dzipipipipipip* or *soiksoiksoiksoik*. **SONG** is a series of variable chip notes. **WING SOUND** is lower pitched than in smaller species but not distinctive.

BEHAVIOR

Flight is graceful and swiftlike, with slow wingbeats interspersed with gliding. Wags and fans tail almost constantly in flight. Prefers high perches; often sits with wings tucked under slightly fanned tail. Highly insectivorous, engaging in long fly-catching bouts, especially in early morning. Takes nectar infrequently at feeders and a variety of flowers, including jícama, agaves. A strikingly unaggressive species; does not defend nectar sources but intimidates smaller species such as Broad-billed for access to flowers. Most sightings in Arizona are of single birds away from feeders, but a few have visited feeding stations intermittently for up to several weeks. No apparent site fidelity outside breeding season; in Arizona, sightings in consecutive years at the same location are rare. Courtship and nesting little studied. **SHUTTLE DISPLAY** consists of short vertical arcs performed directly in front of female with bills almost touching. **NEST** is a cup of soft plant down and spider silk, exterior camouflaged with lichen, bark fragments, other plant debris, usually in an exposed position high in a tree. Nests January to June in northwestern Mexico.

HABITAT

Desert scrub, tropical deciduous forest, riparian corridors; wanders to other habitats, including oak woodland in mountains, after breeding.

DISTRIBUTION

BREEDS from southern Sonora south along Pacific Coast to northwestern Costa Rica. Northern limits of breeding range poorly

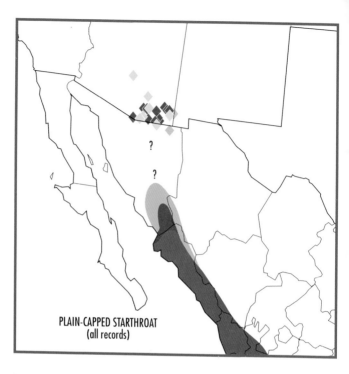

PLAIN-CAPPED STARTHROAT
(all records)

known. In Mexico, nests January to June. **RESIDENT** from northern Sinaloa south. Northern edge of wintering range poorly known. Wanders away from species' breeding range and habitat from late spring through early fall. Retreats south from northern parts of breeding range in late fall, returning in late winter. Irregular post-breeding **VAGRANT** to southeastern Ariz. (Chiricahua, Huachuca, Santa Rita, Whetstone Mts., Patagonia), mostly June to October; several years may pass between sightings. First U.S. record September 1969 in Nogales, Ariz. A single record from Phoenix (October to November 1978) is exceptional. Suspected but unconfirmed in southwestern N.M. (Animas Valley), western Tex.

STATUS AND CONSERVATION

Uncommon at northern edge of breeding range, perhaps threatened by conversion of desert and dry forest habitat into pasture for cattle, exploitation of wild agaves for liquor production (bacanora, mescal, tequila). Much of its life history, ecology, and behavior remain unknown.

Subspecies and Taxonomic Relationships

Northern subspecies *pinicola* ("pine dweller") of northwestern Mexico (Sonora to western Jalisco) has paler underparts and less extensive, redder iridescence in gorget than *leocadiae* (southwestern Mexico to western Guatemala). Most closely related to Long-billed Starthroat, *Heliomaster longirostris*; the two are sometimes separated from the southern starthroats into a separate genus, *Anthoscenus*.

Plumage Variation and Molt

Few differences distinguish the sexes, though young birds may be told from adults by absence of iridescence in gorget, presence of pale feather edges on upperparts. Adults molt June to August, immatures fall through winter.

References

Howell and Webb 1995
Johnsgard 1997
Mlodinow and O'Brien 1996
Russell and Monson 1998
Witzeman 1979

AHAMA WOODSTAR   PLS. 9

lliphlox evelynae
3.5–3.75 in. (9–9.5 cm). Bill length: ♂ 15–17 mm, ♀ 15–18 mm; tail length: ♂ 23–29 mm, ♀ 23–27 mm.

This small, colorful species is an extremely rare visitor to southeastern Florida. Though added to the U.S. list in 1971 based on photos of a living bird, the earliest record was a mummified specimen collected in Miami in 1961 and mislabeled as a *Selasphorus*. More than a decade passed before this specimen was reexamined, correctly identified, and added to the very short list of U.S. records. Its local name in the Bahamas is "god bird."

Description

A slim long-tailed hummingbird with medium-length, slightly decurved bill and extensive cinnamon-rufous in plumage. **ADULT MALE:** Grass green to golden green above. Gorget metallic rose-purple with violet highlights, slightly more violet on chin. Underparts cinnamon-rufous mottled with bright green from lower breast to upper belly, with indistinct paler midline stripe. Sides of neck and upper breast whitish, forming a partial collar. Lower belly whitish, undertail coverts pale rufous. Long, deeply forked tail extends well past wingtips. Central tail feathers dark blue-green, outer feathers narrow, blackish, with broad cinnamon-rufous border on inner web, variable rufous on outer web. **ADULT FEMALE:** Grass green to golden green above; throat and upper breast pale gray to whitish, washed with pale rufous, with faint green spangling at sides; dark cheek crescent contrasts with narrow pale eye-stripe. Underparts rich cinnamon-rufous from lower breast to upper belly, with indistinct paler midline stripe; lower belly whitish. Long narrow tail slightly rounded to double rounded, extends well past wingtips; central feathers bright green to bronze-green, outer pairs banded in grayish rufous, green, and purplish black with rufous tips on R3–5. Undertail coverts pale rufous. **IMMATURE MALE:** Similar to adult female but with more extensive black in outer tail feathers, indistinct rufous feather edges on upperparts. **IMMATURE FEMALE:** Similar to adult female but with indistinct rufous feather edges on upperparts.

SIMILAR SPECIES

Female and immature male **RUFOUS** and **ALLEN'S HUMMINGBIRDS** are more compact, with proportionally shorter bill and tail, no eye-stripe, throat variably spangled with bronze. Tips of outer tail feathers usually white but may be tinged with rufous. Adult females have some rufous at base of R1, few to many metallic orange feathers in center of gorget. Immature males typically have extensive rufous in R1, gorget heavily spangled with bronze with or without scattered metallic orange feathers. Female and immature male **BROAD-TAILED HUMMINGBIRD** have gray face without pale eye-stripe, fine grayish bronze spangling in gorget, broader tail feathers with white tips on R3–5. Female and immature male **RUBY-THROATED HUMMINGBIRD** are more compact, with no rufous in tail, underparts washed grayish green on sides, occasionally with tan or dull cinnamon patch on lower flank or faint cinnamon wash to underparts.

SOUNDS

CALL is a sharp *tit* or *tit-it*, often given in rapid series when excited. **SONG** is a repeated dry *pri'titidee*. Wings and tail make a rustling sound during male's shuttle display.

BEHAVIOR

Takes nectar at a wide variety of flowers, including many common subtropical garden plants such as lantana, porterweed, pentas, and century plants. Male performs a bouncing **SHUTTLE DISPLAY** with tail and gorget extended, accelerating toward the end followed by a rush toward the female before darting away. **NEST** is a cup of soft plant down and spider silk, camouflaged with bits of bark and other plant parts. Nests year-round in the Bahamas.

HABITAT

Gardens, scrub, woodlands, forest edges, mixed pine forest.

DISTRIBUTION

RESIDENT throughout the Bahamas. No apparent seasonal movements. At least 5 individuals have strayed to Florida, all recorded in the southeastern corner of the state: Miami, January 1961

BAHAMA WOODSTAR
(all records)

(specimen); Lantana, Palm Beach Co., August to October 1971; near Homestead, Dade Co., April 1974; Mary Krone Sanctuary, Dade Co., July to August 1981 (male and female). No recent records.

 ## STATUS AND CONSERVATION

A common and adaptable species throughout its range, it is nevertheless vulnerable to hurricanes and the effects of development.

 ## SUBSPECIES AND TAXONOMIC RELATIONSHIPS

Subspecies *evelynae* of northern Bahamas lacks metallic purple forecrown of *lyrura*, resident in the Inaguas. One of a large group of small long-tailed hummingbirds usually called woodstars or sheartails. The Lucifer Hummingbird of the Chihuahuan Desert is its closest North American relative. No hybrids have been reported.

REFERENCES

Fisk 1974
Johnsgard 1983
Owre 1976
Raffaele et al. 1998
Robertson and Woolfenden 1992

LUCIFER HUMMINGBIRD   PLS. 9, 22, 28

Calothorax lucifer

3.5–4 in. (9–10 cm). Bill length: ♂ 19–22 mm, ♀ 21–23 mm; tail length: ♂ 29–33 mm, ♀ 20–28 mm.

A long, deeply forked tail and decurved bill give this specialty of the Chihuahuan Desert one of the most distinctive shapes of any hummingbird in the United States. Though common in parts of Mexico, it is relatively little known in the United States. Its northern stronghold is in Big Bend National Park, where public feeding stations are prohibited, making it one of the more challenging species to see. Populations in Arizona and New Mexico may be increasing. It is closely related to the sheartails, sharing the scissorlike tail shape that gives the group its name. Its sinister-sounding name means "light bearer" in Greek.

Description

A small slim hummingbird with long, black, slightly to moderately decurved bill, short wings, and long narrow tail. **ADULT MALE:** Green to bronze-green above from crown to uppertail coverts. Gorget metallic magenta-purple to violet-purple, extending onto upper breast; feathers at corners elongate and slightly pointed, creating ragged lower border. Sides bronze-green mixed with pale cinnamon, with cinnamon patch on lower flank; whitish midline stripe creates a "vest." Whitish breast and sides of neck create partial collar connecting with pale eye-stripe. Central feathers of deeply forked tail green, outer feathers very narrow, blackish; tail held closed or nearly so when perched, appearing as a sharp spike. **ADULT FEMALE:** Bronze-green to golden green above. Underparts warm white to cream, sides and flanks washed cinnamon-rufous. Throat plain creamy white washed with cinnamon; may show distinct bulge in side view. Broad creamy white to pale cinnamon eye line bordered below by dusky cheek stripe, which often curves around corner of gorget area. Tail forked, feathers narrow. Central feathers green to bronze-green, outer pairs banded in bright rufous, green, and black with white tips. **IMMATURES:** Similar to adult female but with pale feather edges on upperparts. **IMMATURE MALE:** Usually shows first metallic gorget feathers within a few weeks of fledging. **IMMATURE FEMALE:** Shows more extensive white in tail (R2–5) than adult female or immature male.

Similar Species

Most superficially similar hummingbirds with rufous or cinnamon in the plumage, including **CALLIOPE** and **BROAD-TAILED**, have straight bills and much shorter, broader tails. Female and immature male **BLACK-CHINNED HUMMINGBIRD** have straight to slightly decurved bill, shorter tail with no rufous, distinct white spot and narrow indistinct line behind eye. Underparts pale grayish with cinnamon absent or confined to lower flanks. Female and immature male **COSTA'S HUMMINGBIRD** are chunkier, with much shorter, straight to slightly decurved bill, pale grayish underparts, no rufous in very short tail.

Sounds

CALLS include dry chip notes similar to calls of Broad-tailed Hummingbird, given singly or in rapid series when excited, and a musical *tschip* or *tsi-chip*. **SONG** is a weak wheezy squeak, audible only at close range; given by both adult and immature males during territorial defense. Adult male has pointed tip to outer primary that creates slight wing sound, less well developed than in Rufous or Allen's. Tail makes repeated dull cracking sounds during swerving pass at end of dive display; both wings and tail may be involved in loud whirring or rattling sound made during shuttle display.

 ## Behavior

Often assumes hunched posture when perched, with head thrust forward, shoulders rounded. Tail is seldom fanned to show deep fork, even in flight. Agaves, desert honeysuckle, Harvard and Parry penstemon are important nectar sources; other flowers visited include Mexican buckeye, Indian paintbrush, esperanza, desert willow. Avidly takes nectar from bat-pollinated Harvard agave without pollinating flowers. Territorial; males advertise with calls, songs, and displays, chase interlopers. Females defend nest site during breeding season and nectar sources when not nesting. Males often display for females at nest, particularly during building and egg-laying; female may interrupt display by confronting or chasing male. **SHUTTLE DISPLAY** consists of horizontal arcs becoming wider toward end of display, performed in front of female or immature male with gorget extended and tail held vertically or pumped up and down. Courting male often follows with **DIVE DISPLAY**, ascending for 4 to 5 seconds followed by rapid dive, pulling out as he reaches female and swerving past with tail fanned. **NEST** a soft cup of whitish to pale tan plant fibers held together with spider silk and camouflaged with chips of lichen, oak catkins, small leaves, twig fragments, and other plant parts, usually built near ground on large cactus, shrub, or tree. Nests often built on cholla, ocotillo, seed stalk of lechuguilla in Texas and New Mexico, on oak or sycamore in Arizona, northern Sonora. Females may nest close to one another and steal material from other nests. Nests April to September; at least 2 clutches per season.

 ## Habitat

BREEDS in the United States in shrubby desert foothills, steep slopes of dry canyons, desert washes, streamsides with sycamores, and dry oak woodland of Chihuahuan Desert region, 3,800– 5,700 ft. (1,150–1,750 m). May move to higher or lower elevations in late summer to take advantage of nectar sources.

 ## Distribution

BREEDS from western Tex. (fairly common in Big Bend National Park, rare elsewhere in Trans-Pecos), southwestern N.M. (Peloncillo Mts., Guadalupe Canyon), and southeastern Ariz. (Guada-

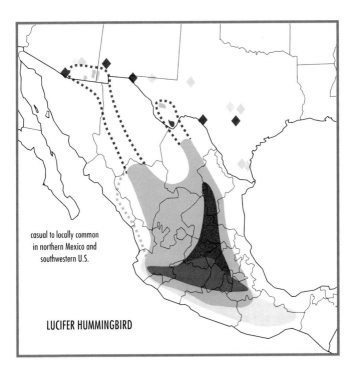

casual to locally common
in northern Mexico and
southwestern U.S.

LUCIFER HUMMINGBIRD

lupe Canyon, Chiri-cahua, Mule, Santa Rita Mts., probably also Huachuca, Whetstone Mts.) south to south-central Mexico. Largest U.S. breeding population centered around Chisos Mts. in Big Bend National Park, rare and local farther west and north. Generally rare and local breeder north of central Mexico. RESIDENT in southern and central Mexico, mainly central plateau. Migrants arrive mid-March to mid-April in Tex., April in N.M., Ariz. Most depart in September; rare October to November. Rare VAGRANTS away from regular haunts have occurred in Edwards Plateau, El Paso, Del Rio, Guadalupe Mts. National Park, Rockport, Beeville, Tex.; Silver City, Gila, N.M.; Tucson, Ariz.

STATUS AND CONSERVATION

Total U.S. population size and breeding density unknown; population in Big Bend National Park estimated to include approximately 100 individuals. Breeding areas in the United States small but well protected from most human impact. Reported regularly in Arizona only since 1970s, possibly related to establishment of feeding stations and increasing number of observers. In the nineteenth century around Mexico City, Lucifer was among several hummingbird species commonly captured to be stuffed and mounted or sold alive as a short-term cage bird. Oldest known banded bird, a male, lived at least 4 years; maximum life span probably much longer. Currently on Partners in Flight WatchList.

SUBSPECIES AND TAXONOMIC RELATIONSHIPS

No subspecies are described. The Lucifer and its closest relative, the Beautiful Hummingbird (*Calothorax pulcher*) of south-central Mexico, are the only members of the genus *Calothorax*, which is part of the diverse woodstar-sheartail group of "flame-throated" hummingbirds. Apparent hybrids with Black-chinned Hummingbird have been observed in western Texas (Big Bend National Park, El Paso) and southern New Mexico (Silver City).

PLUMAGE VARIATION AND MOLT

Length and curvature of pale eye line and dusky cheek stripe of female and immature male vary; some show face pattern similar to that of Black-chinned. Wing molt begins as early as September in adults, later in immatures; molt completed prior to spring migration in northern populations.

REFERENCES

Howell and Webb 1995
Kaufman 1992
Scott 1994

RUBY-THROATED HUMMINGBIRD

Archilochus colubris   PLS. 8, 20, 21, 26, 27, 31

3.25–3.75 in. (8.5–9.5 cm). Bill length: ♂ 14–20 mm, ♀ 16–21 mm; tail length: ♂ 23–31 mm, ♀ 21–29 mm.

The one and only hummingbird in the minds of many, the Ruby-throated is also the only hummingbird that breeds east of the Mississippi River. To reach their eastern nesting grounds each spring, many individuals take a direct but hazardous route across the Gulf of Mexico, flying nonstop over more than 500 miles of open water. The male's metallic scarlet gorget features a contrasting chin strap of velvety black, unlike the solid red gorgets of Broad-tailed and Anna's Hummingbirds. As is the case with most small hummingbirds, males are smaller than females ("reverse" sexual dimorphism). Though the species name seems to refer to a snake, it is more likely a misspelled version of the Arawak word *colibrí* with a Greek suffix.

DESCRIPTION

A small, compact hummingbird with a medium-length straight to slightly decurved black bill, bright green to golden green crown, and long tail. Outer primary (P10) tapers to a narrow rounded tip; inner primaries graduated in width, becoming narrower from outermost (P6) to innermost (P1). **ADULT MALE:** Bright grass green to emerald green above, pale gray to whitish below, becoming green on sides. Gorget mostly ruby red to orange-red, bordered by narrow black band across top edge; corners rounded. Face blackish. White of breast extends around sides of neck, contrasting strongly with gorget and nape. Tail deeply notched; central feathers green, outer feathers narrow and pointed, black with faint violet-purple gloss. Inner primaries modified, lobed on outer web. **ADULT FEMALE:** Bright grass green to golden green above, pale gray to whitish below. Throat unmarked or with variable dusky streaking or spotting at center of gorget. Face dusky, contrasting with throat and white postocular spot. Sides washed gray-green; may show tawny patches on flanks. Notched tail extends slightly beyond wingtips. Central tail feathers green, with or without diffuse dark band at tip. R2 gray-green tipped black; R3 like R2 but narrowly tipped white; R4–5 pointed, broadly tipped white. Inner primaries slightly modified. **IMMATURE MALE:** Resembles adult female, including pointed R5, but with shorter bill, pale buff feather edges. Markings on gorget usually heavier and more extensive. Inner primaries slightly modified. **IMMATURE FEMALE:** Resembles adult female but with pale buff feather edges, small white tip on R2, R5 rounded at tip. Inner primaries unmodified.

SIMILAR SPECIES

BLACK-CHINNED HUMMINGBIRD is duller green above, with dull grayish crown, broad blunt tip to outer primary, longer bill. Adult male has mostly black gorget with metallic violet band at base (hard to see), notched tail with green wash on tips of outer feathers. Females and immature males have shorter, square to slightly notched tail, less contrast between face and throat. Female and immature male **RUFOUS HUMMINGBIRD** show extensive bright rufous in tail, underparts. Female and immature male **COSTA'S HUMMINGBIRD** have shorter tails, inner primaries approximately equal in width, less contrast between face and throat. **ANNA'S HUMMINGBIRD** is chunky, large-headed, with darker gray underparts, primaries approximately equal in width. Adult male has entirely metallic rose red to coppery red gorget with no black border on chin, extensions at corners; crown same color as throat (not visible from some angles). Outer tail feathers medium to dark gray with narrow rounded tips. Female and immature male have broad, rounded outer tail feathers banded in gray-green, dark gray to dull black, white. Female and immature male CUBAN EMERALD are slimmer, with much longer forked tail, orange at base of lower mandible; immature male may show spots or patches of deep emerald green on pale gray to whitish underparts.

Sounds

CALLS include soft *tchew, tchup;* female gives muted *tic-tic* notes while feeding. In territorial encounters, a variety of rapid squeaky twitters, chips, and squeals; male voice is harsher. Nestlings make begging calls, a behavior unknown in other North American hummingbirds. Fledglings make a plaintive *peep.* SONG is a monotonous series of chip notes given at dawn; male also gives a jumbled series of phrases and scratchy notes from a high perch following copulation. Modified inner primaries of adult male produce slightly louder WING SOUND in normal flight than females and immature males, distinctive sounds during territorial and courtship interactions. DIVE NOISE accompanying Dive Display apparently created by sharply pointed outer tail feathers.

Behavior

Tail pumping less consistent than in Black-chinned. Takes nectar from flowers such as salvias, red morning-glory, cardinal flower, jewelweed, trumpet creeper, bee balm, Canadian columbine, coral honeysuckle, even willow catkins when other nectar unavailable. Feeds extensively on Turk's-cap hibiscus, esperanza in fall migration through eastern Mexico. May pierce nectaries of long-tubed flowers to gain access to nectar. Takes insects by flycatching, gleaning. Drinks tree sap from sapsucker wells, acorn cups. Bathes in dew on leaves, fine spray from waterfalls, lawn sprinklers. Sunbathes on perch or stretched out on ground. Male performs U-shaped DIVE DISPLAY for both rival males and prospective mates. Display is a narrow arc beginning 40–50 ft. (12–15 m) above object, accompanied by intensified wing and tail sounds (Dive Noise). SHUTTLE DISPLAY takes place directly in front of perched female, consists of rapid horizontal arcs with gorget feathers erected. Female may be hidden in dense vegetation during displays; signals receptivity with soft *mew* call and tail cocked to side. Male may also perform Shuttle Display for females at nests.

NEST is a soft cup of whitish plant fibers and animal hair held together with spider silk; exterior may be camouflaged with lichen, chips of bark, bud scales, other plant debris. Usually placed on horizontal branch in broad-leafed or coniferous tree, rarely on artificial supports such as windchimes, light fixtures, or electrical wires. May nest 2–3 times per season. Nests mid-April to early October in south, late May to late September in north.

🪸 Habitat

BREEDS in hardwood (maple, birch, oak, poplar), pine, and mixed forest, woodlands, forest edges and clearings, orchards, gardens. Scarce in heavily urbanized and coastal areas. **WINTERS** in shrubby second growth, edges of humid tropical forest, tropical deciduous forest, dry scrub, citrus orchards, gardens. Large concentrations of migrants often utilize groves of oak, hackberry along Gulf Coast in fall migration.

🦃 Distribution

BREEDS in eastern North America north to southern Québec, west to south-central Alberta, eastern edge of Dakotas, Neb., southeastern Kans., eastern and central Okla., eastern Tex.; very rarely in southern tip of Fla. **WINTERS** mainly in tropics from southern Veracruz west across lowlands to southern Sinaloa, to Yucatán Peninsula, Belize, Honduras, western Nicaragua, western Costa Rica. Smaller numbers winter along Gulf Coast of U.S., including southern Fla. Northbound birds may follow Gulf Coast or cross Gulf of Mexico, arriving nearly simultaneously across southern boundary of U.S. in late February to early March. Reaches northern edge of range by mid- to late May. Southward migration appears to be largely overland. Fall migration extends farther inland; common some years in Trans-Pecos Tex. in August and September. Most depart northern edge of range by late August; numbers peak on Gulf Coast of Tex. in mid-September. Adult males migrate earlier than females in both spring and fall; immatures lag behind adults. Few records for eastern Colo., N.M., western Okla., probably more common fall migrant through southern Great Plains than generally recognized. Wintering birds arrive in Costa Rica by early October. **VAGRANT** to Colo. (April, May, July), Calif. (August, September), N.M. (October), Alaska (June), Cuba (fall-winter), Bahamas (fall-winter), eastern Costa Rica (winter), western Panama (winter).

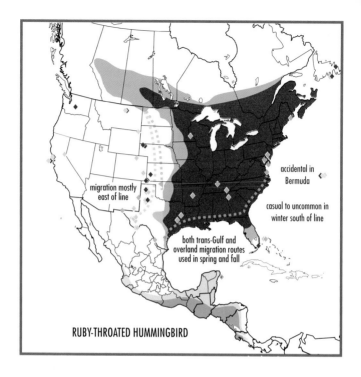

migration mostly east of line

accidental in Bermuda

casual to uncommon in winter south of line

both trans-Gulf and overland migration routes used in spring and fall

RUBY-THROATED HUMMINGBIRD

ili STATUS AND CONSERVATION

Much of the breeding habitat of this species has been altered by human activities, yet overall its status appears secure. Clearing of forest and woodland and widespread spraying of insecticides and herbicides appear to affect local breeding populations. Other unnatural hazards include predation by domestic cats, collisions with windows, cars, transmission towers. Brightly colored insulators on electric fences have lured many hungry birds to death by electrocution. Numerous individuals have been found trapped in the spiny seed heads of burdock, a weed introduced from Europe. Unusual natural predators include tanagers, orioles, large fish, frogs, spiders, dragonflies. Sexes are dramatically different in life span, probably because of the male's smaller size combined with stress of territorial defense and migration. Males have reached at least 7 years of age, females at least 9.

Ruby-throated Hummingbird
spring arrival dates

SUBSPECIES AND TAXONOMIC RELATIONSHIPS

No subspecies are described. Ruby-throated and Black-chinned are closely related east-west counterparts forming a superspecies. The two species may have diverged from a common ancestor during one of several glacial periods that apparently isolated populations of other North American birds. Hybridization with Black-chinned has been reported.

PLUMAGE VARIATION AND MOLT

Dusky markings in gorget of females and immature males are highly variable. Typical pattern in females is fine streaks or spots concentrated centrally, but some have a large irregular blotch of dusky olive on the throat similar to that of immature female Anna's. In immature males, throat markings usually appear as a "five-o'clock shadow" in the shape of the gorget of mature males, though some immature males have lightly marked throats. Immatures usually appear duller on crown and back and may be mistaken for Black-chinned; longer tail and narrow tip to outer primary are best field marks. A few immatures show tawny to cinnamon wash on sides and flanks, dull cinnamon at base of outer tail feathers (similar to *Selasphorus*). Various forms of albinism are common; melanism is rare. Flight feather molt begins late August to early September in adults, late September to early October in immatures. Molt usually complete prior to spring migration.

REFERENCES

Bent 1940
Robinson, Sargent, and Sargent 1996

BLACK-CHINNED HUMMINGBIRD

Archilochus alexandri   **PLS. 7, 20, 21, 26, 27**

3.25–3.75 in. (8.5–9.5 cm). Bill length: ♂ 15–21 mm, ♀ 17–22 mm; tail length: ♂ 23–28 mm, ♀ 24–30 mm.

The western counterpart of the Ruby-throated is abundant and adaptable, exploiting a wide variety of habitats from central Mexico to the southwestern corner of Canada. The colors of both sexes are subdued, with dull green above and dingy gray below. The male's gorget appears entirely black from most angles, its brilliant amethyst violet band visible only when the light strikes it perfectly. The male's most conspicuous feature is a white collar contrasting with the dark head. Both sexes pump and wag the tail almost constantly in flight. The species was named in 1846 in honor of its discoverer, Dr. Alexandre of Mexico, about whom nothing else is known.

DESCRIPTION

A small, compact hummingbird with a medium-length to long, slightly decurved bill, dull grayish crown. Outer primary (P10) broad, blunt, curved; inner primaries graduated in width, becoming narrower from outermost (P6) to innermost (P1). **ADULT MALE:** Dull green to emerald green above, pale gray to whitish below, becoming dull green on sides. Gorget mostly velvety black, with seldom-visible band of metallic amethyst violet (blue-violet to purple) at bottom; corners rounded. White of breast extends around sides of neck, contrasting strongly with all-dark head. Inner primaries modified, pointed at tip with small notch on inner web. **ADULT FEMALE:** Dull green to golden green above, pale gray below. Sides washed gray-green, often with tawny to cinnamon patch on lower flank. Cheek dull gray, lores dusky. Throat unmarked or with variable dusky streaking or spotting at center of gorget. Central tail feathers (R1) green, with or without diffuse dark band at tip. R2 gray-green tipped black; R3 like R2 but narrowly tipped white; R4, R5 pointed, broadly tipped white. Inner primaries show faint notch on inner web. **IMMATURE MALE:** Like adult female, including pointed R5, but with shorter bill, markings on gorget heavier and more extensive, pale buff feather edges visible on upperparts when fresh. Inner primaries show faint notch on inner web. **IMMATURE FEMALE:** Like adult female but with pale buff feather edges visible on upperparts, small white tip on R2, R5 rounded at tip. Inner primaries unmodified.

SIMILAR SPECIES

Female and immature male **RUBY-THROATED HUMMINGBIRD** are brighter green above, especially on crown, with shorter bill and narrower, more pointed tip to outer primaries. Dark face contrasts strongly with whitish throat. Tail slightly longer, distinctly notched, not pumped as consistently. Female and immature male **COSTA'S HUMMINGBIRD** are slightly smaller with shorter bill and tail. Head is proportionally larger, more rounded, with pale gray eyebrow; inner primaries approximately equal in width. Call is a dry *tik*. Female and immature male **ANNA'S HUMMINGBIRD** are chunky and large-headed, darker gray below with subtle scaly appearance to throat and flanks; adult female and immature male usually show rose red to coppery iridescence in gorget. Voice is a sharp *tsip* or *tchik*. Female and immature male **LUCIFER HUMMINGBIRD** have long, narrow, deeply notched to forked tail with rufous at bases of R3–5, rusty cinnamon wash to flanks, slightly to moderately decurved bill.

SOUNDS

CALLS include a soft *tchew*, a variety of mellow *tchip* and *tchup* notes; in aggressive interactions, squeals and twitters. **SONG**, described as a high-pitched warble, is very rarely heard. Modified inner primaries of adult male create dull buzzing whine in flight; softer in immature male and adult female, inaudible in immature female. **DIVE NOISE** is a loud nasal whinny produced by male during Dive Display at bottom of U-shaped arc; probably produced by tail feathers.

BEHAVIOR

Pumps tail almost constantly in hovering flight. Takes nectar from a variety of flowers, including penstemons, agaves, sages, gilias, scarlet creeper, trumpet creeper, ocotillo, chuparosa, scarlet bouvardia, Turk's-cap hibiscus, coral honeysuckle, desert honeysuckle, tree tobacco. Takes insects by fly-catching, gleaning. Drinks tree sap from sapsucker wells, acorn cups. Bathes by dragging belly along surface of water or fluttering in shallow water or on wet leaves. May drink dew to supplement water in nectar. Male performs U-shaped **DIVE DISPLAY**, with low pass near female accompanied by a shrill whinnying sound (Dive Noise). **SHUTTLE DISPLAY**, usually performed in front of female, is accompanied by droning wing sound that varies in intensity in time with movements. **NEST** is a soft cup of whitish plant fibers and animal hair held together with spider silk; exterior may be camouflaged with lichen and plant debris (Arizona eastward) or left mostly bare (California). Nests in a variety of locations from low to high. Females occasionally choose odd sites such as wind chimes, chains, or loops of rope. Nests are often built on remains from previous season. Approximately two-thirds of nesting attempts fail, due primarily to predators. Adults occasionally fall prey to roadrunners and large flycatchers; will mob potential predators such as owls, jays, orioles, tanagers, lizards, and snakes.

HABITAT

BREEDS in deciduous and evergreen oak woodland, riparian forest (willow, cottonwood, hackberry, sycamore, pecan), pinyon-juniper woodland, pine-oak woodland, chaparral, desert washes, canyon bottoms, orchards, urban gardens. Sexes often occur in different densities in breeding habitat; males tend to cluster near nectar sources, while females are scattered or clustered depending on availability of preferred nesting habitat. **WINTERS** in a variety of habitats, including tropical deciduous forest, thorn scrub, tall evergreen tropical forest, gardens.

DISTRIBUTION

BREEDS from south-central Mexico north through western half of Tex. (except eastern Panhandle), extreme southern and western Okla., N.M., Ariz. (absent from most of southwestern corner except Colorado R. corridor), Utah, most of Nev., southern and western Colo., extreme southwestern Wyo., most of Idaho, extreme western Mont., eastern and central Ore., eastern and central Wash., and extreme southern B.C. (Okanagan Valley). Also from northwestern Baja Calif. north along Pacific Coast into Central Valley, foothills of San Joaquin Valley, Calif. One nest record for southwestern Kans. **RESIDENT** from coastal southern Tex. and Rio Grande Valley south into south-central Mexico. **WINTERS**

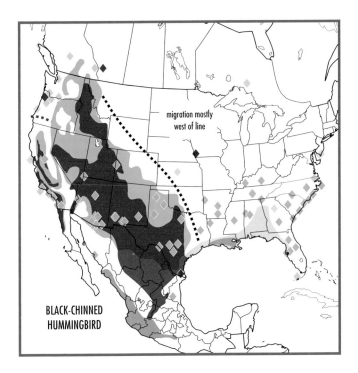

migration mostly
west of line

**BLACK-CHINNED
HUMMINGBIRD**

within resident range and along southwestern Pacific Coast of
Mexico (north to northern Sinaloa). Number of individuals wintering along Gulf Coast to Ga., Fla. appears to be increasing. May
be underreported in Calif. in winter. VAGRANTS recorded in N.C.
(fall–spring), N.J. (fall), S.C. (fall–winter), S.D. (fall), Tenn.
(fall–winter), Ky. (fall–winter), Alta. (July), Ont. (May). Other
northern winter records include Ariz., N.M., Colo., northern and
central Tex., southern Calif.

STATUS AND CONSERVATION

Common, widespread, and tolerant of human activities, altered
habitats. Has benefited from introduction of feeders and nonnative nectar plants, becoming a common urban bird in areas where
it was once uncommon to rare. Threatened riparian habitats in
the West are important for nesting and migration. Population
fluctuations in San Francisco Bay area attributed to loss of exotic
tree tobacco to weed control and flooding. As in Ruby-throated,

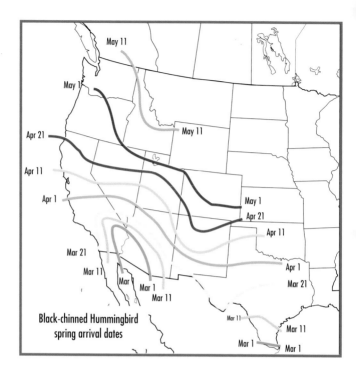

Black-chinned Hummingbird
spring arrival dates

sex ratio of adults is skewed toward females, suggesting higher male mortality. Both males and females have reached at least 8 years of age in the wild.

 SUBSPECIES AND TAXONOMIC RELATIONSHIPS

No subspecies have been named, but distinctly smaller individuals make up breeding populations from southern Texas through central Mexico and a small percentage of migrants through the Southwest. These birds are more readily mistaken for Ruby-throated Hummingbird than are typical Black-chinned. Hybrids have been recorded with Anna's, Costa's, Broad-tailed, Ruby-throated, Lucifer, Allen's, and Blue-throated. Adult male hybrids often show a narrow black chin strap resembling that of Ruby-throated. Hybrids with *Calypte* usually lack metallic iridescent on crown. The Chisos Hummingbird, *Phasmornis mystica* (Ober-holser) is probably a hybrid or oddly plumaged Black-chinned.

PLUMAGE VARIATION AND MOLT

Dusky markings in gorgets of females and immature males are highly variable. Typical pattern in females is fine streaks or spots concentrated centrally, but some have a large irregular blotch of dusky olive on the throat similar to that of immature female Anna's. In immature males, throat markings usually appear as a "five-o'clock shadow" in the shape of the gorget of mature males, though some immature males have lightly marked throats. Adult females will occasionally show one or more randomly placed dark feathers in the gorget area. Leucistic individuals are reported almost every year; partial albinism is fairly common and may be either congenital or acquired. Adults molt flight feathers beginning in September, complete molt by late February. Immatures begin flight feather molt by November, complete molt by mid-April.

REFERENCES

Baltosser and Russell 2000
Banks and Johnson 1961
Bent 1940

NNA'S HUMMINGBIRD   PLS. 6, 20, 21, 26, 27, 31

alypte anna
3.5–4 in. (9–10 cm). Bill length: ♂ 15–19 mm, ♀ 15–20 mm; tail length: ♂ 26–34 mm, ♀ 25–32 mm.

The quintessential urban hummingbird, Anna's Hummingbird has shown remarkable adaptability, allowing it to prosper while extinction claims other species native to California's vanishing chaparral habitats. In recent times it has expanded its range northward and eastward, exploiting exotic flowers in urban and suburban gardens. Though song is now known to be more the rule than the exception among North American hummingbirds, the song of Anna's was among the first to be studied and is still among the best known of all hummingbird songs. The name honors Anna Masséna, Duchess of Rivoli and a patron of the sciences.

DESCRIPTION

A medium-sized chunky hummingbird with medium-length straight black bill, dingy medium to pale gray underparts, medium-length to long tail. Inner primaries all approximately equal width, outer primaries angular at tip. **ADULT MALE:** Bright green to bluish green above. Gorget is rose red to coppery red, with moderate extensions at corners; crown and separate patch behind eye same color as throat. Upper breast medium to pale gray, usually slightly mottled. Pale feather edges give green underparts a scaly appearance; pale midline stripe faint or absent. Long, deeply notched tail extends well beyond wingtips. Outer tail feathers are gray, darker at edges bordering paler translucent patches; R5 narrow, rounded at tip. **ADULT FEMALE:** Bright green to bronze-green above, medium to pale gray below. Gorget markings vary from bronze-gray mottling to a ragged-edged triangle, oval, or diamond of rose red to coppery iridescence. Slightly notched to double-rounded tail extends to or beyond wingtips. Tail feathers broad, rounded; R3–5 banded in dull gray-green, blackish, and white. Bill is straight to very slightly decurved. **IMMATURE MALE:** Resembles adult female but with pale feather edges, heavier mottling in gorget with larger iridescent feathers; R5 broad, rounded, with thin line of black extending into white tip along shaft. **IMMATURE FEMALE:** Very similar to adult female, usually with dull gray mottling in gorget with or without a few iridescent feathers centrally; may have more white in R2. Best distinguished by plumage condition (see Plumage Variation and Molt).

SIMILAR SPECIES

Adult male **COSTA'S HUMMINGBIRD** is smaller, with shorter tail, paler underparts with pale midline stripe creating a distinct "vest"; gorget is deep purple to violet, with longer extensions at corners. Females and immature males have thinner bills, shorter tails that are often pumped or wagged in flight; underparts are paler, plainer. Call note is a dry *tik*. Female and immature male **BLACK-CHINNED HUMMINGBIRD** are slimmer, with longer bills; paler, plainer underparts; inner primaries graduated in width. Tail is usually pumped or wagged in flight. Call note is a soft *tchew* or *tchup*. Adult male **LUCIFER HUMMINGBIRD** is slim with long, distinctly decurved bill; very long, deeply forked tail; rufous wash on underparts.

SOUNDS

CALLS include a sharp *tsip* or *tchik,* given singly, doubled, or in series when agitated, and a rapid *zheega-zheega-zheega* in combat. **SONG** is a series of harsh buzzy notes and chips, often slurred together; typical song pattern is *zhi zhi zhi chur-zwee' dzik dzik.* Song is at least partly learned. Males of isolated population on Guadalupe Island off Baja California sing a simpler song than mainland birds, and a male learned the song of a male Anna's × Calliope hybrid. **DIVE NOISE** accompanying male display is apparently mechanical, produced by air rushing over tail feathers.

Behavior

Typically holds tail still while hovering, unlike Black-chinned and Costa's. Takes nectar at a variety of flowers, including native chaparral currant, fuchsia-flowered gooseberry, wooly blue-curls, pitcher sage, California fuchsia, red bush-penstemon, western columbine, and bush monkeyflower; also exotics such as citrus, tree tobacco, aloes, bottlebrush, and eucalyptus. Feeds extensively on insects, including gnats, midges, and whiteflies, especially during winter. Occasionally observed eating sand and ashes, probably to supply minerals. Adult males defend feeding territories and sing year-round; young males begin singing by late summer, often from concealment. **DIVE DISPLAY** is complex, noisy. Male sings buzzy notes while hovering over the object of the display (female, rival male, other hummingbird species, or even a human), then climbs for 7 to 8 seconds on a wavering trajectory to a height of 65 to 130 ft. (20–40 m) before plunging the same distance in a mere 2 seconds. The dive ends with a shrill squeak (Dive Noise) as the displaying bird passes the object. **SHUTTLE DISPLAY** consists of horizontal arcs above female, with bill pointed toward her, gorget extended, and body horizontal; female often keeps bill pointed toward shuttling male. Perched males threaten intruders by erecting gorget and crown and swaying back and forth, accompanying the flashing iridescence with harsh chatter. Displaying males tend to orient themselves in relation to the sun to give the object of the display the most intense show of color. **NEST** is a soft cup of whitish plant fibers and animal hair held together with spider silk; exterior usually camouflaged with lichen and plant debris, but paint chips, cigarette paper, other artificial materials may be used in urban areas. Male typically takes no interest in nest, but in one extraordinary instance a bird in adult male plumage fed a near-fledging nestling whose mother had disappeared. Nests mid-November to May in California chaparral, October to June in Arizona, mostly February to June in northern parts of range. Has lived to at least 8 years of age.

Habitat

BREEDS in chaparral, coastal scrub, evergreen-oak woodland, riparian woodland, oak savannah, orchards, parks, urban gardens, sea level to 5,700 ft. (1,750 m). **NONBREEDING** birds often move to higher

ANNA'S HUMMINGBIRD

many individuals retreat from northern edge of breeding range in winter, return in early spring

large numbers present in southern Arizona July–October, include migrants from California

rare and irregular north of line July–March

elevations and inland into pine-oak forest, pine-fir forest, mountain meadows, up to 11,000 ft. (3,300 m). Population density and distribution outside coastal southern California dependent in large part on availability of urban habitats.

 ## DISTRIBUTION

RESIDENT from northwestern Baja Calif. along Pacific Coast to southwestern B.C., inland to southern Ariz., southwestern N.M. (Hidalgo Co.). Extremely rare breeder in far western Tex. (2 records). Populations within resident range often fluctuate seasonally. Most individuals disappear from northern edge of range by early winter, returning February–March. **NONBREEDING** birds range south to northern Sinaloa, southwestern Chihuahua, north to western and southern B.C., southeastern Alaska, inland into southern and central N.M., western and central Tex., southwestern Nev. Rare in fall and winter in coastal Tex., La. Nonbreeding individuals may remain as late as early spring, suggesting wide variation in timing of breeding. **MIGRATION** is poorly understood; the species certainly does not migrate in the traditional sense. Year-round presence in some areas may be due to breeding birds being seasonally replaced by migrants from other areas. Large numbers of Anna's in the mountains of Ariz. in nonbreeding season (July to October) have long been assumed to come from Calif., yet of thousands of Anna's banded in Ariz. and Calif., to date only one is known to have traveled between the two states. **VAGRANTS** can occur almost anywhere, most commonly in fall and winter. Records include Ala. (November), interior Alaska (September), Ark. (fall-winter), Colo. (May to December), Fla. (fall-winter), Ga. (fall-winter), Idaho (September to May), Ill. (fall-winter), Kans. (fall-winter), Mich. (December to April), Minn. (fall-winter), Mo. (October to February), Miss. (November to January), Mont. (June to November), N.C. (fall-winter), N.Y. (October to December), Okla. (winter), S.C. (winter), Tenn. (January), northern and eastern Texas (July to March), Utah (fall), Wisc. (August to January), Alta. (June to October), Sask. (July to October).

STATUS AND CONSERVATION

This species has benefited greatly from human activities. Replacement of native chaparral and desert scrub with irrigated gardens and parks has permitted expansion of range north into Canada and east into the Mojave and Sonoran Deserts. Anna's appears to displace Costa's as natural desert gives way to residential and recreational development. Additional study needed to determine how these two species interact in urban habitats.

SUBSPECIES AND TAXONOMIC RELATIONSHIPS

No subspecies are recognized. Anna's and Costa's form a super-species, isolated primarily by habitat preferences. Hybrids with Costa's are fairly common, especially in urban areas of California, Arizona. Hybrids are also recorded with Black-chinned, Calliope, and Allen's. Hybrids with Rufous not confirmed, though perhaps increasingly likely with expansion of Anna's into its range. Male hybrids often sing, though the song may be weak and garbled compared to typical Anna's songs.

PLUMAGE VARIATION AND MOLT

Color of gorget subject to aging effects of sunlight. Feathers emerge rose red, age to coppery bronze, especially at higher elevations in Arizona, where sunlight is more intense. Elongation at corners of gorget more pronounced in older males, becoming more like Costa's. Shape and size of female gorget highly variable, more extensive in older females. Faint wash of rufous sometimes present along shaft near base of outer tail feathers. Adults molt in midsummer, immatures late summer through early fall.

 REFERENCES

Banks and Johnson 1961
Mirsky 1976
Phillips, Marshall, and Monson 1964
Russell 1996
Russell and Monson 1998
Wells, Bradley, and Baptista 1978

COSTA'S HUMMINGBIRD PLS. 5, 20, 21, 26, 27

Calypte costae

3–3.5 in. (7.5–9 cm). Bill length: ♂ 16–17 mm, ♀ 17–18 mm; tail length: ♂ 22–23 mm, ♀ 23–24 mm.

A true desert hummingbird, this species has been edged out of some of its habitat by urbanization and the subsequent invasion of its close relative, Anna's Hummingbird. It thrives in the Mojave and Sonoran Deserts but is uncommon to rare farther east. The "Fu Manchu" gorget of adult males is virtually unmistakable, but females and immature males are easily confused with Anna's or Black-chinned. Much of its life remains a mystery, particularly its travels during the nonbreeding season. Named in honor of Louis Costa, an early collector of hummingbird specimens.

 DESCRIPTION

A tiny compact, large-headed hummingbird with pale gray to whitish underparts, short, thin, straight to slightly decurved black bill; very short tail. Inner primaries all approximately equal width. **ADULT MALE:** Deep green above. Gorget is deep purple to violet, with long extensions at corners that hang down like a mustache or sweep back over shoulders; crown and separate patch behind eye same color as throat. Very pale gray to white breast wraps around side of neck to join whitish eye line, pale eyebrow. Sides green, with whitish midline stripe forming a "vest." Wingtips extend to or beyond tip of short notched tail. Outer tail feathers are gray, darker at edges; R5 narrow, curved inward, tapering to point. **ADULT FEMALE:** Bright green to golden green above, pale gray to whitish below; gorget may be unmarked or show small patch of iridescent violet-purple feathers at lower center. Wingtips extend to or slightly beyond very short, slightly double-rounded tail. Tail feathers rounded; R3–5 banded in dull gray-green, blackish, and white. Thin bill is slightly decurved. **IMMATURE MALE:** Similar to adult female but with broad buffy feather edges when fresh, dusky markings on throat, especially at corners of gorget. Gorget extends downward at corners, often shows extensive patches of metallic purple to violet by late summer. R5 narrower, thin line of black extends into white tip along shaft. **IMMATURE FEMALE:** Resembles adult female but with broad buffy feather edges when fresh, small white tip on R2.

SIMILAR SPECIES

Adult male **ANNA'S HUMMINGBIRD** is larger, with longer tail, dull gray to whitish breast; scaly green underparts lack distinct pale midline. Gorget is rose red to coppery red, with shorter extensions at corners. Females and immature males have longer, heavier bills and longer tails that are seldom pumped or wagged in flight. Underparts are more heavily marked, with scaly pattern on sides and bronze to red iridescent patch in gorget of adult females. Call note is a sharp *tschip* or *tchik*. Female and immature male **BLACK-CHINNED HUMMINGBIRD** are slimmer, with longer bills and tails, inner primaries graduated in width. Call note is a soft *tchew* or *tchup*. Female and immature male **RUBY-THROATED HUMMINGBIRD** are slimmer, with straight bills, longer tails, inner primaries graduated in width. Adult male **LUCIFER HUMMINGBIRD** has long, distinctly decurved bill; very long, narrow, deeply forked tail; rufous wash on underparts.

SOUNDS

CALLS include a weak dry *tik*, given singly or in rapid series when agitated. **SONG** is a thin shrill whistle, *whee-oo*, with rising and falling inflection, given from perch or during display flights. Vocal ability takes several months to develop; males too young to sing the full whistle song may sing a complex song similar to that of Anna's but weaker. Rough rustling sounds heard during dive display and aggressive encounters are believed to be created by the wings or tail.

BEHAVIOR

Tail is pumped or wagged intermittently in flight, similar to Black-chinned. Takes nectar from flowers of many sizes, shapes, and colors, including species adapted for pollination by insects. Desert lavender, wooly blue-curls, wolfberry, fairy-duster, ocotillo, chuparosa, desert honeysuckle, coral-bean, bush-monkeyflower, and penstemons are favorite nectar sources. Visits tree morning-glory and jícama in winter and early spring in western Mexico.

Drinks water when nectar is insufficient to meet needs. Males advertise breeding territory by adopting high, prominent perches and singing. **DIVE DISPLAY** has 3 phases, beginning with 1 or 2 low horizontal passes above or around the object of the display (usually an adult female but occasionally another male or another species of bird). The male then climbs steeply to begin a series of up to 40 high vertical loops directly over the object. Whistle song is given on the descent, loudest at bottom of loop before breaking off in the new ascent. Rougher sounds heard during the display are probably produced by wings or tail. Display terminates in an earthward plunge followed by a short swerving flight away from the object. Male may return quickly to repeat this display or to begin **SHUTTLE DISPLAY**, flying slowly from side to side in front of the female in short looping arcs, occasionally darting toward her. Whistle may accompany this display. Female typically observes displays from perched position, chipping or twittering during the performance. **NEST** is a soft cup of whitish plant fibers, animal hair, and feathers held together with spider silk; exterior may be camouflaged with lichens and plant debris or left mostly bare. Nests in natural desert may be built in dense vines or large woody plants such as paloverde, jojoba, ironwood, ocotillo, desert willow, or on thorny shrubs such as catclaw acacia, pencil cholla, graythorn. Also nests in avocado trees, palms, hackberries, oaks.

Habitat

BREEDS in scrub habitats, dry rocky hillsides covered with cacti and thorny shrubs, and edges of desert washes with dense trees in Sonoran and Mojave Deserts, California chaparral and coastal scrub, oak savannah, dry slopes of foothills, sea level to 4,500 ft. (1,300 m). Also uses urban garden and park habitats and chaparral remnants within developed areas, though less successfully than Anna's Hummingbird. Does well in recently burned chaparral. **NONBREEDING** birds may visit mountain forests up to 6,000 ft. (1,800 m) late summer to fall.

Distribution

Partial migrant. **RESIDENT** throughout Baja Calif., coast and foothills of southern Calif., southern Mojave Desert, northwestern and central Sonora, southwestern Ariz. (north to Lake Havasu), also around desert cities (Phoenix, Tucson, Yuma). Part of population breeding within resident range retreats south in winter. **BREEDS** north to central Calif. (Sacramento, Owens Valley), southern Nev., east to central Ariz., southern Ariz.-N.M. border (Guadalupe Canyon, Peloncillo Mts.), south to south-central

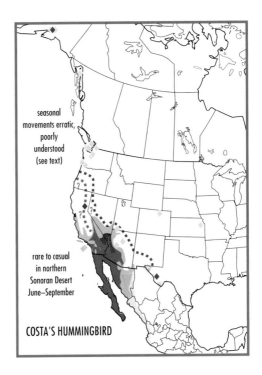

seasonal movements erratic, poorly understood (see text)

rare to casual in northern Sonoran Desert June–September

COSTA'S HUMMINGBIRD

Sonora. Rare and local in breeding season in extreme southwestern Utah, San Francisco Bay area north to western Ore. **WINTERS** from southern Sonora south along Pacific Coast to Nayarit, Jalisco. **SPRING MIGRANTS** arrive in Calif., Ariz. February to April (later in north). Post-breeding birds may move south along Pacific Coast of Mexico, north into Pacific Northwest, or inland into high valleys and uplands of southeastern Ariz., southwestern N.M., eastern Sonora, southern Chihuahua, returning to lower elevations October to December. **VAGRANTS** reported in Alaska (July to October), Kans. (November), western Tex. (September to January, April), central and southern Tex. (January to March), western Wash. (August to October), Colo. (May), Alta. (August), B.C. (April to June).

STATUS AND CONSERVATION

Range has fluctuated within historic times, with expansion of nonbreeding range in California, breeding range in Arizona, New Mexico. Urbanization, agriculture, and fire suppression are destroying or changing the character of its habitat in many areas. California coastal scrub habitat has been virtually wiped out by development. In northwestern Mexico, conversion of native desert scrub to pastures of exotic bufflegrass reduces availability of nectar, nest sites. Less adaptable to urban habitats and feeding stations than Anna's, which has replaced it in many areas.

Subspecies and Taxonomic Relationships

No subspecies are recognized. The genus *Calypte* once included the Bee Hummingbird *(Mellisuga helenae)* of Cuba, which has matching iridescence in gorget and crown and long Costa's-like extensions at the corners of its gorget. The two current members of the genus are very close relatives. Hybrids between Costa's and Anna's are common, especially in urban areas. Hybrids have also been reported with Blue-throated, Black-chinned, Calliope, and Broad-tailed.

Plumage Variation and Molt

Rare females may acquire male-like gorget; distinguished from immature males by molt stage, entirely green or dusky crown, absence of mature male tail feathers. Molt is poorly understood; may vary between populations. In Arizona, adults molt summer to early fall, immatures fall to winter.

References

Baltosser and Scott 1996
Banks and Johnson 1961
Wells, Bradley, and Baptista 1978

CALLIOPE HUMMINGBIRD PLS. 4, 18, 19, 24, 25

Stellula calliope

2.75–3.25 in. (7.5–8 cm). Bill length: ♂ 13–15 mm, ♀ 14–16 mm; tail length: ♂ 19–21 mm, ♀ 21–23 mm.

The smallest of all breeding birds in the United States, an adult male Calliope Hummingbird weighs less than a penny. His gorget of wine red streaks over a white background is unique, one reason this species is traditionally placed in its own genus. The slightly larger female resembles a tiny short-tailed female Broad-tailed. The species name is Greek for "beautiful voice" and may refer to the muse of epic poetry, in either case a seemingly inappropriate name for a bird of limited vocal ability.

DESCRIPTION

A very small hummingbird with a short black bill and very short tail with unique spade-shaped central feathers that widen significantly from a narrow base before tapering abruptly to a point (best developed in adults). Wingtip broad, blunt, curved. **ADULT MALE:** Bright green above, creamy white below with green wash on sides and flanks. Gorget consists of wine red to reddish purple iridescence over white background; individual feathers white basally, ranging in shape from round or broadly oval and nearly flat at center of gorget to very long, narrow, pointed, and convex at corners. Face is dull grayish, with slightly darker cheek, whitish mustachial stripe beginning at base of upper mandible. Wingtips extend to or beyond tip of very short, slightly notched tail. Tail feathers dull gray variably edged in cinnamon-rufous basally; R1 narrow at base, becoming wider toward tip before abruptly tapering to a spade-shaped point. **ADULT FEMALE:** Bright grass green to golden green above, creamy white below washed with cinnamon-rufous on sides, flanks, and across lower breast. Gorget usually evenly stippled to spangled with dusky to brownish bronze, rarely with a few larger spangles at lower center reflecting dull wine red. Face dull grayish with slightly darker cheek. Slightly notched tail usually falls short of wingtips. Central tail feathers green with or without narrow rufous edges at base; R3–5 (rarely R2–5) tipped white, usually with narrow edges of cinnamon-rufous basally. Undertail coverts washed pale cinnamon, paler at tips. Outer primary (P10) broad, blunt-tipped. **IMMATURE MALE:** Similar to adult female but usually with more heavily marked gorget, often with random spots, streaks, or patches of wine red iridescence. R1 always narrowly edged in dull cinnamon-rufous at base (difficult to see). **IMMATURE FEMALE:** Similar to adult female but with indistinct pale feather edges on upperparts. R1 green with blackish tip, no rufous edges at base; large white tip on R3, usually small white tip on R2.

SIMILAR SPECIES

BUMBLEBEE HUMMINGBIRD has extremely short bill (shorter than remainder of head). In all plumages tail is banded in rufous, black, and white and extends slightly beyond wingtips. Outer primary (P10) narrow, rounded at tip. Adult male has solid rose-magenta gorget with no white showing through. Female and immature male show more extensive rufous in tail, narrower, straighter outer primaries. Female and immature male **BROAD-TAILED HUMMINGBIRD** are much larger, with longer bill and tail, more rufous in outer tail feathers, and narrower, straighter primaries. **RUFOUS** and

ALLEN'S HUMMINGBIRDS are slightly larger, with longer bill and tail, richer rufous wash to underparts, more rufous in outer tail feathers, and narrower, straighter primaries.

Sounds

Generally quiet, especially so in migration. **CALLS** include a soft *tchip*, weak twittering during territorial encounters. Dive Display ends with metallic *tzing* or *pzzt-zing*, possibly vocal, and weak raspberry-like *pfft*, probably created by braking action of wings or tail.

Behavior

Tail is often cocked upward, perpendicular to body, while hovering at flowers or feeders. Takes nectar from a wide variety of plants, including red currant, Indian paintbrush, orange honeysuckle, western columbine, skyrocket, Rocky Mountain beeplant. Often takes nectar from flowers within inches of the ground. Takes insect prey mostly by fly-catching from an exposed perch. Feeds regularly at sapsucker wells. Males most assertive on breeding grounds. Displays are more often directed at females than rival males, which are usually chased. **DIVE DISPLAY** is U- or J-shaped, punctuated at bottom of arc with *pzzt-zing*. In **SHUTTLE DISPLAY**, male hovers in front of and slightly above female, with wings buzzing loudly. Female may vocalize frequently during display or respond by joining male in spinning aerial dance with bills locked. Displays and chases may be accompanied by fanning of long rays of male's gorget into a dramatic sunburst. **NEST** is a well-insulated cup of soft plant fibers held together with spider silk; exterior camouflaged with bits of bark, lichen chips, moss. Built in a pine, fir, spruce, or hemlock, usually sheltered by an overhanging branch, often atop a pine cone. Site may be reused, with new nest built on top of old. Nesting females will attack squirrels, other potential predators. Nests late April to mid-August.

Habitat

BREEDS in montane conifer forests, in willows along streams, aspen thickets, and older second growth following fires or clear-cutting, 4,000–11,000 ft. (1,200–3,400 m), rarely as low as 500 ft. (185 m). **WINTERS** from low-elevation thorn forest to humid pine forest in southwestern Mexico. **MIGRATES** through both montane and lowland habitats.

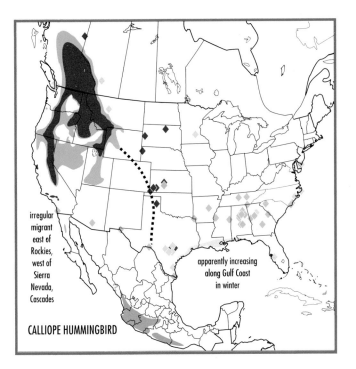

irregular migrant east of Rockies, west of Sierra Nevada, Cascades

apparently increasing along Gulf Coast in winter

CALLIOPE HUMMINGBIRD

Distribution

BREEDS from northern Baja Calif. (Sierra San Pedro Martir), southern Calif. (San Bernardino, San Jacinto, San Gabriel Mts.) north through northwestern Nev., northern Idaho, to southeastern B.C., southwestern edge of Alta., east to western Mont., western Wyo., central Utah. **WINTERS** in southwestern Mexico, along Gulf Coast west to northwestern Fla. (mostly southern La.), rarely in Southwest (western Tex., Ariz.). **SPRING MIGRATION** is mainly through higher elevations along Pacific Flyway. Northbound migrants arrive in southern Calif. March to April, reach Ore., Wash., B.C. in early to mid-April. Smaller numbers pass through mountains of Southwest late March to May. **FALL MIGRATION** utilizes both Pacific and Rocky Mtn. Flyways and wider range of elevations, including mountains and desert riparian corridors. Rare to uncommon in western Colo. late June to August, rare July to August in eastern Colo., western Kans. Uncommon to abundant in mountains of central N.M., central and southern Ariz. July to September, rare

October to December. Rare July to September in western Tex., casual farther east to coast. **VAGRANTS** recorded in northern Ala. (November), Ark. (November to December), central Fla. (March to April), northern Ga. (winter), Kans. (July to August), Minn. (November to December), Okla., N.C. (October to March), Neb. (June to August), N.J. (November), S.C. (December to April), S.D. (August), eastern and central Tex., Tenn. (November to April), Sask. (July to August).

 ## STATUS AND CONSERVATION

In absence of natural fires, sunny openings in forest canopy left by small-scale clear-cutting may be of benefit in stimulating growth of nectar plants and shrub habitat for nesting. Survival of migrants may be enhanced by feeders when natural nectar is scarce. Has reached at least 6 years of age in the wild, 12 years in captivity.

 ## SUBSPECIES AND TAXONOMIC RELATIONSHIPS

The sole member of its genus, the Calliope Hummingbird is most closely related to the Broad-tailed and Bumblebee Hummingbirds, more distantly to Rufous and Allen's. Hybrids have been recorded with Anna's, Costa's, Rufous, and Broad-tailed.

 ## PLUMAGE VARIATION AND MOLT

Rufous edges at base of R1 always present in immature male, always absent in immature female, highly variable in adult female. Adult females rarely show a small patch of iridescent wine red feathers at the lower center of the gorget. Normal male gorget may flash violet-blue or green along edges of elongated feathers. Adult male collected in western Mexico in early spring had violet-purple gorget streaks; plumage was otherwise normal, with no characteristics suggesting hybrid origin. Some adult males have diffuse whitish tips on R4–5, perhaps an indicator of youth. Little is known of molt in this species, though in both adults and immatures it appears to take place largely or completely on the wintering grounds.

REFERENCES

Banks and Johnson 1961
Bent 1940
Calder and Calder 1994

this heloisa

2.75–3 in. (7–7.5 cm). Bill length: ♂ 11–13 mm, ♀ 11–14 mm; tail length: ♂ 18–19 mm, ♀ 19–20 mm.

This tiny hummingbird has not been reported north of Mexico since two females were collected in the Huachuca Mountains of southeastern Arizona in July 1896. These specimens were originally described as a new species, Morcom's Hummingbird (*Atthis morcomi*), because of slight differences in color from the southern subspecies of the Bumblebee. Though its nearest known range is far south of the Arizona border, more recent visitors of this species may have gone unnoticed because of its close resemblance to the Calliope Hummingbird and the general difficulty in distinguishing among hummingbirds with rufous in the plumage. Formerly known as Heloise's Hummingbird.

DESCRIPTION

A very small hummingbird with a very short black bill; tail banded in rufous, black, and white on the outer feathers. **ADULT MALE:** Bright bronze-green to bronze above, white below with rufous wash on sides and flanks overlaid with bronze on lower flanks. Gorget solid deep rose-magenta with flashes of violet, corners elongate, slightly pointed as in Lucifer Hummingbird. Lores and cheeks grayish. Slightly rounded tail extends past wingtips. R1 rounded at tip, sides nearly parallel, bronze-green with or without narrow rufous edges at base. R2 has broad rufous edges at base, tip green and black with or without small white spot. R3–5 broadly banded in rufous, black, and white. Outer primary (P10) narrows abruptly near tip, creating flight sound (see Sounds). **ADULT FEMALE:** Grass green or golden green to bronze-green above, creamy white below washed with pale cinnamon-rufous on sides, flanks, and across lower breast; gorget creamy white spangled with brownish bronze, often with a few larger dull magenta spangles at lower center. Tail similar to that of adult male except with slightly less rufous; no rufous edges on R1; undertail coverts white, often with buffy wash. Outer primary (P10) narrow, rounded at tip. **IMMATURE MALE:** Similar to adult female but with more heavily marked gorget, pale feather edges on upperparts. Gorget extends downward at corners. **IMMATURE FEMALE:** Similar to adult female but with pale feather edges on upperparts.

Similar Species

CALLIOPE HUMMINGBIRD is slightly larger, with longer bill, proportionally shorter tail, brighter green upperparts. Tail of adult male solid dark gray or faintly edged in rufous, with little or no white on R3–5; wingtips usually extend slightly beyond tail. Gorget is narrow wine red to purple spangles and streaks over white background. Females and immature males have proportionally shorter, notched to double-rounded tail with little or no obvious rufous, less obvious spade shape to R1. Outer primary (P10) broad, blunt-tipped. **RUFOUS** and **ALLEN'S HUMMINGBIRDS** are larger, longer billed, with bright rufous wash to face, sides, flanks, undertail coverts. **LUCIFER HUMMINGBIRD** is larger, slimmer, with long decurved bill and long narrow tail.

 ## Sounds

CALLS include high-pitched chips and twitters similar to those of Calliope or Broad-tailed. **SONG** is a thin whining whistle, *sseeuuuu*, fading out near end. Narrowed outer primaries of adult male create beelike buzzing in flight; structure less well developed in immature male.

 ## Behavior

A relatively little known species. Slow, steady flight resembles that of a large bee, perhaps helping it escape detection by larger species whose territories it parasitizes. A retiring species not prone to confrontation. Often feeds at flowers with shorter corolla tubes, including many pollinated by insects. May feed within inches of the ground. **NEST** is undescribed. Breeding season of northern populations unrecorded, probably spring to early summer.

 ## Habitat

Edges of cloud forest and montane pine forest, pine-oak woodland, 5,000–10,000 ft. (1,500–3,000 m).

 ## Distribution

RESIDENT in Sierra Madre from southern Chihuahua and southern Tamaulipas south to central and southern Mexico. Two females collected in Huachuca Mts. on 2 July 1896. No other U.S. records.

BUMBLEBEE HUMMINGBIRD

STATUS AND CONSERVATION

Little known, even in Mexico. May be vulnerable to logging of
mountain forests, replacement of diverse native trees with a few
commercially valuable species.

SUBSPECIES AND TAXONOMIC RELATIONSHIPS

In northern subspecies *margarethae*, male gorget is slightly
darker, female and immature male have whiter tips to outer tail
feathers than do eastern and southern *heloisa*. *Atthis* is very
closely related to *Selasphorus* and *Stellula*, and these 3 genera
may eventually be lumped together.

PLUMAGE VARIATION AND MOLT

Variation in amount of white at tips of rectrices does not seem
consistently related to age or sex; further study needed. Molt of

northern populations poorly known. Adults molt in summer, immatures winter to spring.

REFERENCES

Bent 1940
Howell and Webb 1995
Johnsgard 1997
Phillips et al. 1964
Züchner 1999d

BROAD-TAILED HUMMINGBIRD PLS. 3,18, 24, 25

Selasphorus platycercus

3.75–4.25 in. (9.5–11 cm). Bill length: ♂ 16–19 mm, ♀ 17–20 mm; tail length: ♂ 30–35 mm, ♀ 27–33 mm.

The common nesting hummingbird of the Rocky Mountains, this species is found from Wyoming and central Idaho south to Guatemala. The silvery wing trill of adult males, like the ringing of tiny bells, is a familiar sound of summer in the Rockies. One of the earliest spring migrants, it often arrives on its alpine breeding grounds long before the snow has melted. A female banded in southern Colorado is the oldest known wild hummingbird in North America, having reached at least 12 years of age. The species name means "broad tail" in Greek.

DESCRIPTION

A medium-sized hummingbird with a long tail and medium-length straight black bill. **ADULT MALE:** Brilliant grass green to emerald green above, white below with gray-green "vest" and tawny wash on flanks. Gorget brilliant hot pink to rose red, contrasting vividly with white breast. Cheeks, edges of chin feathers dull olive-gray; lores dusky. Tail is long, extending well past wingtips. R1 pointed, usually all green, rarely dusky. R2 green or green and black, with narrow to broad rufous edge on outer web. R3–4 blackish with faint violet-purple sheen, outer web narrowly edged in rufous. R5 narrow, rounded, all dark or with smudgy whitish tip. **ADULT FEMALE:** Bright grass green above, white below washed with pale rufous on sides and flanks. Gorget usually evenly stippled to spangled with dusky to bronze, rarely with a few larger spangles at lower center reflecting dull rose pink to reddish bronze. Face dull olive-gray with slightly darker cheek, dusky lores. Long tail shows rufous in R2–5, often mottled with black or green; white tips on R3–5 (narrow on R3, sometimes faint pale edge at tip of R2). Undertail coverts creamy white washed with cinnamon-buff at base. Outer primary (P10) tapers to narrow tip. **IMMATURE MALE:** Resembles adult female but with sides washed green or rufous and green; gorget usually more heavily marked. Tail feathers typically more pointed, especially R1–3; rufous in R3–5 lightly to heavily mottled with black or dull green, concentrated along shaft of feather. **IMMATURE FEMALE:** Similar to adult female but usually with pale feather edges on upperparts, less rufous in R2–5, white tips on R2–5.

SIMILAR SPECIES

Adult male **RUBY-THROATED HUMMINGBIRD** lacks wing trill, has ruby red throat with narrow black chin strap, dark lores and cheeks, forked tail without rufous. Adult male **ANNA'S HUMMINGBIRD** lacks wing trill, has rose red to coppery red throat and crown, pale to medium gray upper breast, distinctly scaly underparts, whitish midline indistinct or absent, dull gray notched tail. Female and immature male **RUFOUS** and **ALLEN'S HUMMINGBIRDS** are slightly smaller, with proportionally shorter bill and tail; underparts more intensely washed with rufous, more extensive rufous in tail feathers, particularly R2 and R5. Female and immature male **CALLIOPE HUMMINGBIRD** are smaller with very short bill and tail; wingtips extend to tail tip or slightly beyond; rufous in tail limited to narrow edges near base. Outer primaries broad, curved, blunt-tipped. Female and immature male **LUCIFER HUMMINGBIRD** have unspotted throat, curving dusky "sideburns," longer, moderately to strongly decurved bill; very long tail is narrow, deeply notched to forked.

SOUNDS

CALLS include bright *chip* and *tschip* notes, less harsh than Rufous, richer and more emphatic than Calliope. **WING SOUND** of adult male is a bright silvery trill, created by modified outer primaries. Immature and molting males are silent, but there is evidence that the sound can be deliberately muffled. Flight displays and wing sound may substitute for song in this species.

BEHAVIOR

A mild-mannered species that is easily dominated by migrating Rufous and even occasionally by much smaller Calliope. Visits a wide variety of flowers, including barrel columbine, claret cup cactus, New Mexican locust, scarlet bouvardia, twinberry honeysuckle, skyrocket, Indian paintbrush, larkspurs, penstemons, manzanitas, currants, willow catkins on breeding grounds; ocotillo, Parry penstemon in migration through lower elevations;

sages, currants, and butterfly bush on wintering grounds in Mexico. Often forages in open mountain meadows. Excellent memory, capable of discriminating between new and previously visited flowers. Takes sap from wells drilled by sapsuckers. Forages for invertebrate prey by fly-catching and gleaning; eats aphids, gnats, spiders, other small arthropods. Early arrivals on breeding grounds subsist on invertebrates and sap until first flowers bloom. **DIVE DISPLAY** begins with ascent to height of 35–75 ft. (12–25 m) followed by power dive, pulling out in front of female, rival male, even nonhummingbirds; accompanied by wing trill; males on territory repeat display frequently throughout the day. **SHUTTLE DISPLAY** ("whisking display") is performed for perched female; male appears to be bouncing back and forth in front of female on a long rubber band. Male often ascends over territory to scan vegetation below for elusive female. **NEST** is a soft cup of whitish plant fibers and animal hair held together with spider silk; exterior camouflaged with lichens, moss, plant debris. Material may be recycled from old nests or stolen from nests of other birds. Built near bottom of canopy in conifer or broad-leafed tree, often under shelter of overhanging branch. Nest may be attached to side of branch to achieve maximum protection from above. Female often adds significant additional material during incubation. Nests late May to mid-August in Colorado, April to August in Southwest. Typically 1 brood per year in central Rocky Mountains but probably 2 broods in warmer areas.

Habitat

BREEDS in mountain forests and woodland, edges of meadows; conifer forest, pine-oak woodland, pinyon-juniper, willow thicket along streams, aspen groves. May move to lower elevation habitats, including tropical deciduous forest and gardens, in winter.

Distribution

BREEDS Wyo. and central Idaho south to Guatemala. **RESIDENT** from southern Sonora and Chihuahua south. An early migrant; arrives in Ariz. and N.M. by late February. A male hybrid with White-eared Hummingbird inherited this early migration schedule, arriving in Ariz. up to 6 weeks earlier than male White-eared. Migratory population **WINTERS** within resident range in Mexico, also in small numbers along Gulf Coast. **VAGRANTS** recorded in northern Ark. (November to December), Del. (winter), Fla. (January to February), Ga. (fall-winter), Ill. (November), Ind. (winter), Kans. (June to September), Mich. (August to winter), Miss. (fall-win-

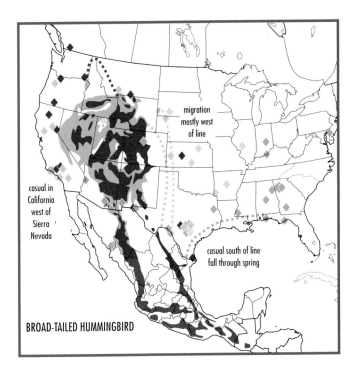

migration mostly west of line

casual in California west of Sierra Nevada

casual south of line fall through spring

BROAD-TAILED HUMMINGBIRD

ter), Neb. (August to September), N.J. (November), Ore. (May to August), S.D. (June to September), eastern and central Tex., Wash. (August), B.C. (July).

STATUS AND CONSERVATION

Common in the Rocky Mountains and Sierra Madre Occidental of Mexico. Feeders increase exposure to hazards such as predators, pesticides, windows.

SUBSPECIES AND TAXONOMIC RELATIONSHIPS

Though the Broad-tailed is in the same genus as Rufous and Allen's, recent DNA studies suggest that it may be as closely related to Calliope. Despite its wide geographic range and sedentary habits in Mexico and Guatemala, no subspecies have been identified.

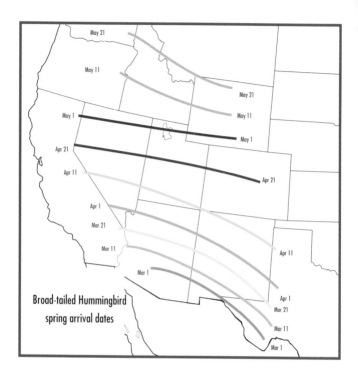

Broad-tailed Hummingbird
spring arrival dates

PLUMAGE VARIATION AND MOLT

Color, pattern, and even shape of adult male tail feathers are highly variable, as is pattern of rufous, black, and green in tails of immature males. A few adult females show a patch of iridescent rose- red feathers at lower center of gorget. Adults molt February to April, immatures molt March to June. A "late-blooming" species. Immature males often do not show metallic gorget feathers until late in fall migration. Second-year males are often in wing and gorget molt during migration in May.

REFERENCES

Banks and Johnson 1961
Calder and Calder 1992

elasphorus rufus

3.5–4 in. (9–10 cm). Bill length: ♂ 15–18 mm, ♀ 17–19 mm; tail length: ♂ 26–29 mm, ♀ 24–28 mm.

The fiery color of this small hummingbird matches its temperament. It is a common fall migrant in the Rocky Mountains, with a pugnacious nature that makes it a less-than-welcome guest at some feeding stations. The Rufous breeds farther north than any other hummingbird and travels phenomenal distances each year between its summer and winter homes. It is an important pollinator in the cool cloudy climate of the Pacific Northwest, where cold-blooded insect pollinators are at a disadvantage. This was likely the first hummingbird encountered by humans who crossed the Bering land bridge approximately 20,000 years ago.

DESCRIPTION

A small hummingbird with medium-short all-black bill and extensive rufous in plumage. **ADULT MALE:** Back varies from solid rufous or rufous with scattered green spangles (typical) to more than half green; crown bright green. Underparts creamy white with rufous "vest." Gorget brilliant scarlet to orange, appearing golden or even yellow-green from some angles. Cheeks and eyebrows dull rufous, lores dusky. Black-tipped rufous tail is long, extending past wingtips. Pointed tail feathers become progressively narrower from R1 to R5, which resembles a steak knife. R2 distinctly notched on inner web near tip. **ADULT FEMALE:** Bright green above, white below strongly washed with rufous on sides, flanks, and undertail coverts, extending onto edges of rump. Face and sides of gorget washed rufous. Gorget creamy white to ivory, lightly to heavily spangled with green to bronze (concentrated along sides); iridescent red-orange to coppery feathering in center of gorget varies from a few small spangles to dense ragged-edge triangle or diamond. Rounded tail extends past wingtips, shows extensive rufous in R2–5; R2 usually shows shallow indentation near tip, narrow green band separating rufous base from black tip. R5 narrow. **IMMATURE MALE:** Similar to adult female but usually with gorget more heavily marked, often with large mirrorlike gorget feathers in patches throughout gorget area or concentrated in lower center of throat. R2 rufous and black, without green. **IMMATURE FEMALE:** Resembles adult female but with fewer and smaller gorget markings (center of throat may be unmarked white), broader outer tail feathers with less rufous, small white tip on R2.

Adult males with mostly or entirely rufous backs are unmistakable; however, a small percentage of adult males have extensive green on the back, complicating separation from **ALLEN'S HUMMINGBIRD**. Typical adult male Allen's has no notch at tip of R2, narrower tail feathers overall, with R5 extremely narrow and stiletto-like. Adult female and immature Rufous are generally indistinguishable from Allen's in the field but may be separated by close examination of tail characteristics in hand or in photos. Female and immature male **BROAD-TAILED HUMMINGBIRD** are larger with slightly longer bill, grayish face, broader tail feathers with less rufous and more extensive green, paler rufous wash on underparts; no rufous in R1, on rump or uppertail coverts. Female and immature male **CALLIOPE HUMMINGBIRD** have shorter bill, much shorter tail with small amount of rufous, mostly on edges of feathers; metallic gorget feathers of immature male rose to wine red, elongate and narrow at corners of gorget. Outer primaries broad, blunt-tipped. Female and immature male **BUMBLEBEE HUMMINGBIRD** have much shorter bill, short tail with less rufous; metallic gorget feathers of immature male rose to wine red (if present). Female and immature male **LUCIFER HUMMINGBIRD** are slender, with unspotted throat, curving dusky "sideburns," longer, moderately to strongly decurved bill; very long tail is narrow, deeply notched to forked. **BAHAMA WOODSTAR** has very long forked tail; females have unspotted throats.

SOUNDS

CALLS include an emphatic *tchip, zeek zee'kik,* and *zeee' zik'iti-zik'iti-zik'iti* in combat. This species does not sing. **WING SOUND** of adult male is a shrill metallic whine, created by narrow pointed tips of outer primaries. Immature males and females have less modified primary tips and do not produce a distinctive sound. Flight displays and wing sound may substitute for song.

BEHAVIOR

Highly aggressive and territorial, even in migration. Regularly drives larger hummingbirds from nectar sources. Visits a variety of plants with short to medium-length flowers, including columbines, fireweed, skyrocket, bee-balm, Indian paintbrushes, larkspurs, honeysuckles, red currant, salmonberry, Rocky Mountain bee-plant. Takes sap from wells drilled by sapsuckers. Early arrivals on breeding grounds feed mainly on insects until flowers begin to bloom. **DIVE DISPLAY** of males is oval or U-shaped, accompanied by a series of *dit-dit-dit-deeer* dropping in pitch, followed by popping sounds probably made by tail feathers. SHUTTLE DISPLAY is a series of horizontal figure eights, more three-dimensional than in many species; may be directed at competitors for nectar as well as potential mates. Female may join male in joint "swinging" display flight prior to mating. NEST is a soft thick-walled cup of plant down and moss held together with spider silk and camouflaged with lichens, moss, and plant debris. Site is usually in dense branches of a conifer such as Sitka spruce, western red cedar, or Douglas-fir, often built on foundation of previous year's nest. Probably only one nesting attempt per season in northern part of range unless first nest fails early. Incubation lasts 15 to 17 days; nestlings fledge in approximately 3 weeks. Nests March to July; fledglings appear by late May.

HABITAT

BREEDS in forest openings, edges, and brushy second growth in conifer and mixed conifer-hardwood forests, including coastal temperate rain forest. WINTERS in a variety of habitats in western and southern Mexico, from scrubby second growth and thorn forest to high oak and pine-oak forests. Northern wintering birds prefer gardens with feeders, winter-blooming flowers, and dense vegetation for shelter.

DISTRIBUTION

BREEDS from coastal southeastern Alaska south through southern Yukon, most of B.C., southwestern Alta., Wash., northwestern and central Idaho, western Mont., most of Ore., extreme northwestern Calif. Early onset of southward migration and highly territorial behavior have led to mistaken reports of breeding as far south as N.M. and Ariz. WINTERS from coastal southern Calif. and Gulf Coast (mostly La., Miss., Ala., Tex.) south to south-central Mexico. Northernmost winter residents mostly coastal, spreading into interior farther south. Spring migration mostly through Pacific Flyway (rare in spring east of Calif.); fall migration split between Pacific and Rocky Mtn. Flyways. Spring migration appears to be undertaken in short segments to avoid overreaching northern limit of spring flowers. Adult males generally migrate earlier than females in both spring and fall. Males arrive in Wash. late February to early March, reach northern edge of range in southeastern Alaska by early May. Southbound males pass through western Colo. late June to early August. Adult females appear within 1 to 2 weeks of adult males. Migration of immatures is latest and most drawn out; first individuals typically 1 to 2 weeks behind adult females, last may pass through a month after the last

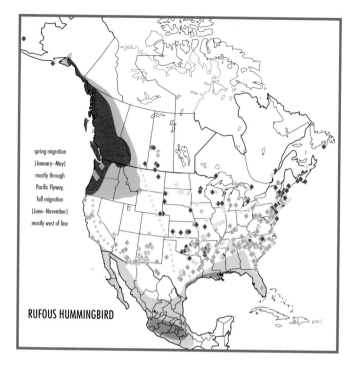

spring migration
(January–May)
mostly through
Pacific Flyway,
fall migration
(June–November)
mostly west of line

RUFOUS HUMMINGBIRD

adult females. Strongly prone to wandering during fall migration; reported from all states east of Rocky Mtns. and most Canadian provinces. Widespread **VAGRANT** in fall and winter in eastern U.S. and Canada. Could appear almost anywhere; usually discovered at feeders.

STATUS AND CONSERVATION

Population declines have been noted over parts of breeding range, for reasons still unclear. Extensive logging within both breeding and wintering ranges would be expected to increase nectar availability, opening sunny clearings that support favorite flowers; this does not seem to have had positive effects on populations, however. Feeders supplement natural food supplies but expose birds to dangers such as windows, cats, and pesticides. Short nesting season and perilous migration may limit ability of populations to rebound from declines due to habitat destruction. Currently on Partners in Flight WatchList.

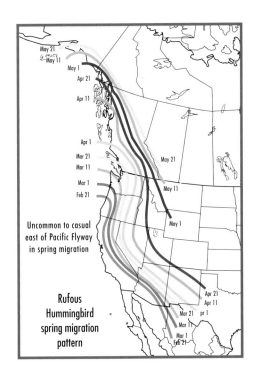

May 21
May 11
May 1
Apr 21
Apr 11
Apr 1
Mar 21
Mar 11
Mar 1
Feb 21

May 21
May 11
May 1

Uncommon to casual
east of Pacific Flyway
in spring migration

Rufous
Hummingbird
spring migration
pattern

Apr 21
Apr 11
pr 1
Mar 21
Mar 1
Mar 1
Feb 21

SUBSPECIES AND TAXONOMIC RELATIONSHIPS

No subspecies are described. Its closest relative is Allen's Hummingbird, so close that some authors have suggested lumping them into a single species. The two overlap very narrowly along the border between Oregon and California. Distinguishing hybrids involving Rufous from those involving Allen's is more challenging than most hybrid questions. Hybrids between Rufous and Calliope are well described, but reported Rufous × Allen's and Rufous × Anna's are controversial. Most reports of the latter combination probably refer to Anna's × Allen's, but recent expansion of breeding range of Anna's may increase the likelihood of this combination.

PLUMAGE VARIATION AND MOLT

Adult males are highly variable in amount of green iridescence on upper back, from almost immaculate rufous to a scattering of green feathers to entirely green with rufous rump and uppertail coverts. Females tend to acquire more iridescence in gorget with each molt. Gorgets of older females may be almost entirely orange-red. Occasional immature female may show heavy spangling in gorget, resembling immature male. Adults molt December to February; immatures begin molting shortly after arrival on wintering grounds, often extending into spring migration.

 REFERENCES

Banks and Johnson 1961
Calder 1993
Stiles 1974

ALLEN'S HUMMINGBIRD PLS. 1, 18, 24, 25

Selasphorus sasin

3.2–3.6 in. (8–9 cm). Bill length: ♂ 15–20 mm, ♀ 16–21 mm; tail length: ♂ 22–26 mm, ♀ 22–27 mm.

This close relative of the Rufous Hummingbird has one of the most restricted breeding ranges of any North American hummingbird, for it is confined to the Pacific Coast from southern California to southern Oregon. Though its habitat has been heavily altered by human activities, it has managed to adapt to urban and suburban environments. Its natural history is closely linked with several endemic Pacific Coast plants, some of which are threatened or endangered. Though known to stray eastward in fall migration, this species is probably underreported because of the extreme difficulty of distinguishing it from Rufous Hummingbird. The species was named in honor of California bird collector Charles A. Allen.

 DESCRIPTION

A small hummingbird with medium-short to medium-length all-black bill and extensive rufous in plumage. Similar in all respects to and very difficult to distinguish from Rufous Hummingbird. **ADULT MALE:** Brilliant green above with green crown, rufous rump and uppertail coverts, white below with rufous "vest"; back is more than half green. Gorget brilliant scarlet to orange, appearing golden or even yellow-green from some angles. Cheeks and eyebrows dull rufous, lores dusky. Rufous-and-black tail is long, extending past wingtips. Sharply pointed tail feathers all tipped black, narrow, becoming progressively narrower from R1 to R5, which is extremely narrow and stiletto-like. R2 tapers smoothly to a point. Bill is medium-short. **ADULT FEMALE:** Bright green above, white below washed with rufous on sides and flanks extending onto edges of rump. Face and sides of gorget washed rufous. Gorget creamy white to ivory, lightly to heavily spangled with green to bronze (concentrated along sides); iridescent red-orange to coppery feathering in center of gorget varies from a few small spangles to dense ragged-edge triangle or diamond. Rounded tail extends past wingtips, shows extensive rufous in R3–5; R2 usually shows no indentation near tip, R5 very narrow. Outer primary (P10) tapers to narrow, rounded tip. **IMMATURE MALE:** Similar to adult female but usually with gorget more heavily marked, often with large mirrorlike gorget feathers in patches throughout gorget area or concentrated in lower center of throat. **IMMATURE FEMALE:** Similar to adult female but typically with fewer and smaller gorget markings (center of throat may be unmarked white), broader outer tail feathers with less rufous, small white tip on R2.

SIMILAR SPECIES

Adult male **RUFOUS HUMMINGBIRD** may have back more than half green; tail feathers are broader, with abrupt taper of R2 creating a distinct notch on the inner web. On close examination, adult female and immature male Rufous usually show broader tail feathers and subtle indentation near tip of R2. Female and immature male **BROAD-TAILED HUMMINGBIRD** are larger with grayish face, much broader tail feathers with more extensive green. Female and immature male **CALLIOPE HUMMINGBIRD** have shorter bill; much shorter tail shows small amount of rufous, mostly on edges of feathers. Female and immature male **BUMBLEBEE HUMMINGBIRD** have much shorter bill, metallic gorget feathers rose to wine red (if present); very short tail has less rufous. Female and immature male **LUCIFER HUMMINGBIRD** are slender, with unspotted throat, curving dusky "sideburns," longer, moderately to strongly decurved bill; very long tail is narrow, deeply notched to forked.

SOUNDS

CALLS similar to those of Rufous but often softer; include *zeek zee'kik* and *zeee' zik'iti-zik'iti-zik'iti*. **WING SOUND** of adult male is metallic whine created by sharp points on outer primaries. Various sounds heard during male's courtship display, including an explosive rattle, are likely made by wings and tail. Flight displays and wing sound may substitute for song in this species.

BEHAVIOR

Both sexes territorial, though typically less aggressive than Rufous. Feeding behavior similar to that of Rufous. Utilizes eucalyptus and other introduced plants for nectar in addition to native species such as twinberry honeysuckle, bush-monkeyflower, fuchsia-flowered gooseberry. **DIVE DISPLAY** of male is J-shaped, beginning with a "pendulum display" of repeated shallow vertical arcs above object of display (female or rival male) followed by wavering ascent and rapid descent. **SHUTTLE DISPLAY** consists of short looping flights toward and away from the object with tail fanned and gorget flared. **NEST** is a soft cup of whitish plant fibers and animal hair held together with spider silk; camouflaged with chips of lichen and plant debris. Nests February to July.

Habitat

BREEDS in moist coastal and riparian forest and woodland, including introduced eucalyptus, sea level to 1,000 ft. (300 m). Males prefer open shrubby areas for breeding territories, while females prefer more densely vegetated sites with tree cover for nesting. **WINTERS** in forest edge and clearings in southern Mexico. Resident populations gravitate to groves of blooming eucalyptus in winter.

Distribution

BREEDS from coastal southern Calif. (Orange Co., northern San Diego Co.) north to southern Ore., including Channel Is.; range overlaps slightly with that of Rufous. Subspecies *sasin* **WINTERS** in south-central Mexico; nonmigratory *sedentarius* and a few individuals of subspecies *sasin* winter in southern Calif., north to Santa Barbara. Migratory subspecies arrives on northern breeding grounds between January and March, departs by September. Southward migration is over a more eastern route for some individuals, where they are greatly outnumbered by virtually indistinguishable Rufous. Rare but regular in southern Ariz., very rare and seldom confirmed in N.M., western Tex., Utah, Nev. Rare in winter on Gulf Coast; a few fall-winter records from eastern states, including Del., Fla., Ga., La., Mass., Miss., N.J., eastern Tenn., Tex., Va.

Status and Conservation

The range of Allen's Hummingbird is one of the most restricted of any northern hummingbird but appears to be expanding in southern California. The nonmigratory race, once confined to the Channel Islands, has spread from the Palos Verdes Peninsula north to Ventura County and south to northern San Diego County This expansion may be linked to increase in irrigated

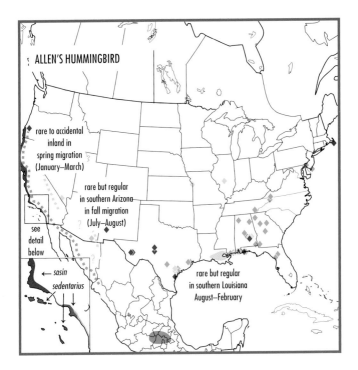

ALLEN'S HUMMINGBIRD

rare to accidental
inland in
spring migration
(January–March)

rare but regular
in southern Arizona
in fall migration
(July–August)

see
detail
below

sasin

sedentarius

rare but regular
in southern Louisiana
August–February

landscaping with exotic flowering plants and naturalization of nonnative eucalyptus and tree tobacco. These changes have also supported population growth and range expansion of the larger and more aggressive Anna's Hummingbird, however. Feral populations of exotics such as eucalyptus trees and tree tobacco may also compete with rarer plants for the birds' pollination services. Breeding range of the migratory subspecies closely matches that of orange bush-monkeyflower, a plant unique to the Pacific Coast. Other plants pollinated by Allen's Hummingbird include the endangered western lily and several endemic plants of California's Channel Islands.

SUBSPECIES AND TAXONOMIC RELATIONSHIPS

The subspecies *sedentarius* apparently originated on the Channel Islands and colonized the mainland between 1939 and 1968. It has recently spread along the coast north to Ventura County, south to northern San Diego County. Though this subspecies is essentially nonmigratory, an Allen's specimen from Louisiana was identified as *sedentarius*. Lengths of wing and tail are between those of subspecies *sasin* and Rufous Hummingbird, bill averages longer than either. Hybrids have been reported with Rufous, Black-chinned, and Anna's.

PLUMAGE VARIATION AND MOLT

Shape and pattern of rectrices variable by age and sex but also individually, complicating separation from Rufous even in hand. Occasional immature female may show heavy spangling in gorget, resembling immature male. Molt takes place September to January.

REFERENCES

Banks and Johnson 1961
Mitchell 2000
Stiles 1974

ACKNOWLEDGMENTS

A book such as this would not be possible without the hard work and dedication of many friends and colleagues in the birding, ornithological, and hummingbird communities. Pete Dunne acted as the catalyst to get the project rolling. His confidence in my knowledge and ability has been a major motivational force. My husband, colleague, and co-founder of the Southeastern Arizona Bird Observatory, Tom Wood, took on additional responsibilities both at home and at work to free my time for research and writing, in addition to providing field assistance, inspiration, and feedback as the manuscript progressed. My editor at Houghton Mifflin, Lisa White, showed great patience and forbearance as the project dragged on longer than any of us had hoped.

I am deeply grateful for the friendship and support of Dale and Marian Zimmerman, Millicent S. "Penny" Ficken, and Clay and Pat Sutton, who placed their wealth of knowledge and experience in ornithology and publishing at my disposal. Their work has been an inspiration, and I appreciate their insightful comments on the manuscript.

This project also benefited greatly from the input of the hummingbird specialists and bird banders who reviewed all or part of the work in progress, many of whom were generous with their time and expertise in the field as well: Barbara Carlson, Ross Hawkins, Don Mitchell, Fred Moore, Nancy Newfield, Mark Newstrom, Brent Ortego, Dave Patton, Bob and Martha Sargent, and Ellie Womack. Much of the detailed information that made this guide possible was collected and made available by members of the hummingbird banding community, including Fred Bassett, Linda Beall, Steve and Debbie Bouricius, Bill Calder, Susan Campbell, Bennet Carver, Bob Daly, Ross Dawkins, David and Linda Ferry, J. Cam Finlay, Perk Floyd, Troy Gordon, Bill Hilton Jr., Karen Lundy, Art and Hanna Richard, Lee Rogers, Steve and

Ruth Russell, Glen Swartz, Deanna Turnage-Smith, George West, Susan Wethington, Brenda Wiard, and Ruth Yoder. Among the enthusiastic volunteers and dedicated professionals who have assisted in the Southeastern Arizona Bird Observatory's hummingbird studies are Barbara Alberti, Hank Brodkin, Ken Charters, Erin Hodges, Tim Hodges, Dave Krueper, Bob Jones, Norma Jones, Burt Jones, Mitzi Jones, Stan Lilley, Dan McCready, Wendy Hakes McCready, Dutch Nagle, Pat Nagle, Jon Samuelson, K. Alison Schaaf, Jean Segerstrom, Lisa Walraven, Wezil Walraven, and Alan Whalon. Miscellaneous field assistance in various locations was provided by John Berree, Alan Craig, Miriam Davey, Forrest Davis, Clayton Fogle, Chris Van Voorhies Hurt, Eduardo Gomez Limón, David Hedges, Linda Hedges, Francie Jeffries, John Karges, David McKay, Jorge Montejo, Narca Moore-Craig, Susie Nowell, Clay and Pat Sutton, Tom Sylvest, Rick and Lynne Taylor, Leslie Van Epps, Beth Wood, and Craig Zalk.

Field observations were greatly facilitated by those rare, generous individuals who routinely extend hospitality to both hummingbirds and birders at their private feeding stations, including Tom and Edith Beatty, Jesse Hendrix, Wally and Marion Paton, and Walter and Sally Spofford. Examination of specimens was critical to creating thorough, accurate species accounts. Ornithological collections (and staff) consulted during research for this guide include the Field Museum, Chicago (David Willard, Mel Traylor); Museum of Natural Science at Louisiana State University, Baton Rouge (J. V. Remsen Jr., Steve Cardiff, Donna Dittmann); the Moore Laboratory of Ornithology at Occidental College, Los Angeles (John Hafner, Janice Grancich); San Diego Natural History Museum (Phil Unitt); Natural History Museum of Los Angeles County (Kimball Garrett, Kathy Molina); Academy of Natural Sciences, Philadelphia (Leo Joseph); and the American Museum of Natural History, New York (Paul Sweet).

The "freshness" of the data used in compiling this book is largely thanks to the Internet, which has made possible instant sharing of information via virtual communities such as HUM-NET (created by Van Remsen) and BIRDWG05 (Arizona–New Mexico discussion group, one of several BirdChat offshoots created by Chuck Williamson). Members of these and other cyber-communities who generously shared their sightings and other observations include Jorn Ake, David Arbour, John Arvin, Lyn Atherton, Steve Backes, Helen Baines, Tracey Banowetz, Lynn Becnel, Paulette Biles, Yvonne Bordelon, Winston Caillouet, Clifford A. Cathers, Bob Chapman, Olga Clifton, Paul Conover, Nigel Crook, Miriam Davey, Terry Davis, Michael Delesantro,

Dennis Demcheck, Susanna Dempsey, Paul Dickson, Sidney Doll, Les Eastman, Jane Edwards, Ted Eubanks, Karen Fay, Mike Feighner, Frank Fekel, Carol Foil, Fran Foley, Bill Fontenot, Dot Freeman, Steve Ganley, Keith Graves, Cathy Green, Gerry Green, John Green, Elizabeth Guidry, Marty Guidry, Carolyn Haluska, Jay Hand, Marjorie Hastings, Jim Hays, Rich Hoyer, Jim Ingold, Ann Johnson, Roy Jones, Scott Knaus, Arlene Koch, Ray Koppi, Kathryn Lance, David L'Hoste, Beth Maniscalco, Lori Markoff, Mary Martin, Karen McBride, Paul McKenzie, Blake Maybank, Marty Michener, David Muth, Jerry Oldenettel, Fernando Ortiz-Crespo, Mary Anne Owen, Margaret Owens, Dick Palmer, Melissa Pappas, Rob Parsons, Noel Peyton, Gary Phillips, Judy Pike, Timothy Price, John Pushcock, Bette Reincke, Bryant Roberts, Lisa Robichaux, Ron Rovansek, David Sarkozi, Charlotte Seidenberg, John Sevenair, Leanna Shaberly, Margret Simmons, Jim Sinclair, Patricia Snider, Cliff Statler, John Sylvest, Martha Tarafa, Karen Taylor, Rick Taylor, David Tracy, Cathy Troy, Sandy Turner, Vicki Vance, Christine Van Cleve, Richard Wagner, Peggy Wang, Alan Weisman, Ronni Welsh, Jana Whittle, Rob Yaksich, and Mary Zimmerman. Very special thanks to Tom Sylvest and Stacy Jon Peterson, who have put a great deal of work into compiling records of individual birds reported on HUMNET. Assistance in researching the status of Cuban Emerald and Florida records was provided by Bruce H. Anderson, Reed Bowman, Paul Conover, Harry Hooper, Rob Protz, Nedra Sekera, P. William Smith, Glen Woolfenden, and Craig Zalk.

The accuracy and completeness of the maps was greatly improved with the help of the following regional reviewers: Bruce H. Anderson, Larry Arnold, Jim Arterburn, Kelly B. Bryan (Texas Parks and Wildlife Department), Paul Conover, Troy Corman (Arizona Breeding Bird Atlas), J. Cam Finlay, Ted Floyd (Great Basin Bird Observatory), Brush Freeman, Bill Grossi, Rick Hallowell, Mark Klym (Texas Parks and Wildlife Department), Greg Lasley, Mark Lockwood, Steve Mlodinow, Mike Patterson, Dan Reinking (Sutton Avian Research Center), and Shirley Sturts. Draft range and migration maps were prepared with the able and enthusiastic assistance of Lanny Chambers; they received their final form from Larry O. Rosche.

I also thank the following for enriching my life and imagination with their passions and gifts in the arts and sciences: Edward Abbey, Ian Anderson, Douglas Adams, Florence Merriam Bailey, Robert Bateman, Charles Bendire, Arthur Cleveland Bent, John Bonham, Graham Chapman, John Cleese, Charles Darwin, Charles Lutwidge Dodgson, Dian Fossey, Aretha Franklin, Emperor Frederick II, Louis Agassiz Fuertes, Theodor S. Geisel,

Terry Gilliam, David Gilmour, Jane Goodall, Matt Groening, Connie Hagar, Jim Henson, Frank Herbert, Eric Idle, John Paul Jones, Terry Jones, Gary Larson, Edward Lear, Aldo Leopold, Margaret Morse Nice, Jimmy Page, Margaret Parker, Irene Pepperberg, Roger Tory Peterson, Robert Plant, Alexander Skutch, Jessie Maye Smith, Chris Smithers, David Snow, George Miksch Sutton, Dora Sylvester, Richard Thompson, Alfred Russell Wallace, Roger Waters, and Robert Allen Zimmerman.

GLOSSARY

accidental. In birding terminology, a species whose occurrence in an area is extremely rare and unexpected. See also **casual, rare, vagrant.**

arid. Referring to an area low in annual rainfall.

arthropod. An invertebrate with a hard exoskeleton and jointed legs; includes insects and spiders.

auriculars. The feathers over the external ear opening, located on the cheek.

belly. The lower part of the underside, below the breast.

[?]. The area including chin, throat (gorget), and breast, sometimes extending onto upper belly.

biogeography. The study of the geographic distribution of living things.

breast. The upper part of the underside, between throat and belly.

casual. In birding terminology, a species whose occurrence in an area is infrequent but at somewhat regular intervals. See also **accidental, rare, vagrant.**

Central America. The region from southern Mexico (south of the Isthmus of Tehuantepec) to southern Panama.

cheek. The area on the side of the head below and behind the eye. See also **face, auriculars.**

chin. The area immediately below base of the lower mandible; the upper part of the throat or gorget.

common name. See **English name.**

crissum. The undertail coverts taken together as one feature of the plumage.

crown. The area beginning at the base of the bill and extending backward across the top of the head; divided into forecrown and hindcrown.

dimorphism, sexual. See **sexual dimorphism.**

double-rounded. Tail shape in which the outer and inner pairs of feathers are shorter than those in between.

emargination (emarginate). An abrupt change in contour, as in a notched or scalloped edge.

endangered. In danger of extinction without immediate protective measures.

endemic. A species restricted to a given area.

English name. The standardized name accepted by English-speaking ornithologists; also known as common name.

exituc. In ecology, refers to a species of animal or plant, not native to an area, that has been either deliberately or accidentally introduced from another region.

extinction. The permanent disappearance of a species or subspecies. See also **endangered, threatened.**

eye line. An area of contrasting color directly behind the eye; also called postocular line, eye stripe.

eyebrow. The narrow area immediately above the eye, extending forward over the lore and backward over the postocular area; also known as superciliary line.

face. The side of the head, including the cheek, lore, eyebrow, and postocular area.

family. A taxonomic category into which genera are grouped by broad similarities in anatomy, physiology, behavior, and ecology. See also **subfamily, genus, species, subspecies.**

female-plumaged. In species exhibiting sexual dimorphism, refers to the similar plumage of females and immature males.

femoral tuft. The fluffy feathers around the base of a hummingbird's legs.

flame-throated. Refers to a group of small hummingbirds in which adult males have brilliant, metallic iridescence in a discrete area on the throat (gorget).

flank. The lower side, between the base of the wing and the base of the tail.

fledgling. A young bird that has left the nest but is not yet independent.

flight feathers. The broad, stiff feathers of the wing that make flight possible; divided into primaries (outer) and secondaries (inner).

fly-catching. Capturing flying insects in midair.

flyway. A route followed by birds during migration.

forecrown. The front part of the crown.

forked. Tail shape in which outer pairs of feathers are much longer than inner pairs, creating a deep indentation.

genera. See **genus.**

genus (plural genera). The taxonomic category just above species; closely related species are grouped together in the same genus, while genera are grouped into subfamilies and families. See **family, species.**

gleaning. Hunting for insects or other prey by searching bark, leaves, and other surfaces and hiding places.

gorget. The area of iridescent color on the throat of many adult male hummingbirds; also this same area in females and immature males.

graduated. Tail shape in which central pair of feathers is significantly longer than outer pair.

habitat. The environment in which an animal or plant lives.

hybrid. Offspring produced by the mating of different species.

immature. A young bird that is independent but has not completed the molt into adult plumage.

insectivorous. Refers to an animal that eats insects and other invertebrates.

invertebrate. Any complex animal without a backbone. See also **arthropod.**

iridescence (iridescent). Shimmering, often metallic-looking colors created by refraction and reinforcement of light waves as they reflect off structural elements.

lichen. A plantlike association of fungi and algae that often grows on rocks or tree bark in crusty, leafy (foliose) or finely branching mosslike (dendroid) forms.

lore. The area directly in front of the eye.

malar stripe. An area of contrasting color along the jaw line between the cheek and throat or gorget.

mandible, upper or lower. The halves of the bill, which may be different colors.

melanin. The basic pigment in the feathers, hair, skin, and scales of animals, usually black, gray, or brown in color but capable of creating other colors through refraction and interference effects.

metallic. Intensely iridescent, as in the gorget and crown color of many male hummingbirds.

migration. Annual movements between one region or habitat and another; may be latitudinal (north-south) or elevational.

molt. The normal cycle of loss and replacement of feathers.

montane. Refers to mountains.

morphology. The study of the physical forms of animals and plants.

moustachial stripe. An area of contrasting color at the lower leading edge of the cheek slightly above the jaw line. See also **malar stripe.**

nape. The area at the back of the head, between the crown and upper back.

North America. Properly, the land mass and nearby islands north of the Isthmus of Tehuantepec in southern Mexico; in the context of field guides, this usually refers to the continental United States and Canada.

notched. Tail shape in which the central pair of feathers is slightly shorter than the outer pairs.

order. A taxonomic category into which families are grouped. See also **family, genus, species.**

ornithology. The scientific study of birds.

photoperiod. The relative lengths of day and night, which vary seasonally;

believed to trigger migration and breeding in temperate zone hummingbirds.

platelet. A flattened disk; in the iridescent feathers of hummingbirds, melanin platelets create iridescent colors.

plumage. The feathers of a bird considered as a whole.

postocular (stripe/spot). The area beginning immediately behind the eye, above the cheek.

primary. One of the outer 10 flight feathers of the wing, those attached to the bones of the "hand"; numbered from inner to outer (P1 to P10).

rare. In birding terminology, a bird of very uncommon but regular occurrence in one area that may be common elsewhere. See also **accidental, casual, endangered, threatened, vagrant.**

rectrices (singular rectrix). The tail feathers, arranged in five pairs numbered from central to outer (R1 to R5).

rectrix. See **rectrices.**

riparian. Related to rivers and streams.

rounded. Tail shape in which feathers become slightly shorter from inner to outer pairs.

rump. The area at the base of the tail, sometimes including the uppertail coverts.

scientific name. A two-part label identifying a particular species; often called Latin name.

secondary. One of the shorter inner flight feathers of the wing, those attached to the bones of the "forearm."

sexual dimorphism. Physical characteristics distinguishing males from females, usually most apparent at maturity. See also **female-plumaged.**

sibling species. One of a pair or group of closely related species.

site fidelity. The tendency of birds to return to the same nesting, wintering, or migratory stopover locations each year.

sky island. Any of several mountain ranges in Arizona, New Mexico, Texas, and adjacent northern Mexico that are isolated from each other by desert valleys and act as stepping stones for migrating birds between the southern Rocky Mountains and the Sierra Madre of Mexico.

soft parts. The visible skin around the eyes, at the corners of the mouth, and on the feet and legs.

song. Vocalizations that serve to establish and maintain territory and advertise for mates; usually more complex and variable than calls.

Southwest. The region from western Texas west to southeastern California and north to the southern portions of Colorado, Utah, and Nevada.

species. A population of organisms that are distinct from others in appearance, behavior, geographic distribution, and/or habitat and seldom or never interbreed with populations of similar organisms.

subadult. A young bird nearing maturity but still exhibiting immature characteristics.

subfamily. Genera and species are placed in subfamilies based on less obvious and less fundamental characteristics than those that define families.

subgenus. A division of genus, usually related to characteristics common to some but not all species within a genus.

subspecies. A division of species, usually related to visible characteristics common to members of populations separated by range or habitat; also called race.

superspecies. A grouping of two or more closely related species; each species in such a group is called a sibling species.

taxonomy (taxonomic). The science of the classification of living things; also, the arrangement of species, genera, families, and orders to reflect evolutionary relationships.

threatened. In long-term danger of extinction if current trends continue.

throat. The area between the base of the bill and the breast. See also **gorget.**

underparts. The breast and belly, with or without the throat, sides, and undertail coverts.

undertail coverts. The soft feathers that form a triangle on the underside of the tail.

upperparts. The back, rump, and uppertail coverts, with or without the crown and central rectrices.

uppertail coverts. The soft feathers covering the base of the tail feathers dorsally.

vagrant. A bird that has wandered outside its normal area of occurrence. See also **accidental, casual, endangered, rare, threatened.**

vent. The external opening through which waste and reproductive products pass; cloaca.

LIST OF NECTAR PLANTS

COMMON NAME	SCIENTIFIC NAME	FAMILY
Agave	*Agave* spp.	Agavaceae
Agave, Harvard	*Agave harvardiana*	Agavaceae
Aloe	*Aloe* spp.	Asphodelaceae
Amaryllis	*Hippeastrum* spp.	Amaryllidaceae
Bee Balm	*Monarda didyma*	Lamiaceae
Bee-plant, Rocky Mountain	*Cleome serrulata*	Capparidaceae
Blue-curls, Wooly	*Trichostema lanatum*	Lamiaceae
Bottlebrush	*Callistemon* spp.	Myrtaceae
Bougainvillea	*Bougainvillea* spp.	Nyctaginaceae
Bouvardia, Scarlet	*Bouvardia ternifolia*	Rubiaceae
Buckeye, Mexican	*Ungnadia speciosa*	Sapindaceae
Buckeye, Red	*Aesculus pavia*	Hippocastanaceae
Bush-Monkeyflower, Orange	*Mimulus (Diplacus) aurantiacus*	Scrophulariaceae
Bush-Penstemon	*Keckiella* spp.	Scrophulariaceae
Butterfly Bush	*Buddleia* spp.	Verbenaceae
Cactus, Claret Cup	*Echinocereus triglochidiatus*	Cactaceae
Cactus, Holiday	*Schlumbergera* spp.	Cactaceae
Canna	*Canna indica*	Cannaceae
Cardinal Flower	*Lobelia cardinalis*	Campanulaceae
Century Plant	*Agave* spp.	Agavaceae
Chestnut, Horse	*Aesculus hippocastanum*	Hippocastanaceae
Cholla	*Opuntia* spp.	Cactaceae
Chuparosa	*Justicia californica*	Acanthaceae
Columbine, Barrel	*Aquilegia triternata*	Ranunculaceae
Columbine, Canadian	*Aquilegia canadensis*	Ranunculaceae
Columbine, Canary	*Aquilegia chrysantha*	Ranunculaceae
Columbine, Western	*Aquilegia formosa*	Ranunculaceae
Coral-bean	*Erythrina* spp.	Fabaceae

COMMON NAME	SCIENTIFIC NAME	FAMILY
Creeper, Scarlet	*Ipomoea cristulata, hederifolia*	Convolvulaceae
Creeper, Trumpet	*Campsis radicans*	Bignoniaceae
Cuphea (Mexican Cigar)	*Cuphea* spp.	Lythraceae
Currant, Chaparral	*Ribes malvaceum*	Grossulariaceae
Currant, Red	*Ribes sanguineum*	Grossulariaceae
Cypress, Standing	*Ipomopsis rubra*	Polemoniaceae
Esperanza (Yellow Bells)	*Tecoma stans*	Bignoniaceae
Eucalyptus	*Eucalyptus* spp.	Myrtaceae
Fairy Duster	*Calliandra* spp.	Fabaceae
Fairy-duster, Baja	*Calliandra peninsularis*	Fabaceae
Firebush	*Hamelia patens*	Rubiaceae
Fireweed	*Epilobium angustifolium*	Onagraceae
Four-o'-clock	*Mirabilis jalapa*	Nyctaginaceae
Fuchsia, California	*Zauschneria (Epilobium) californica*	Onagraceae
Gilia	*Ipomopsis* spp.	Polemoniaceae
Gooseberry, Fuchsia-flowered	*Ribes speciosum*	Grossulariaceae
Heliconia	*Heliconia* spp.	Heliconiaceae
Hibiscus, Sultan's Turban	*Malvaviscus arboreus*	Malvaceae
Hibiscus, Tropical	*Hibiscus rosa-sinensis*	Malvaceae
Hibiscus, Turk's-cap	*Malvaviscus drummondii*	Malvaceae
Honeysuckle, Coral	*Lonicera sempervirens*	Caprifoliaceae
Honeysuckle, Desert	*Anisacanthus* spp.	Acanthaceae
Honeysuckle, Japanese	*Lonicera japonica*	Caprifoliaceae
Honeysuckle, Mexican	*Justicia spicigera*	Acanthaceae
Honeysuckle, Orange	*Lonicera ciliosa*	Caprifoliaceae
Honeysuckle, Twinberry	*Lonicera involucrata*	Caprifoliaceae
Honeysuckle, White	*Lonicera albiflora*	Caprifoliaceae
Ice Cream Bean Tree	*Inga* spp.	Fabaceae
Iris, Rocky Mountain	*Iris missouriensis*	Iridaceae
Jewelweed, Touch-me-not	*Impatiens capensis (biflora), pallida*	Balsaminaceae
Jicama	*Ipomoea bracteata*	Convolvulaceae
Larkspur	*Delphinium* spp.	Ranunculaceae
Lantana	*Lantana* spp.	Verbenaceae
Lavender, Desert	*Hyptis emoryi*	Lamiaceae
Lechugilla	*Agave lechugilla*	Agavaceae
Lily, Western	*Lilium occidentale*	Liliaceae
Lobelia, Mexican	*Lobelia laxiflora*	Campanulaceae
Locust, New Mexican	*Robinia neomexicana*	Fabaceae
Madrone, Arizona	*Arbutus arizonica*	Ericaceae

COMMON NAME	SCIENTIFIC NAME	FAMILY
Madrone, Baja	*Arbutus peninsularis*	Ericaceae
Madrone, Pacific	*Arbutus menziesii*	Ericaceae
Madrone, Texas	*Arbutus xalapensis*	Ericaceae
Manzanita	*Arctostaphylos* spp.	Ericaceae
Mistletoe, Tropical	*Psittacanthus* spp.	Loranthaceae
Monkeyflower, Cardinal	*Mimulus cardinalis*	Scrophulariaceae
Morning-glory, Red	*Ipomoea coccinea*	Convolvulaceae
Morning-glory, Tree	*Ipomoea arborescens*	Convolvulaceae
Ocotillo	*Fouquieria splendens*	Fouquieriaceae
Olive, Mexican	*Cordia boissieri*	Boraginaceae
Orchid Tree	*Bauhinia* spp.	Fabaceae
Paintbrush, Indian	*Castilleja* spp.	Scrophulariaceae
Penstemon	*Penstemon* spp.	Scrophulariaceae
Penstemon, Arizona	*P. pseudospectabilis*	Scrophulariaceae
Penstemon, Bearded	*Penstemon barbatus*	Scrophulariaceae
Penstemon, Bridges	*Penstemon bridgesii*	Scrophulariaceae
Penstemon, Fendler	*Penstemon fendleri*	Scrophulariaceae
Penstemon, Harvard	*Penstemon harvardii*	Scrophulariaceae
Penstemon, Parry	*Penstemon parryi*	Scrophulariaceae
Penstemon, Red Bush	*Keckiella cordifolia*	Scrophulariaceae
Penstemon, Superb	*Penstemon superbus*	Scrophulariaceae
Pentas	*Pentas lanceolata*	Rubiaceae
Poinciana, Royal	*Delonix regia*	Fabaceae
Porterweed	*Stachytarpheta* spp.	Verbenaceae
Powderpuff	*Calliandra* spp.	Fabaceae
Rose of Sharon	*Hibiscus syriacus*	Malvaceae
Sage, Gregg	*Salvia greggii*	Lamiaceae
Sage, Mountain	*Salvia regla*	Lamiaceae
Sage, Pineapple	*Salvia elegans*	Lamiaceae
Sage, Pitcher	*Salvia spathacea*	Lamiaceae
Sage, Scarlet	*Salvia splendens*	Lamiaceae
Sage, Texas or Tropical	*Salvia coccinea*	Lamiaceae
Salmonberry	*Rubus spectabilis*	Rosaceae
Shrimp Plant	*Justicia brandegeana*	Acanthaceae
Skyrocket	*Ipomopsis aggregata*	Polemoniaceae
Thistle, Arizona	*Cirsium arizonicum*	Asteraceae
Tobacco, Tree	*Nicotiana glauca*	Solanaceae
Vine, Cypress	*Ipomoea quamoclit*	Convolvulaceae
Willow (Catkins)	*Salix* spp.	Salicaceae
Willow, Desert	*Chilopsis linearis*	Bignoniaceae
Wolfberry	*Lycium* spp.	Solanaceae

Resources for Hummingbird Watchers

Books, Magazines, and Videos

Hummingbirds: The Sun Catchers
by Jeff and April Sayre
NorthWord Press 1996
> The amazing lives of hummingbirds plus profiles of North American species, illustrated with beautiful photos.

The World of the Hummingbird
by Harry Thurston
Sierra Club Books 1999
> A poet and award-winning nature writer explores the lives and travels of these remarkable birds.

Ruby-throated Hummingbird
by Robert Sargent
Stackpole Books 1999
> An in-depth look at the most familiar of North American hummingbirds, by a prominent hummingbird bander and founder of the Hummer/Bird Study Group.

Attracting and Feeding Hummingbirds
by Sheri Williamson
T.F.H. Publications 2000
> An introduction to creating a backyard hummingbird haven; illustrated with color photos of hummingbirds, flowers, feeders, etc.

Hummingbird Gardens: Attracting Nature's Jewels to Your Backyard
by Nancy L. Newfield and Barbara Nielsen
Houghton Mifflin 1996
> Real-life examples of successful backyard hummingbird habitats in six major regions of the United States and Canada, with sample garden designs and lists of nectar plants for each region.

Wildlife Viewing Guides
published by Falcon Press
A series of concise guides to the best wildlife viewing areas in each state; developed in cooperation with Defenders of Wildlife.

A Birder's Guide to Southeastern Arizona
by Richard Cachor Taylor
American Birding Association 1995 (updated 1999)
The best resource for planning a visit to this hummingbird lover's paradise. Includes site descriptions, maps, and a seasonal bar-graph checklist of over 400 bird species, including 16 hummingbirds.

WildBird
Subscription Department
P.O. Box 52898
Boulder, CO 80323-2898
A full-sized magazine featuring colorful articles, photo features, and an annual hummingbird issue (May). Available on newsstands or by subscription.

Bird Watcher's Digest
P.O. Box 110
Marietta, OH 45750
(800) 879-2473
Though small in format (the size of *Reader's Digest*), *BWD* is packed with articles and feature columns by some of America's best-known birders. Available on newsstands or by subscription.

Dances with Hummingbirds (video)
Nature Science Network
Video of hummingbirds in flight set to music; includes a second segment interpreting the species and behavior seen in the first segment.

Watching Hummingbirds (video)
Nature Science Network
More on hummingbird behavior from the creator of *Dances with Hummingbirds*.

WEB RESOURCES (SEE ALSO ORGANIZATIONS)

Hummingbirds!
www.hummingbirds.net
A variety of information about North American hummingbirds, including species profiles, frequently asked questions, migration maps, product reviews, reprints of scientific papers, and an extensive bibliography. Created by Lanny Chambers.

Birding the Americas Trip Report and Planning Repository
www.3.ns.sympatico.ca/ns/maybank/Trips.htm
   An archive of firsthand reports on birding trips in North, Central, and South America plus additional travel planning information, collected and maintained by Blake Maybank.

ORGANIZATIONS AND AGENCIES

The Hummingbird Society
P.O. Box 394
Newark, DE 19715
   (800) 529-3699
   Web site: www.hummingbirdsociety.org
   A nonprofit organization dedicated to international understanding and conservation of hummingbirds.

Cornell Laboratory of Ornithology
P.O. Box 11
Ithaca, NY 14581
   Web site: www.ornith.cornell.edu
   Sponsors Project FeederWatch, a volunteer program monitoring wintering birds. Publishes a quarterly magazine and newsletter for members.

American Bird Conservancy
1250 24th Street NW, Suite 400
Washington, DC 20037
   (202) 778-9666
   Web site: www.abcbirds.org
   A nonprofit organization dedicated to preserving the unique bird life of the Americas, including neotropical migrants such as hummingbirds.

American Birding Association
P.O. Box 6599
Colorado Springs, CO 80934
   (719) 578-9703
   Web site: www.americanbirding.org
   A nonprofit organization dedicated to recreational birding and bird conservation. Publishes a magazine, newsletters for adults and students, and a series of bird-finding guides and checklists.

National Audubon Society
700 Broadway
New York, NY 10003
   (212) 979-3000
   Web site: www.audubon.org

One of the oldest national conservation organizations, founded in 1905 to protect birds, other wildlife, and their habitats. Local and regional chapters throughout the United States are excellent resources for local birding and conservation information.

National Wildlife Federation
8925 Leesburg Pike
Vienna, VA 22184
(703) 790-4000
Web site: www.nwf.org
This national conservation organization is involved in a wide variety of educational activities, including a certification program for backyard wildlife habitat.

Hummer/Bird Study Group
P.O. Box 250
Clay, AL 35048-0250
(205) 681-2888
Web site: www.hummingbirdsplus.org
A nonprofit organization dedicated to the study and preservation of hummingbirds and other migratory birds. Conducts research and educational activities in the Southeast; migration banding station at Fort Morgan, Alabama, is open to visitors.

Cape May Bird Observatory
Center for Research and Education
600 Route 47 North
Cape May Court House, NJ 08210
(609) 861-0700
Web site: www.njaudubon.org/abtnjas/cmbo.html
A division of the New Jersey Audubon Society dedicated to conservation, research, and education. Staff and volunteer naturalists offer walks, workshops, and other activities year-round, including hummingbird walks in late summer and early fall. Center features demonstration gardens for hummingbirds, butterflies, etc.; hummingbird flowers and other wildlife-friendly plants available for purchase spring through fall.

Southeastern Arizona Bird Observatory
P.O. Box 5521
Bisbee, AZ 85603-5521
(520) 432-1388
Web site: www.sabo.org
A nonprofit organization dedicated to the conservation of the birds of southeastern Arizona. Offers activities year-round, including hummingbird workshops in late summer. Hummingbird banding sessions on the San Pedro River (April to September) are open to the public. Web site includes frequently asked questions

about hummingbirds, photo feature on hummingbird banding, links to books and other resources.

Lady Bird Johnson Center
4801 La Crosse Avenue
Austin, TX 78739-1702
(512) 292-4200
Web site: www.wildflower.org
Founded by Lady Bird Johnson, this organization promotes the cultivation, appreciation, and conservation of native wildflowers. Offers educational activities and publications and acts as a clearinghouse for information on sources for wildflower seed and nursery stock.

USGS Patuxent Wildlife Research Center
Bird Banding Laboratory
12100 Beech Forest Road
Laurel, MD 20708-4037
(301) 497-5790
(800) FAR-BAND to report banded birds
Web site: www.pwrc.usgs.gov/bbl/
Jointly administers the North American Bird Banding Program with the Bird Banding Office of the Canadian Wildlife Service.

FEEDER MANUFACTURERS

Aspects, Inc.
P.O. Box 408
Warren, RI 02885
(888) ASPECTS (277-3287)
Web site: www.aspectsinc.com

Best-1 Hummingbird Feeder
P.O. Box 998
Poteet, TX 78065
(800) 772-3604

Droll Yankees
27 Mill Road
Foster, RI 02825
(800) 352-9164
Web site: www.drollyankees.com

Nature's Best
P.O. Box 730
Bracketville, TX 78832
(800) 454-2473
Web site: nbhummingbird.com

BIBLIOGRAPHY

American Ornithologists' Union. 2000. *A.O.U. Check-list of North American Birds,* seventh edition [with supplements]. www.aou.org/aou/birdlist.html.

Anderson, J. O., and G. Monson. 1981. Berylline Hummingbirds nest in Arizona. *Continental Birdlife* 2:56-61.

Andrews, R., and R. Righter. 1992. *Colorado Birds: A Reference to Their Distribution and Habitat.* Denver, Colo.: Denver Museum of Natural History.

Arriaga, L., R. Rodriguez-Estrella, and A. Ortega-Rubio. 1990. Endemic hummingbirds and madrones of Baja: are they mutually dependent? *Southwestern Naturalist* 35:76–79.

Audubon mailing list archives. list.audubon.org/archives.

Baltosser, W. H. 1986. Nesting success and productivity of hummingbirds in southwestern New Mexico and southeastern Arizona. *Wilson Bulletin* 98:353–367.

Baltosser, W. H. 1989. Nectar availability and habitat selection by hummingbirds in Guadalupe Canyon. *Wilson Bulletin* 101:559–578.

Baltosser, W. H., and P. E. Scott. 1996. Costa's Hummingbird (*Calypte costae*). No. 251 in *The Birds of North America,* A. Poole and F. Gill, eds. Philadelphia: The Birds of North America, Inc.

Baltosser, W. H., and S. M. Russell. 2000. Black-chinned Hummingbird (*Archilochus alexandri*). No. 495 in *The Birds of North America,* A. Poole and F. Gill, eds. Philadelphia: The Birds of North America, Inc.

Banks, R. C., and N. K. Johnson. 1961. A review of North American hybrid hummingbirds. *Condor* 63:3–28.

Baptista, L. F., and K.-L. Schuchmann. 1990. Song learning in the Anna Hummingbird. *Ethology* 84:15–26.

Beavers, R. A. 1977. First specimen of Allen's Hummingbird, *Selasphorus sasin* (Trochilidae), from Texas. *Southwestern Naturalist* 22:285.

Bent, A. C. 1940. Life Histories of North American Cuckoos, Goat-suckers, Hummingbirds and Their Allies. United States National Museum Bulletin 176:1-506.

Bleiweiss, R., J. A. Kirsch, and J. C. Matheus. 1997. DNA hybridization evidence for the principal lineages of hummingbirds (Aves: Trochilidae). *Molecular Biology and Evolution* 14:325–343.

Brown, R. W. 1956. *Composition of Scientific Words*. Washington, D.C.: Smithsonian Institution Press.

Browning, M. R. 1978. An evaluation of the new species and subspecies proposed in Oberholser's *Bird Life of Texas. Proceedings Biological Society of Washington* 91:85–122.

Buchmann, S. L., and G. P. Nabhan. 1996. *The Forgotten Pollinators*. Washington, D.C.: Island Press.

Bündgen, R. 1999a. Blue-tailed Emerald. In *Handbook of the Birds of the World*, Vol. 5, Barn-owls to Hummingbirds, J. del Hoyo, A. Elliot, and J. Sargatal, eds. Barcelona: Lynx Edicions.

Bündgen, R. 1999b. Cuban Emerald. In *Handbook of the Birds of the World*, Vol. 5, Barn-owls to Hummingbirds, J. del Hoyo, A. Elliot , and J. Sargatal, eds. Barcelona: Lynx Edicions.

Calder, W. A. 1993. Rufous Hummingbird *(Selasphorus rufus)*. No. 53 in *The Birds of North America*, A. Poole and F. Gill, eds. Philadelphia: The Birds of North America, Inc.

Calder, W. A., and L. L. Calder. 1992. Broad-tailed Hummingbird *(Selasphorus platycercus)*. No. 16 in *The Birds of North America*, A. Poole, P. Stettenheim, and F. Gill, eds. Philadelphia: The Birds of North America, Inc.

Calder, W. A., and L. L. Calder. 1994. Calliope Hummingbird *(Stellula calliope)*. No. 135 in *The Birds of North America*, A. Poole and F. Gill, eds. Philadelphia: The Birds of North America, Inc.

Calder, W. A., and S. M. Hiebert. 1983. Nectar feeding, diuresis, and electrolyte replacement of hummingbirds. *Physiological Zoology* 56: 325–334.

CalPhotos. www.dlp.cs.berkeley.edu/photos/.

Canadian Wildlife Service Ontario Region. Wildspace: Ruby-throated Hummingbird. www.on.ec.gc.ca/wildlife/wildspace/life.cfm?ID=RTHY.

Chavez-Ramirez, F., and A. Moreno-Valdez. 1999. Buff-bellied Hummingbird *(Amazilia yucatanensis)*. No. 388 in *The Birds of North America*, A. Poole and F. Gill, eds. Philadelphia: The Birds of North America, Inc.

Clyde, D. P. 1972. Anna's Hummingbird in adult male plumage feeds nestling. *Condor* 74:102.

Colorado Field Ornithologists. Colorado Bird Records Committee. www.cfo-link.org/cbrchome.html.

Cornell Laboratory of Ornithology, National Audubon Society. 2001. Christmas Bird Count Database. birdsource.cornell.edu/cbc/index.html.

Cruickshank, H. G. 1964. A Cuban Emerald Hummingbird. *Florida Naturalist* 37:23, 32.

Ferguson, Douglas C., Chuck E. Harp, Paul A. Opler, Richard S. Peigler, Michael Pogue, Jerry A. Powell, and Michael J. Smith. 1999. Moths of North America. Jamestown, ND: Northern Prairie Wildlife Research Center Home Page. www.npwrc.usgs.gov/resource/distr/lepid/moths/mothsusa.htm.

Fisk, E. J. 1974. Second United States record of a Bahama Woodstar. *American Birds* 28:855.

Garrido, O. H., and A. Kirkconnell. 2000. *A Field Guide to the Birds of Cuba*. Ithaca, N.Y.: Cornell University Press.

Gentry, H. S. 1998. *Gentry's Río Mayo Plants*. Revised and edited by P. S. Martin, D. Yetman, M. Fishbein, P. Jenkins, T. R. Van Devender, and R. K. Wilson. Tucson: University of Arizona Press.

Georgia Hummer Study Group. Winter Hummingbird Sightings. www.gahummer.org/winter_hummingbird_reports.htm.

Gill, F. B. 1994. *Ornithology*, 2nd ed. New York: W. H. Freeman and Co.

Glaciation and Pleistocene Biogeography. www.georgian.edu/~wootton/biogeog6.htm.

Gordon, Troy. 1999. Wedge-tailed Sabrewing Hummingbirds at El Cielo Biosphere Reserve, Tamaulipas, Mexico. web.missouri.edu/~multgord/mohummers.htm.

Gordon, Troy. 2000. Missouri's Hummingbirds. web.missouri.edu/~multgord/mohummers.htm.

Grant, K. A., and V. Grant. 1968. *Hummingbirds and Their Flowers*. New York: Columbia University Press.

Gustafson, M. E., and J. Hildenbrand. 1999. Bird Banding Laboratory Home Page, ver 12/01/99. www.pwrc.usgs.gov/bbl/.

Hainebach, K. 1992. First records of Xantus' Hummingbird in California. *Western Birds* 23:133–136.

Hallowell, Rick. 2001. Costa's Hummingbird Nests in Ridgecrest, California. www.ridgecrest.ca.us/~hallowel/hummers/.

Howell, S. N. G., and S. Webb. 1995. *A Guide to the Birds of Mexico and Northern Central America*. New York: Oxford University Press.

Johnsgard, P. A. 1983. *Hummingbirds of North America*. Washington, D.C.: Smithsonian Institution Press.

Johnsgard, P. A. 1997. *Hummingbirds of North America*, second ed. Washington, D.C.: Smithsonian Institution Press.

Jones, E. G. 1992. Color variation in maturing male Rufous Hummingbirds. *North American Bird Bander* 17:119–120.

Jones, E. G. 1993. Throat patterns of female Rufous Hummingbirds. *North American Bird Bander* 18:13–14.

Kaufman, K. 1990. *Advanced Birding*. Boston: Houghton Mifflin.

Kaufman, K. 1992. Lucifer Hummingbird identification. *American Birds* 46:491–494.

Kaufman, K. 2000. *Birds of North America* (Kaufman Focus Guide). Boston: Houghton Mifflin.

Kuban, J. F., J. Lawley, and R. L. Neill. 1983. The partitioning of flowering century plants by Black-chinned and Lucifer Hummingbirds. *Southwestern Naturalist* 28:143–148.

McKenzie, P. M., and M. B. Robbins. 1999. Identification of male Rufous and Allen's hummingbirds, with specific comments on dorsal coloration. *Western Birds* 30: 86–93.

MacKinnon H., Barbara. 1992. *Checklist of the Birds of the Yucatán Peninsula/Listado de Aves de la Península de Yucatán*. Mérida: Amigos de Sian Ka'an.

Maybank, Blake. 2001. Birding the Americas Trip Report and Planning Repository. www3.ns.sympatico.ca/ns/maybank/Trips.htm.

Meisenzahl, K. 1998. Second record of the Green Violet-ear for Oklahoma. *Bulletin of the Oklahoma Ornithological Society* 31:24–25.

Merns, B., and R. Merns. 1992. *Audubon to Xantus: The Lives of Those Commemorated in North American Bird Names*. London: Academic Press.

Minnesota Ornithologists Union Species Distribution Maps. www.biosci.cbs.umn.edu/~mou/birdref.html.

Mirsky, E. N. 1976. Song divergence in hummingbird and junco populations on Guadalupe Island. *Condor* 78:230–235.

Mitchell, D. E. 2000. Allen's Hummingbird (*Selasphorus sasin*). No. 501 in *The Birds of North America*, A. Poole and F. Gill, eds. Philadelphia: The Birds of North America, Inc.

Mlodinow, S. G., and M. O'Brien. 1996. *America's 100 Most Wanted Birds*. Helena, Mont.: Falcon Press.

Monroe, B. L., Jr., and C. G. Sibley. 1993. *A World Checklist of Birds*. New Haven: Yale University Press.

Munz, P. A. 1961. *California Spring Wildflowers*. Berkeley: University of California Press.

Munz, P. A. 1963. *California Mountain Wildflowers*. Berkeley: University of California Press.

Nahuatl Source Materials. www.umt.edu/history/NAHUATL/SOURCES.html.

Newfield, N. L. 1983. Records of Allen's Hummingbird in Louisiana and possible Rufous × Allen's hybrids. *Condor* 85:253–254.

Newfield, N. L. 2001. Possible anywhere: Green Violet-ear. *Birding* 33:114–121.

Niehaus, T. F., C. L. Ripper, and V. Savage. 1984. *A Field Guide to Southwestern and Texas Wildflowers*. Boston: Houghton Mifflin.

Oberholser, H. C. 1974. *The Bird Life of Texas*. Austin: University of Texas Press.

Owre, O. T. 1976. Bahama Woodstar in Florida: first specimen for continental North America. *Auk* 93:837–838.

Park Science Highlights. National Park Service. www2.nature.nps.gov/parksci/vol19(1)/05highlights.htm.

Parrish, J. R. 1988. Kleptoparasitism of insects by a Broad-tailed Hummingbird. *Journal of Field Ornithology* 59:128–129.

Paul Conover's Hummingbird Identification Pages. www.users.talstar.com/conover.

Patterson, M. 1990. Green-backed *Selasphorus* Hummingbirds in Clatsop County, Oregon. *Oregon Birds* 16 (3): 218–221. home.pacifier.com/~mpatters/bird/humm/HUMMREPORT.html.

Peterson, R. T., and E. L. Chalif. 1973. *A Field Guide to Mexican Birds*. Boston: Houghton Mifflin.

Peterson, Stacy Jon. 2001. Trochilids Web Page. www.geocities.com/trochilids/.

Pettingill, O. S., Jr. 1970. *Ornithology in Laboratory and Field,* 4th ed. Minneapolis: Burgess Publishing Co.

Phillips, A. R. 1975. The migration of Allen's and other hummingbirds. *Condor* 77:196–205.

Phillips, A., J. Marshall, and G. Monson. 1964. *The Birds of Arizona*. Tucson: University of Arizona Press.

Powers, D. L. 1996. Magnificent Hummingbird (*Eugenes fulgens*). No. 221 in *The Birds of North America,* A. Poole and F. Gill, eds. Philadelphia: The Birds of North America, Inc.

Powers, D. L., and S. Wethington. 1999. Broad-billed Hummingbird (*Cynanthus latirostris*). No. 430 in *The Birds of North America,* A. Poole and F. Gill, eds. Philadelphia: The Birds of North America, Inc.

Pulich, W. M. 1968. The occurrence of the Crested Hummingbird, *Orthorhyncus cristatus exilis,* in the United States. *Auk* 85:322.

Pytte, C., and M. S. Ficken. 1994. Aerial display sounds of the Black-chinned Hummingbird. *Condor* 96:1088–1091.

Raffaele, H., J. Wiley, O. Garrido, A. Keith, and J. Raffaele. 1998. *A Guide to the Birds of the West Indies*. Princeton, N.J.: Princeton University Press.

Ridgley, R. S. 1976. *A Guide to the Birds of Panama*. Princeton, N.J.: Princeton University Press.

Robertson, W. B., and G. E. Woolfenden. 1992. *Florida Bird Species: An Annotated List*. Florida Ornithological Society Special Publication No. 6.

Robinson, T. R., R. R. Sargent, and M. B. Sargent. 1996. Ruby-throated Hummingbird (*Archilochus colubris*). No. 204 in *The Birds of North America,* A. Poole and F. Gill, eds. Philadelphia: The Birds of North America, Inc.

Russell, S. M. 1996. Anna's Hummingbird (*Calypte anna*). No. 226 in

The Birds of North America, A. Poole and F. Gill, eds. Philadelphia: The Birds of North America, Inc.

Russell, S. M., and G. Monson. 1998. *The Birds of Sonora.* Tucson: University of Arizona Press.

Russell, S. M., and R. O. Russell. 1994. Lucifer Hummingbirds banded in southeastern Arizona. *North American Bird Bander* 19:96–98.

Schuchmann, K.-L. 1999. Antillean Crested Hummingbird. In *Handbook of the Birds of the World,* Vol. 5, Barn-owls to Hummingbirds, J. del Hoyo, A. Elliot, and J. Sargatal, eds. Barcelona: Lynx Edicions.

Scott, P. E. 1994. Lucifer Hummingbird *(Calothorax lucifer).* No. 134 in *The Birds of North America,* A. Poole and F. Gill, eds. Philadelphia: The Birds of North America, Inc.

Scott, P. E. 1999. Xantus's Hummingbird. In *Handbook of the Birds of the World,* Vol. 5, Barn-owls to Hummingbirds, J. del Hoyo, A. Elliot, and J. Sargatal, eds. Barcelona: Lynx Edicions.

Skutch, A. 1973. *The Life of the Hummingbird.* New York: Crown.

Skutch, A. 1999. *Trogons, Laughing Falcons, and Other Neotropical Birds.* College Station: Texas A&M University Press.

Sprunt, A., Jr. 1954. *Florida Bird Life.* New York: Coward-McCann and National Audubon Society.

Stevenson, H. M., and B. H. Anderson. 1994. *The Birdlife of Florida.* Gainesville: University Press of Florida.

Stiles, F. G. 1974. Age and sex determination in Rufous and Allen hummingbirds. *Condor* 74:25–32.

Stiles, F. G. 1982. Aggressive and courtship displays of the male Anna's Hummingbird. *Condor* 84:208–225.

Stiles, F. G. 1999a. Green Violet-ear. In *Handbook of the Birds of the World,* Vol. 5, Barn-owls to Hummingbirds, J. del Hoyo, A. Elliot, and J. Sargatal, eds. Barcelona: Lynx Edicions.

Stiles, F. G. 1999b. Green-breasted Mango. In *Handbook of the Birds of the World,* Vol. 5, Barn-owls to Hummingbirds, J. del Hoyo, A. Elliot, and J. Sargatal, eds. Barcelona: Lynx Edicions.

Stiles, F. G., and A. F. Skutch. 1989. *A Guide to the Birds of Costa Rica.* Ithaca, N.Y.: Cornell University Press.

Stimson, L. A. 1944. An emerald hummingbird at Miami, Florida. *Florida Naturalist* 17:33–34.

Sutton, G. M. 1972. *At a Bend in a Mexican River.* New York: Paul S. Eriksson, Inc.

Swarth, H. S. 1904. Birds of the Huachuca Mountains. *Pacific Coast Avifauna* 4.

Tamm, S., D. P. Armstrong, and Z. J. Tooze. 1989. Display behavior of male Calliope Hummingbirds during the breeding season. *Condor* 91:272–279.

Tarbutton, B., and D. Clapp. 1998. First record of the Green Violet-ear for Oklahoma. *Bulletin of the Oklahoma Ornithological Society* 31:21–24.

Texas Bird Records Committee. www.members.tripod.com/~tbrc/tindex.htm.

U.S. Geological Survey, Northern Prairie Wildlife Research Center. Northern Prairie Biological Resources. www.npwrc.usgs.gov/resource/resource.htm.

Wagner, H. O. 1945. Notes on the life history of the Mexican Violet-ear. *Wilson Bulletin* 57:165–187.

Wagner, H. O. 1957. The molting periods of Mexican hummingbirds. *Auk* 74:251–257.

Wauer, R. H. 1973. *Birds of Big Bend National Park and Vicinity.* College Station: Texas A&M University Press.

Wauer, R. H. 1992. *A Naturalist's Mexico.* College Station: Texas A&M University Press.

Weller, A. A. 1999a. Rufous-tailed Hummingbird. In *Handbook of the Birds of the World,* Vol. 5, Barn-owls to Hummingbirds, J. del Hoyo, A. Elliot, and J. Sargatal, eds. Barcelona: Lynx Edicions.

Weller, A. A. 1999b. Cinnamon Hummingbird. In *Handbook of the Birds of the World,* Vol. 5, Barn-owls to Hummingbirds, J. del Hoyo, A. Elliot, and J. Sargatal, eds. Barcelona: Lynx Edicions.

Weller, A. A. 1999c. Azure-crowned Hummingbird. In *Handbook of the Birds of the World,* Vol. 5, Barn-owls to Hummingbirds, J. del Hoyo, A. Elliot, and J. Sargatal, eds. Barcelona: Lynx Edicions.

Weller, A. A. 1999d. Violet-crowned Hummingbird. In *Handbook of the Birds of the World,* Vol. 5, Barn-owls to Hummingbirds, J. del Hoyo, A. Elliot, and J. Sargatal, eds. Barcelona: Lynx Edicions.

Weller, A. A. 1999e. Berylline Hummingbird. In *Handbook of the Birds of the World,* Vol. 5, Barn-owls to Hummingbirds, J. del Hoyo, A. Elliot, and J. Sargatal, eds. Barcelona: Lynx Edicions.

Wells, S., R. A. Bradley, and L. F. Baptista. 1978. Hybridization in *Calypte* hummingbirds. *Auk* 95:537–549.

Wells, S., and L. F. Baptista. 1979a. Breeding of Allen's Hummingbird on the southern California mainland. *Western Birds* 10:83–85.

Wells, S., and L. F. Baptista. 1979b. Displays and morphology of an Anna × Allen hummingbird hybrid. *Wilson Bulletin* 91:524–532.

Weydemeyer, W. 1971. Injured Calliope Hummingbird lifted by another. *Auk* 88:431.

Williamson, S. L. 2000. Blue-throated Hummingbird (*Lampornis clemenciae*). No. 531 in *The Birds of North America,* A. Poole and F. Gill, eds. Philadelphia: The Birds of North America, Inc.

Witzeman, J. 1979. Plain-capped Starthroats in the United States. *Continental Birdlife* 1:1–3.

Zimmerman, D. A. 1973. Range expansion of Anna's Hummingbird. *American Birds* 27:827–835.

Züchner, T. 1999a. Wedge-tailed Sabrewing. In *Handbook of the Birds of the World*, Vol. 5, Barn-owls to Hummingbirds, J. del Hoyo, A. Elliot, and J. Sargatal, eds. Barcelona: Lynx Edicions.

Züchner, T. 1999b. Amethyst-throated Hummingbird. In *Handbook of the Birds of the World*, Vol. 5, Barn-owls to Hummingbirds, J. del Hoyo, A. Elliot, and J. Sargatal, eds. Barcelona: Lynx Edicions.

Züchner, T. 1999c. White-eared Hummingbird. In *Handbook of the Birds of the World*, Vol. 5, Barn-owls to Hummingbirds, J. del Hoyo, A. Elliot, and J. Sargatal, eds. Barcelona: Lynx Edicions.

Züchner, T. 1999d. Bumblebee Hummingbird. In *Handbook of the Birds of the World*, Vol. 5, Barn-owls to Hummingbirds, J. del Hoyo, A. Elliot, and J. Sargatal, eds. Barcelona: Lynx Edicions.

PHOTO CREDITS

BILL BEATTY: 111 R4
ROBERT A. BEHRSTOCK: 71 L3, 71 R3, 75 R1, 83 L1, 83 L2, 111 L2, 111 R2, 247
KELLY B. BRYAN: 77 L4, 77 R4, 109 R1
JIM BURNS: 73 R1, 95 R2, 109 L1
FRANK CLELAND/GNASS PHOTO IMAGES: 1, 14, 53 L3, 53 L4, 53 R1, 53 R4, 55 L3, 55 L4, 57 L1, 57 R1, 61 L4, 61 R1, 63 L2, 63 L3, 63 L4, 63 R1, 63 R2, 63 R3, 71 R2, 81 R2, 81 R3, 234
DON DESJARDIN: 51 L1
RICH DITCH: 22
RON ERWIN: 65 L3, 65 L4, 255
CLAYTON FOGLE: 51 R1, 51 R2, 53 L1, 55 L1, 69 L2, 69 L4, 73 L3, 79 R1, 81 L3
RUSSELL AND MARTHA HANSEN: 61 L1, 65 L2, 69 R1, 71 L1, 71 L2, 71 R1, 73 R4
WILLIAM HAWK: 69 L1
KEVIN KARLSON: 67 L4, 67 R4, 81 R4
G. C. KELLEY: 59 L1, 79 L4, 81 R1
PHIL KELLY: 83 L4
GREG LASLEY: 67 R2, 83 R1, 83 R4, 95 R4
GREG W. LASLEY/KAC PRODUCTIONS: 65 R1
MASLOWSKI WILDLIFE PRODUCTIONS: 59 L3, 65 R2, 111 L1, 242
CHARLES W. MELTON: ix, 40, 42 top, 51 L2, 59 R3, 65 L1, 111 L3
ANTHONY MERCIECA: vii, 51 L3, 55 R1, 67 L2, 69 R2, 75 R2, 81 L2, 83 L3, 83 R3, 89 R4, 111 R1, 112–113, 257
ELINOR OSBORN PHOTOGRAPHY: 111 R3
RALPH PAONESSA: 42 middle, 63 L1, 73 R3
STEVE PRCHAL: 111 L4
SID AND SHIRLEY RUCKER: ii–iii, 65 R3, 71 L4, 71 R4, 77 L1, 77 L2, 77 R2, 115
HUGH P. SMITH: 49, 51 L4, 53 L2, 61 L3, 61 R2, 75 L2
ROBERT A. SUTTON: 75 L1
CONNIE TOOPS: 57 L2, 81 L1, 231

INDEX

We provide the page number on which each species account begins and (in bold face) the number of the plate(s) that portray the species. Maps and photographs are placed within the species accounts.

THE PETERSON SERIES®

PETERSON FIELD GUIDES®

BIRDS

ADVANCED BIRDING North America 97500-X
BIRDS OF BRITAIN AND EUROPE 0-618-16675-0
BIRDS OF TEXAS Texas and adjacent states 92138-4
BIRDS OF THE WEST INDIES 0-618-00210-3
EASTERN BIRDS Eastern and central North America 91176-1
EASTERN BIRDS' NESTS U.S. east of Mississippi River 93609-8
HAWKS North America 67067-5
    HUMMINGBIRDS North America 0-618-02496-4
      WESTERN BIRDS North America west of 100th meridian
      and north of Mexico 91173-7
      WESTERN BIRDS' NESTS U.S. west of Mississippi
      River 0-618-16437-5
       MEXICAN BIRDS Mexico, Guatemala, Belize, El
       Salvador 97514-X
       WARBLERS North America 78321-6

FISH

PACIFIC COAST FISHES Gulf of Alaska to Baja California 0-618-00212-X
ATLANTIC COAST FISHES North American Atlantic coast 97515-8
FRESHWATER FISHES North America north of Mexico 91091-9

INSECTS

INSECTS North America north of Mexico 91170-2
BEETLES North America 91089-7
EASTERN BUTTERFLIES Eastern and central North America
    90453-6
WESTERN BUTTERFLIES U.S. and Canada west of 100th
    meridian, part of northern Mexico 79151-0

MAMMALS

MAMMALS North America north of Mexico 91098-6
ANIMAL TRACKS North America 91094-3

ECOLOGY

EASTERN FORESTS Eastern North America 92895-8
CALIFORNIA AND PACIFIC NORTHWEST FORESTS 92896-6
ROCKY MOUNTAIN AND SOUTHWEST FORESTS 92897-4
VENOMOUS ANIMALS AND POISONOUS PLANTS) North America north of
    Mexico 93608-X

PETERSON FIELD GUIDES® continued

PLANTS

EDIBLE WILD PLANTS Eastern and central North America 92622-X

EASTERN TREES North America east of 100th meridian 90455-2

FERNS Northeastern and central North America, British Isles and Western Europe 97512-3

MEDICINAL PLANTS AND HERBS Eastern and central North America 98814-4

MUSHROOMS North America 91090-0

PACIFIC STATES WILDFLOWERS Washington, Oregon, California, and adjacent areas 91095-1

ROCKY MOUNTAIN WILDFLOWERS Northern Arizona and New Mexico to British Columbia 93613-6

TREES AND SHRUBS Northeastern and north-central U.S. and southeastern and south-central Canada 35370-X

WESTERN TREES Western U.S. and Canada 90454-4

WILDFLOWERS OF NORTHEASTERN AND NORTH-CENTRAL NORTH AMERICA 91172-9

SOUTHWEST AND TEXAS WILDFLOWERS 93612-8

EARTH AND SKY

GEOLOGY Eastern North America 0-618-16438-3

ROCKS AND MINERALS North America 91096-X

STARS AND PLANETS 93431-1

ATMOSPHERE 97631-6

REPTILES AND AMPHIBIANS

EASTERN REPTILES AND AMPHIBIANS Eastern and central North America 90452-8

WESTERN REPTILES AND AMPHIBIANS Western North America, including Baja California 93611-X

SEASHORE

SHELLS OF THE ATLANTIC Atlantic and Gulf coasts and the West Indies 0-618-16439-1

PACIFIC COAST SHELLS North American Pacific coast, including Hawaii and the Gulf of California 18322-7

ATLANTIC SEASHORE Bay of Fundy to Cape Hatteras 0-618-00209-X

CORAL REEFS Caribbean and Florida 0-618-00211-1

SOUTHEAST AND CARIBBEAN SEASHORES Cape Hatteras to the Gulf Coast, Florida, and the Caribbean 97516-6

PETERSON FLASHGUIDES™

ETERSON FIELD GUIDES can be purchased at your local bookstore
or by calling our toll-free number, (800) 225-3362.

hen referring to title by corresponding ISBN number,
eface with 0-395, unless title is listed with 0-618.